Gunfight at the Eco-Corral

Gunfight
at the Eco-Corral

Western Cinema and the Environment

Robin L. Murray and Joseph K. Heumann

University of Oklahoma Press : Norman

Library of Congress Cataloguing-in-Publication Data

Murray, Robin L.
    Gunfight at the eco-corral : western cinema and the environment /
Robin L. Murray and Joseph K. Heumann.
        p. cm.
    Includes bibliographical references and index.
        ISBN 978-0-8061-4246-3 (pbk.:alk.paper)   1. Western films—History
and criticism.   2. Ecology in motion pictures.   3. Nature in motion pictures.   4. Environmental protection and motion pictures.   I. Heumann,
Joseph K.   II. Title.
    PN1995.9.W4M87 2011
    791.43'65878—dc23

                                                        2011028909

The paper in this book meets the guidelines for permanence and durabil-
ity of the Committee on Production Guidelines for Book Longevity of
the Council on Library Resources, Inc. ∞

Contents

Illustrations

Preface and Acknowledgments

Gunfight at the Eco-Corral grew out of our reintroduction to Clint Eastwood's *Pale Rider,* a blatantly anti-hydraulic-mining film and a remake of *Shane.* The movie effectively and powerfully critiques hydraulic mining by illustrating its horrific environmental consequences in a series of scenes documenting how hydraulic cannons erupt in explosive blasts of water that destroy the landscape, eroding topsoil and literally uprooting trees on hillsides to more easily access the gold that lies beneath. But *Pale Rider* takes its critique further and also includes literal critiques by characters in the film and a resolution that replaces this catastrophic mining technique with a more sustainable approach that nurtures community and preserves the earth. This message seemed clear to us and served as our first eco-cinematic publication, "*Pale Rider:* Environmental Politics, Eastwood Style" in the 2005 issue of *Jump Cut.*

What stood out for us, however, was how few reviewers noted this obvious environmental message on display in *Pale Rider,* a message Eastwood himself describes in several interviews. In one for Turner Classic Movies, for example, he exclaims: "They just literally mow the mountains away, you know, the trees and everything. . . . All that was outlawed in California some years ago, and they still do it in Montana and a few places" (Steinberg). And in an interview with Christopher Frayling, Eastwood explains: "It was outlawed way back, even before ecological concerns were as prevalent as they are today. So we play on that in the film. It's kind of an ecological statement" (135).

Eastwood's statements left us wondering if other American Westerns also served as ecological statements, playing on contemporary environmental concerns while drawing on an authentic environmental history that includes devastating techniques and strategies (such as hydraulic mining) to extract and exploit resources. After screening hundreds of American mainstream, independent, and B Westerns, our suspicions were verified. Although all highlight the landscape as both setting and, to a certain extent, character, many Westerns also more blatantly draw on the environmental history Eastwood so clearly critiques. This book is a product of that extensive study. Films as diverse as Gene Autry and Roy Rogers musicals, early John Wayne B movies, or revisionist cinematic wonders such as *McCabe and Mrs. Miller* are grounded in an American environmental history bent on exploiting resources in the name of progress.

Current Westerns continue to draw on the drive for resources that is at the center of many earlier movies. A truly American film genre, the Western is regaining its status. The popular and critical success of the remake of *True Grit* (2010) demonstrates the resurgence of this genre that builds on Americans' hunger for their history and the promise of progress provided there. Although the narrative of *True Grit* focuses primarily on a revenge plot, it also highlights both a savage landscape that invites the "taming" civilization can provide and, in the characters of Rooster Cogburn (Jeff Bridges) and Mattie Ross (Hailee Steinfeld), illustrates the pioneer spirits necessary to settle the Wild West.

Rango (2011), however, most deliberately addresses environmental issues as it both elucidates the environmental history surrounding water rights in the Desert Southwest and critiques current water-rights practices in the Las Vegas area. In an obvious homage to *Chinatown* noted by critics from *Time Magazine* to *Salon.com*, *Rango* explores a hero's attempts to "save a parched Old West–style town from the depredations of water barons and developers" (O'Hehir). With help from a variety of anthropomorphized western characters, Rango (Johnny Depp) successfully returns water to the desert, defeating the water-baron mayor (Ned Beatty) and rehabilitating his henchman, Rattlesnake Jake (Bill Nighy).

Rango illustrates the continuing influence of the Western and its environmental underpinnings. The film's historical narrative, however, is also connected with the contemporary world Rango seems to leave behind when he is thrown out of his human family's car, for the mayor seeks to recreate a desert paradise similar to Las Vegas and its surrounding golf courses, a connection that reinforces the enduring effects of both the genre and the environmental history that grounds it. By both integrating innovative CGI and animation techniques from Industrial Light and Magic and translating the film's narrative to a video game format, *Rango* also effectively demonstrates the ongoing effects of the Desert Land Act and the exploitation of water rights it sometimes encouraged.

In *Gunfight at the Eco-Corral,* we acknowledge both the legacy and future of the American Western in relation to environmental history.

We would also like to acknowledge those who supported us throughout the process of research and drafting this text. Our department chairs, Dana Ringuette from English and Mark Borzi from Communication Studies, both supported the semester sabbatical we each received in 2007 that allowed us to begin drafting this text. We would also like to thank our research group for motivating us to continue work during later stages of this project: Dagni Bredesen, Terri Fredrick, Chris Hanlon, Ruth Hoberman, Jeannie Ludlow, and Angela Vietto kept us accountable during weekly research reports, providing the support needed to complete manuscript revisions. Most importantly, we would like to thank our editor, Jay R. Dew, for his support and professionalism throughout this project. Our experience with the University of Oklahoma Press has been enjoyable because of his dedication to this project.

In addition to these individuals, we would like to acknowledge two journals that previously published portions of the book's narrative. Portions of chapter 2 were published as "Mining Westerns: Seeking Sustainable Development in *McCabe and Mrs. Miller*," *Journal of Ecocriticism* 2.2 (July 2010). Also, a portion of chapter 6 was previously published as "Passage as Journey in Sherman Alexie's *Smoke Signals:* A Narrative of Environmental Adaptation," *Jump Cut* 52 (Summer 2010).

Gunfight at the Eco-Corral

Introduction

We fear your success. This was a pretty country you took away from us—but you see how dry it is now. It is only good for red ants, coyotes, and cattlemen.

Quanah Parker, July 4, 1898

Perhaps the two most iconic Westerns of the 1950s, *The Searchers* (1956) and *Shane* (1953), have invited a variety of critical readings, most of which highlight the conflicts between the side of right (aligned with the hero in each movie) and that of a misguided antagonist (American Indians and corporate ranchers, respectively) as well as those between civilization and savagery.[1] The homesteaders conquer their enemies in both films, with the help of a hero who seems to embody elements of both a civilized and savage world. In both the hero must return to a savage wilderness because he sees himself as unfit for the civilized (better) world. What is missing from these readings, however, is a closer look at the historical context behind the dramatic narratives that drive the films and their heroes. The real battle in *Shane* and *The Searchers,* and in many Westerns, is not between the little guy and

3

the big guy or even between civilization and savagery. Instead, these films draw on environmental battles that are ongoing and potentially devastating for what we think of as the American West. We argue that Westerns like these call for environmental readings based in ecological dichotomies that break down when considered in relation to the historical and cultural contexts of the films and their settings.

In *The Searchers,* for example, numerous scenes call for an explicit eco-critical reading. The ability of the Comanche to live off the desert is contrasted with white settlers' intentions to turn what they see as a wasteland into something good and fine. Discussions of how whites must understand American Indians can coax life out of animals and the environment in ways they have not yet learned are always emphasized by Ethan Edwards, who harbors both an intense hatred and an abiding respect for his Comanche enemies' survival strategies.

In *Shane* the conflict is not between white settlers and American Indians, but between white homesteaders and white ranchers. Here the conflict is skewed against the open-range method and in favor of raising cattle, as well as grain and vegetables, in fenced-in enclosures, which is deemed better for the cattle, the agriculture that sustains them, and the environment. Joe Starrett (Van Heflin), the chief homesteader in the film, tells Shane (Alan Ladd): "In case you wanted to know, that's Ryker's [Emile Meyer] spread all over there. He thinks the whole world belongs to him. The old-timers can't see it yet, but runnin' cattle on an open range can't go on. It takes too much space for too little results. Those herds aren't any good. They're all horns and bone. Cattle that is bred for meat and fenced in and fed right, that's the thing." According to Starrett then, open-range ranching is inefficient and wasteful, destroying more land than is necessary and resulting in marginal beef; grain-fed cattle, in contrast, are fat and happy and cause little damage to the environment. For Starrett and the other homesteaders, "This is farming country, a place for people to bring up their families. Who's Ryker to run us away from our own homes? He only wants to grow beef, and we want to grow families, to grow them good and strong, the way they were meant to be grown. God didn't make all this country just for one man like Ryker."

Rufus Ryker, however, believes his free-range ranching is better not only for him and his way of life but also for the environment. Asserting that he has earned his right to ranch an open landscape, Ryker resents how easily homesteaders usurp it: "When I came to this country, you weren't much older than your boy. We had rough times. Me and other men that are mostly dead now. I got a bad shoulder yet from a Cheyenne arrowhead. We made this country, we found it and we made it, with blood and empty bellies. Cattle we brought in were hazed off by Indians and rustlers. They don't bother you much any more because we handled 'em. We made a safe range out of this. Some of us died doing it, but we made it. Then people move in who never had to rawhide it through the old days." But he also resents the environmental consequences of the homesteaders' presence: "They fence off my range and fence me off from water. Some of them plough ditches, take out irrigation water. So the creek runs dry sometimes and I gotta move my stock because of it. And you say we have no right to the range. The men that did the work and ran the risks have no rights?" Both Starrett and Ryker believe that they have the right to the land not only because they have earned it—either through hard work or law—but also because their respective ranching method coincides best with the landscape, preserving the land as well as fattening the cattle. Each of these examples seems to rest on conflicting views of how best to manage the wilderness.

THEORETICAL APPROACHES TO THE WESTERN

Fundamentally then, definitions of the Western genre, no matter what the approach, seem to rest on an examination of contradictions or dichotomies and binary oppositions—a garden versus a desert, civilization versus wilderness, or those who are civilized versus those who are savage—in relation to structure, history, and/ or culture (depending on the approach). Yet these approaches— and the works representing them—rarely examine dichotomies in relation to historicized views of environmental degradation or sustainable development. And these dichotomies are seldom explored through an exclusively eco-critical lens, even though most Westerns call for such a reading since environmental issues are pivotal to the films' narratives and histories.

The genre is typically defined in relation to a binary of some kind, but the environmental dichotomies broached in both *The Searchers* and *Shane* are either absent from discussions or peripheral to a primary argument. Andrew Tudor, for example, defines the Western in its simplest terms as "a film [or literary work] set in the western United States between 1860 and 1900 and involving as its central theme the contrast between garden and desert" (4), but this contrast is rarely approached from an eco-critical perspective. It also denies the fact that the West was not a "desert" needing such a transformation for its original inhabitants—the American Indians. Instead, Tudor identifies three approaches to analyzing and defining genres—structural, historical, and/or cultural—all of which define or redefine particular binaries like that between garden and desert.

The first approach, which originates in structuralism, involves listing a genre's iconography, stock characters, typical themes, and central narrative patterns. From this approach, genre patterns are analyzed like language: there is an identifiable grammar and syntax. For example, John G. Cawelti's *Six-Gun Mystique* and its sequel and Will Wright's *Sixguns and Society: A Structural Study of the Western* provide structural generic readings of the Western in film and literature. Cawelti's original text serves as "an attempt to define what sort of characters, actions, settings and themes made the western into a recognizable popular genre" (3), while his sequel continues such a structuralist approach, this time with the infusion of some aspects of critical theory and cultural studies. Wright's study approaches Westerns in relation to the mythology underlying them and compares myth to language, explaining that myths and mythology consist of "an abstract structure through which the human mind imposes a necessary order and a symbolic content through which the formal structure is applied to contingent, socially defined experience" (11).

Another approach to the Western attempts to situate genres more carefully within their historical and cultural context. To find out how a genre achieved public popularity and to analyze the influence this had on studio production, this approach asks questions such as: What were the feedback mechanisms between a studio's production output and the American audience's interest in a particular genre? Was each genre's success dependent on its ability to tap major cultural anxieties prevalent at that time? Alf H. Walle's *Cowboy Hero and Its Audience: Popular Culture as Market Derived Art,* for example, combines "the deterministic focus of business thought with classic determinist models from the humanities," making it possible "to employ a wealth of focused theories from consumer research that predicts how and why people behave the way they do when they embrace goods and services" (4). Garth Jowett's *Film: The Democratic Art* takes a close look at audience in relation to film genres and periods. This 1976 work prompted new studies in film history that examined questions regarding spectatorship and the interactive relationships between movies and their audiences.

A third approach to analyzing major film categories links changes in genres over time to fundamental changes in culture. So, for example, when the Western went into decline in the 1970s, this may mean that American society had become tired of cowboys and the frontier. Or it might mean that the basic story needed to be made relevant in a different way, as when *Unforgiven* (1992) commented on cowboy violence and expanded the participation of women and racial others in the West. Richard

Slotkin's *Gunfighter Nation: The Myth of the Frontier in Twentieth-Century America* and Jane Tompkins's *West of Everything: The Inner Life of Westerns* (both from 1992) take this approach and link Western films and fiction to cultural contexts.

Slotkin argues that the frontier myth rested on both progressive and populist schools of American ideology. According to him, "The 'progressive' style . . . reads the history of savage warfare and westward expansion as a Social Darwinian parable, explaining the emergence of a new managerial ruling class and justifying its right to subordinate lesser classes to its purposes." In contrast, the populist style rests on premises that "combined the agrarian imagery of Jeffersonianism and the belief in economic individualism and mobility characteristic of pre–Civil War 'free labor' ideology. Progress in the populist style is measured by the degree to which the present state of society facilitates a broad diffusion of property, of the opportunity to 'rise in the world,' and of political power" (22).

For Tompkins: "The arch-images of the genre—the gunfight, the fistfight, the chase on horseback, the figure of the mounted horseman outlined against the sky, the saloon girl, the lonely landscape itself—are culturally pervasive and overpowering. They carry within them compacted worlds of meaning and value, codes of conduct, standards of judgment, and habits of perception that shape our sense of the world and govern our behavior without our having the slightest awareness of it" (6). Her work examines how and why the Western and its generic elements have had an influence on Americans' beliefs, both in general and in relation to specific works. John H. Lenihan's 1985 text, *Showdown: Confronting Modern America in the Western Film,* also examines Westerns in relation to their historical context, primarily focusing on films after World War II as responses to "the changing contemporary issues and outlooks in America" since the war.

ENVIRONMENTAL HISTORY AND THE WESTERN

Yet that historical context rests on environmental concerns still debated today: Is sheep herding more damaging to the environment than cattle ranching? Do western lands sustain imported cattle as readily as buffalo? Were homestead farmers the cause of the Dust Bowl years, or was the destruction of the plains an inevitable consequence of overgrazing? In retrospect, we can reexamine Westerns in relation to the environmental issues they debate.

In *The Sea of Grass* (1947), for example, Jim Brewton (Spencer Tracy) argues that cattle grazing serves the land better than homestead farming, an argument Lenihan takes seriously in his study of the film's narrative, citing Brewton's statement that "heavy rains destroy the plowed soil" after the homesteaders farm the land. Brewton, Lenihan contends, had "prove[n] his contention that God ordained the 'sea of grass' for buffalo and cattle" (100). He compares *The Sea of Grass* to Pare Lorentz's *The Plow that Broke the Plains* (1936), a New Deal documentary with both a conservationist and communal message. We disagree with Lenihan's reading.

In stark contrast *The Sea of Grass* foregrounds a "frontier empire-builder" rather than an agent for community building, so the film, and Lenihan's reading of it, begs questions about the validity of Brewton's claims about homesteaders' more environmentally destructive methods. Instead of taking these claims and the film's narrative structure at face value, we suggest that both invite an eco-critical reading that demystifies the dichotomies between cattle ranchers and homesteaders in the 1880s Southwest on which beliefs about the superiority of cattle ranching rest.

Donald Worster foregrounds the environment as one of his four themes in a new western history. For him, a new history reveals truths about the consequences of western conquest, "driving out myth and self-deception, as we face unblinkingly the fact that from its earliest days the fate of the western region has been one of furnishing raw materials for industrialism's development" (*Under Western Skies* 14). According to Worster, the study of the West has come to be allied "with the emerging field of environmental history, an alliance that has encouraged doubts about the role of capitalism, industrialism, population growth, military expenditures, and aimless economic growth in the region—that questions whether they have really blazed a trail to progress" (15). In studies of cowboy ecology, water rights, and grassland culture, for example, Worster applies an environmental-historical approach to the West's development, revealing the ecological consequences of unfettered notions of progress. His work expands definitions of conquest defined by historians like Patricia Nelson Limerick to include not only resources but also the longtime environmental effects of their exploitation.

With such a precedent in environmental history as grounding, it seems inevitable that recent historical readings of the Western would also consider the environment as an important theme. Yet only a few texts reading these films through a historical lens address environmental history as one element affecting the movies and their interpretations of history. J. E. Smyth's *Reconstructing American Historical Cinema: From* Cimarron *to* Citizen Kane, for example, seems to promise a new view of history similar to Worster's in conjunction with historical film, for it seeks to legitimize historical film as history and rereads gender, race, and cultures in a sampling of them.

But Smyth does not address environmental repercussions of westward expansion illustrated by the movies represented in the text, including *Cimarron* (1931), *The Last of the Mohicans* (1936), and *The Plainsman* (1936). He argues "that a filmic writing of American history flourished in Hollywood from 1931 to 1972" and seeks to "reconstruct a critical understanding of classical Hollywood's American historical cycle and its engagement with professional and popular history, traditional and revisionist

historical discourse, and modern history" (19). Smyth shows us
that these films provide what he calls "a critical revisionism," but
he stops short of extending that revisionist approach to environmental history.

Scott MacDonald's *The Garden in the Machine: A Field Guide
to Independent Films about Place* highlights "the history and geog-
raphy of the *depiction* [emphasis Macdonald's] of place, in literature, painting, and photography and especially film and video"
(xxi). MacDonald's text includes a chapter, "Re-envisioning
the American West," in relation to Wayne Franklin's outline
of American narrative forms: "the discovery narrative," "the
exploratory narrative" (89), and "the settlement narrative" (90).
He examines several independent films that, as MacDonald puts
it, "revivify . . . our sense of place in all its complexity—that
is, . . . evoking something of the original discoverers' wonder at
where we are, something of the original explorers' excitement in
transforming the possible into the actual, and something of the
original settlers' understanding of the practical failures of their
surround—while at the same time recognizing the problematic
moral, environmental, and political implications of five centuries of European involvement in the Western Hemisphere" (91).
MacDonald's work, however, concentrates on visual and narrative representations of place as they valorize Franklin's narrative
descriptions; he applies his lens to contemporary independent
films from the 1970s forward rather than traditional Westerns;
and he avoids elucidating environmental consequences in the
movies he explores.

Although Smyth's text looks through a revisionist lens at a
variety of historical films, not just Westerns, Scott Simmon's *The
Invention of the Western Film: A Cultural History of the Genre's First
Half-Century* highlights both the Western and the American West
as historical and cultural artifacts. Simmon argues that the "cultural baggage carried by Western films should allow them to be
unpacked through a cultural history, by which I mean examining
film aesthetics within a wide context of literature and visual arts,

of social histories and the eras depicted and of the years when the films were produced, and of the ideologies propounded by the films" (xiv). He asserts that the Western gained prominence when film narratives highlighted both American Indians and an explicitly American landscape. Simmon, then, does take landscape into consideration, but only as a setting that differentiates US films from those of France and Italy (9). As his title suggests, he offers a cultural history of the Western rather than a redefinition of history or a historiography, so his work addresses Worster's new history of the West even less than does Smyth.

Still, some works read Westerns through an eco-critical lens. Janet Walker's edited American Film Institute anthology, *Westerns: Films through History,* and Deborah A. Carmichael's *The Landscape of Hollywood Westerns: Ecocriticism in an American Film Genre* both, to differing degrees, apply notions of environmental history like those of Worster to these films. Walker draws on arguments that resemble those of Smyth, insisting that, as Jim Kitses and Andre Bazin explain, "the western is history" (qtd. in Walker 1). For Walker, the Western is history not only because of the films' setting but also "by virtue of the period in which a given film was produced" (2). She argues in her introduction against those who would claim that the Western is a-historical and includes a series of essays in her volume that reread history in these films, typically through a postmodern lens like that Worster applies. Despite this revisionist approach to the film as history, however, none of the essays Walker includes examine environmental history and its influence on the Western. Although these works confront history in relation to the film, they fall short of an eco-critical reading like that of Worster.

Our text aligns best with that of Deborah Carmichael. Her edited anthology successfully explores the intersection between environmental history and the Western. Although most of the essays explore the connection between land and American cultural mythmaking rather than environmental history, others (including our own contribution, "Hydraulic Mining, Then and

Now: The Case of *Pale Rider*") move beyond the place of landscape in films addressing the American West. In *The Landscape of
Hollywood Westerns,* chapters like John Shelton Lawrence's "Western Ecological Films: The Subgenre with No Name," Peter C.
Rollins's "Tulsa (1949) as an Oil Field Film: A Study of Ecological
Ambivalence," and to a certain extent Mary Pinard's "Haunted
by Waters: The River in American Films" provide eco-critical
readings of Westerns grounded in environmental history, readings more focused on the genre than those in David Ingram's
Green Screen: Environmentalism and Hollywood Cinema. The text
also extends definitions of the Western to include readings of
films set in the West but more influenced by, rather than defined
by, the genre, including *Chinatown* and *The Grapes of Wrath.*

This book builds on work begun with Carmichael's anthology (and in our own mining piece). By focusing on environmental issues discussed in traditional Westerns, our study offers a
space in which we can read these films through this eco-critical
lens and make the history behind the environmental debates
found in them transparent. Such a lens opens up the reading of
literary and filmic texts to what Cheryl Glotfelty calls "ecological approach[es]." Glotfelty argues that "environmental literary
studies" grew out of Frederick O. Waage's *Teaching Environmental Literature: Materials, Methods, Resources* and then blossomed in
the 1990s, beginning with Harold Fromm's MLA special session
"Ecocriticism: The Greening of Literary Studies" in 1991. Her
introduction to *The Ecocriticism Reader* defines eco-criticism as
"the study of the relationship between literature and the physical environment" (xviii) and then poses questions asked by eco-
critics and theorists.

Several of Glotfelty's questions apply to this book: "How has
the concept of wilderness changed over time? . . . What view
of nature informs U.S. Government reports, corporate advertis-
ing, and televised nature documentaries, and to what rhetorical effect? What bearing might the science of ecology have on
literary studies? . . . What cross-fertilization is possible between

literary studies and environmental discourse in related disciplines such as history, philosophy, psychology, art history, and ethics?" (xix). Cross-fertilizing film studies with environmental history offers an inroad to the Western grounded in both historical and environmental contexts.

Eco-criticism has developed according to three distinctive stages identified by Glotfelty: examination of representations of nature and the natural world in literature and popular culture, recuperation of neglected works of nature writing, and a more theoretical phase that looks at how discourse has defined humans as separate from nature, how oppression of women is linked with the domination of nature, how ecology can serve "as a metaphor for the way poetry functions in society" (xxiv), and how deep ecology (which critiques anthropocentrism) might influence literary study. This project examines representations of nature in Westerns, broadens definitions of nature writing to include film, and reads some of these movies through a theoretical and historical lens to show how (and with what results) ecology has affected the western film, especially in relation to US western history. Our approach aligns with second-wave inquiry in eco-criticism, as Lawrence Buell defines it in *The Future of Environmental Criticism:* "The exegesis of environmental subtexts through historical and critical analyses that employ ready-to-hand analytical tools of the trade together with less familiar ones eclectically derived from other disciplinary bailiwicks and . . . the identification or reinterpretation of such thematic configurations as pastoral, eco-apocalypticism, and environmental racism" (130).

Most eco-critics valorize an essential view of nature and the natural world, one that excludes a situated postmodern perspective. "Postmodern natures," views of nature that suggest its representation is relative, are often seen as problematic. In *Reinventing Nature,* for example, the majority of the essays suggest that readers should fear the consequences of viewing nature through a postmodern lens. Gary Lease's introduction claims, "Postmodern answers, to date, have ignored certain actors and obscured certain questions" (vii). Donald Worster's "Nature and the Disorder of History" argues that postmodern historians are excessively relativistic and that they distort reality. N. Katherine Hayles's "Searching for Common Ground" insists that the "deconstructionist paradigm, if accepted broadly, would . . . destroy environmentalism, since the environment is just a social construction" (viii). And Stephen R. Kellert's "Concepts of Nature East and West" asserts, "The deconstructionist notion that all cultural perspectives of nature possess equal values is both biologically misguided and socially dangerous" (103).

Eco-critics seem to suggest that immersing perceptions of nature in their historical context would "distort reality." In fact, any form of relativism—viewing nature relative to history, culture (which Ruth Benedict describes as human "personality writ large" [223]), or individual perceptions—seems to be seen as problematic. For these eco-critics, the consequences of viewing nature and the natural through a postmodern lens become frightening because such a perspective paralyzes the viewer, eradicating any possibility of socially or environmentally conscious activism. These eco-critics, then, take an a-historical view of nature.

Patrick Murphy, Dana Phillips, and others argue that relative views of nature and its representations need not silence it. By empowering nature at the local, culturally and historically situated level, its essential value can be valorized. Phillips describes a movement from modernist dualistic thought to a postmodern world of representation (205, 206). Murphy contends in a 1999 *PMLA* forum that in a postmodern eco-criticism, "Environments . . . are seen instead as a fundamental feature of the ideological horizons of literary works" (1099). Phillips's view of postmodernism, unlike those espoused in either the Western Literary Association discussion or *Reinventing Nature,* does not lead to a lack of agency or inability to take an activist stance toward the environment. Instead, he concludes in "Is Nature Necessary?" that postmodern thought offers a way to "green our society" from a local level. Phillips asserts: "Unmaking history seems to me to be the sober prospect postmodernism offers us, and is more difficult than making it. The special difficulty of unmasking what used to be called natural history is compounded by our ignorance of human complicity in it, and revising it is going to take more than just good writing or vigorous demonstration. But thinking and working our way through the past, and the perhaps unthinkable, impossible future of nature, may be our last best hope for building dwelling thinking here and now" (222).

Our approach looks to Buell, Phillips, and contemporary postmodern and environmental-justice eco-critics for a way to reveal environmental themes and aesthetics obscured by the technology presenting them. By unmasking history, we seek to illuminate the eco-critical perspectives behind the films presented here and highlight how changing views of land use and water and mineral rights are manifested in their representations of environmental issues. Ultimately, we seek to offer a new lens to look at the American Western in relation to what used to be called natural history. We also offer what we see as a better way to film the West in response to current views of history and ecology, views that disprove the theories revealed in movies from the 1900s forward.

Phillips's plea to unmask history gains force in relation to Serpil Oppermann's eco-centric postmodern approach. Oppermann asserts: "Representations of nature . . . project an effect of reality but do not merely represent the *real* material condition of nature. [They] create a model of reality that fashions our discourses and shapes our cultural attitudes to the natural environment" (112). But he also demonstrates the power of a postmodern theory that does not erase its referent, in this case nature, arguing, "it is the postmodern . . . that unravels the destructive social and cultural matrices that make environmental degradation possible" (115). To reinforce his claim, he cites Arran E. Gare's assertion in *Postmodernism and the Environmental Crisis* that "Poststructuralism not only exposes the structures which make environmental destruction appear inevitable and which constitute people as the agents of this destruction; it has been called upon to explain why environmentalists are failing in their struggle, and to show them how to be more effective" (75, qtd. in Oppermann, 115).

By taking a "polysemic and multivocal" approach to texts (117), Oppermann's study aligns with the primary goal of our work to situate Westerns and explore their relationship to environmental history. Paralleling our own goals, his approach to texts "critically assess[es] the ways in which nature has been defined, constructed, interpreted, recontextualized, reflected, represented or misrepresented" and "explore[s] the problematic relations between culture [as Euro-American personality writ large] and the environment in their literary [and filmic] contexts" (117). His approach also "draws attention to the linguistic manipulations behind the discursive constitution of nature at the bottom of which lies human oppression of the nonhuman world resulting in the environmental degradation" found in constructions of ideals like progress as linear development and destruction of nature and the wilderness (117). And Oppermann's approach seeks to "contest . . . the dominant ideological discourses behind various representations of nature" (118). Our work attempts to unmask history, drawing attention to linguistic and visual manipulations to analyze their consequences and, ultimately, offer a better way.

Our work points to the experiences Joni Adamson had when teaching American Indian literatures in a freshman writing course at the University of Arizona, experiences that unmasked the history driving the narratives in relation to her American Indian students' personal historical memories. She noted that discussions of works like Leslie Silko's *Ceremony* would turn from "the abstract, aesthetically beautiful concept of 'the earth in balance,' ... to ... the ways in which Tayo's mother represents the high rates of teenage pregnancy, the high rates of suicide, the high rates of alcohol abuse, and the high numbers of alcohol-related automobile accidents that occur in communities that have been racially marginalized and impoverished by the U.S. government's reservation system" (xv).

These discussions highlight the importance of the environmental-justice movement in discussion of the Western. Like Adamson's students, we seek to unmask the environmental degradation and racial injustice behind the narrative and aesthetic of a variety of Westerns. According to Adamson, further class responses revealed how what the United Church of Christ called environmental racism affected these students' daily lives, from open-pit uranium mines and their toxic runoff to unfettered visions of progress. She asserts that these disasters are a product of "unchecked development that rely for their authority on privileged Western notions of objective truth and control of nature, and that sanction the sacrifice of people and their surrounding environments, thereby constituting the philosophical bases of contemporary environmental racism" (xx).

Applying an environmental-justice approach in combination with an eco-centric postmodern approach may reveal contemporary environmental racism like that which "sanction[s] the sacrifice of people and their surrounding environments," and which is evident in the majority of the Westerns we viewed. Issues made transparent and addressed by environmental-justice studies in the American West rest on centuries of environmental racism and exploitation resulting from "unchecked development" that continues. The "Sonoran Desert Conservation Plan," a 2002 Environmental Justice E.I.S. Paper, illustrates the continuing effects of environmental racism. It examines "whether low and/or minority neighborhoods are or have been disproportionately affected by the impacts of pollutants in air or water, whether they are or have been disproportionately affected by land use decisions, and whether they are or have been disproportionately affected financially by environmentally-related governmental decisions" (3). These same issues are examined in Westerns focusing on ranching and farming, water rights, mining techniques, land rush and the oil frontier, railroad epics, and those examining American Indians and adaptation. But these can best be revealed through what Oppermann calls an eco-centric postmodern lens and, we hope, addressed in relation with environmental justice.

Such an eco-critical lens gives the Western genre a richer and more culturally and historically situated reading that reveals the ideology behind representations of nature within each film. We have chosen a selection of films to highlight the variety of ways environmental issues are addressed in Westerns from the 1920s through the present. These address mining with a conflict between corporate and community miners; water rights, usually with a similar conflict but in conjunction with elements from New Deal programs; American Indian versus Anglo-American worldviews; land-rush issues that set up "sod busters" in conflict with ranchers; exploration for oil and the various bifurcations on which it rests; and several conflicts that contrast cattle ranchers with various groups, including farmers and sheep ranchers. They all also rest on differing views of progress, sometimes in relation to technology. We assert, then, that the binaries represented in these films typically blur when examined more closely, and such blurring demonstrates the complexity of environmental history and environmental degradation.

In chapter one, our book first seeks to unearth the environmental history that focused on ranching and then reveals its complexity in relation to Westerns that draw on the conflict between cattle ranchers and farmers, and cattle and sheep ranchers, in relation to cultural and historical contexts. The question for us is how these films respond to the historical contexts they seem to replicate as well as those in which they are immersed.

Our second chapter offers eco-critical readings of mining films that both perpetuate and complicate the dichotomy between two "classes" of miners—corporate versus individual "tin pan" miners. Films highlighting copper, gold, and silver mining grapple with environmental issues like toxic-waste runoff and actual exploitation of the land and its resources by mining itself as well as the more traditional "big guys" versus "little guys" conflict.

Chapter three explores water rights in relation to the big guys versus little guys dichotomy found in a variety of Westerns. This chapter provides a space in which to explore a variety of Westerns highlighting water rights in relation to the historical, cultural, and regional contexts with which they interact.

In chapter four we examine representations of the land rush in Westerns and in relation to conflicts over oil that arise when western lands are opened for mass settlement. Questions regarding land exploitation are illustrated by changes in the environment, but they seem to go untreated, at least explicitly. Environmental consequences of oil production, which serves as one outcome of the onslaught of settlers, remain unquestioned. This discussion provides a space in which these consequences can be "mined" in conjunction with filmic representations of the rush for land and the rush for progress.

Chapter five highlights one of the most influential technological developments and its influence on the American West— the railroad. Although other advances that resulted from the land rush certainly altered the western environment, the transcontinental railroad in particular affected the region's ecology and milieu most dramatically. Trains changed ranching, for example, shortening the duration of cattle drives and lessening losses of beeves along the way. In Westerns, railroads also lead to the elimination of the buffalo. The railroad serves to accelerate both populist and progressive versions of progress rather than change

The wilderness becomes an urban landscape in *How the West Was Won*

or eliminate it. Trains speed up settlement, communication, economic growth, and, inevitably, environmental destruction, not only in the historic American West but also in the films that represent it.

Chapter six provides a space to explore the American Indian worldview in relation to environmental adaptation as it is constructed in various films. Although American Indians seem to be constructed as "innocents" with less maturity than Euro-Americans in most of these movies, their view of landscape and land use is represented as more environmentally conscious than that of Euro-Americans. *Dances with Wolves* (1990) has been frequently discussed as a revisionist Western offering a space for American Indian voices, but other films address the Indian question in less obvious ways. Many others construct American Indians as an "other" who must be destroyed or vanquished for civilization to prosper, but even films like *The Searchers* include a more sympathetic look at them and environmental adaptation when scrutinized more fully. Most importantly, when American Indians take over the role of filmmaker, as in *Smoke Signals,* their own unique evolutionary and comic narratives can be revealed.

Our last chapter synthesizes our arguments and suggests alternative ways to address the West's environment and both avoid and heal its degradation. Since the Desert Southwest is the fastest growing part of the United States, consequences of such progress are still increasing, building on the transformation of a wilderness into an urban landscape connected by a cloverleaf of interstate highways like that in the conclusion of *How the West Was Won* (1962). Our approach to eco-criticism parallels these alternatives and joins together environmentalism and "wise use" approaches to reading filmic texts. So when faced with a classic as misguided in its environmental politics as *Shane* or *The Searchers,* or B Westerns from singing cowboys like Gene Autry or Roy Rogers, eco-criticism offers a solution—a reading that draws on traditional approaches but marries them to environmentalism.

CHAPTER 1

Don't Fence Me In

Ecology and Free-Range and Fenced Ranching in *Shane* and *Sea of Grass*

A cowboy never takes unfair advantage.

A cowboy never betrays a trust.

A cowboy always tells the truth.

A cowboy is kind to small children, to old folks, and to animals.

A cowboy is free from racial and religious prejudice.

A cowboy is helpful and when anyone's in trouble, he lends a hand.

A cowboy is a good worker.

A cowboy is clean about his person and in thought, word, and deed.

A cowboy respects womanhood, his parents, and the laws of his country.

A cowboy is a patriot.

> Gene Autry, "The Ten Commandments of the Cowboy," 1939

The range war, popularized in Hollywood Westerns, is full of gunplay, fistfights, ambushes, family disintegration, class warfare, and the destruction of native populations and wildlife. Westerns foregrounding range wars, however, may also provide a view of the variety of films tackling dichotomies between differing approaches to cattle ranching, between cattle ranchers and farmers, and between cattle and sheep ranchers, especially in relation to the environment that sustains them. See, for example, *Shane* and *The Sea of Grass*. *Shane* holds a place in classic film history, while *The Sea of Grass* is all but lost despite its stars, Katherine Hepburn and Spencer Tracy, and its director, Elia Kazan. And the two films come out on opposite sides of the conflict. *Shane* supports the views of small farmers and ranchers, who see fencing as the best way to save the land and raise better crops and cattle. *The Sea of Grass* asserts that sodbusters (homestead farmers) have ruined the land and that ranchers like Jim Brewton (Spencer Tracy) would have preserved the grasses and the environment that sustains them. The questions for us, however, is, when viewed through an eco-centric postmodern lens, how do these films, and others dealing with similar conflicts, respond to the historical contexts they seem to replicate as well as those in which they are immersed? And what do those responses suggest about representations of nature in relation to free-range versus fenced ranching?

We assert that historical and ecological studies since the 1970s have actually disproved all of the theories revealed in these films as well as in the ecological research of the 1940s and 1950s. Instead, ecologists and historians from the 1980s forward demonstrate that no matter what the method, ranching and farming left an indelible and destructive mark on the land. Despite the recent consensus, such ecological readings suggest, however, that filmic representations of ranching and an open range still rest on bifurcations between ranching and farming methods, chiefly because they perpetuate a myth rather than an accurate representation of the American West.

Open Range (2003) is a case in point. Years after research negated the ecology behind free-range ranching, the film argues vehemently (and violently) for that method and against enclosed

Sea of cattle crossing the railroad tracks in *Red River*

farms and ranches, especially private-property rights and barbed wire. The film's heroes, Charley Waite (Kevin Costner) and Boss Spearman (Robert Duvall), battle a town whose citizens have been forced to support a large ranch owner who restricts any other cattle crossing his "privately owned" land. The rancher has bullied the town so strongly that the first business in view when Charley and Spearman arrive there is a store that sells barbed wire and advertises the fact on its front façade. The conflict seems clear and its result relentlessly unjust: Charley and Spearman suffer the loss of many of their trail crew. But they fight back and win, so their worldview in favor of the open range is validated.

From the film's bucolic opening to its triumphant conclusion, free-range ranching is both valorized and romanticized as an integral element of the frontier. It opens with views of cattle on a broad range and a sky darkened by a coming storm. Waving grass and pastoral music reinforce the peaceful scene, a serenity unbroken by thunderstorms or a cowboy cheating at cards. The tone changes only after the chief conflict of the film—that between free-range and fenced cattle ranching—comes into play. When Mose (Abraham Benrubi), one of their two hands, does not return from town, Charley and his boss go after him and immediately come up against opposition to their way of ranching. They see the sign for the fencing and barbed-wire company as they enter town. They are told that the area's chief property owner, Denton Baxter (Michael Gambon), and his men "don't take to free grazers or free grazing."

Boss Spearman counters with wisdom that seems to line up with the American ideal of freedom: "Are we moving on?" he asks. "We always do once we graze off a place." And when Baxter's men attempt to scatter his herd, Spearman decides to fight back—"one man telling another where he can go; that's another thing," he proclaims. After Mose and his dog are killed, and Button (Diego Luna), another hand, is injured, Spearman and Charley seek revenge and seem to be fighting for a valorous way of life as well. They are associated with only positive qualities: friendship (between themselves and their crew), loving relationships with pets (their own dog and one they save from drowning in a storm), pragmatic gentility embodied by Sue Barlow (Annette Bening), and both courage and ingenuity in their battle with Baxter, the sheriff, and his men (against incredible odds). Corporate ranchers like Baxter, however, are constructed as corrupt villains who kill for property rather than ideals.

Ultimately, *Open Range* comes out in favor of free-range grazing and all of the ideal qualities it represents in the film. Fenced ranching, in contrast, is associated with corrupt, land-grabbing corporate ranchers like Baxter. The film, however, oversimplifies arguments for and against free-range ranching and harks back to research from the 1920s through the 1950s that both valorized and contradicted that method. More importantly, it reinforces a mythology resting on American ideals of the western frontier.

The film's argument in favor of free-range ranching rests on this mythology rather than on contemporary land-use research.

Open Range, then, serves as an effective case in point, introducing and illustrating the debate between free-range and fenced ranching that continues despite research demonstrating the adverse effects both methods had on the environment of the West. From here, the roots of this ecological debate can be explored with a reading of an iconic silent Western, *Tumbleweeds* (1925). Then a close examination of two films with opposing perspectives on the range war, *Sea of Grass* and *Shane,* in relation to documents from the period demonstrates the same conflicting viewpoints on the environmental effects of different forms of ranching. Finally, an exploration of Westerns responding to the Johnson County War from the 1980s forward, a period in which environmentalists had a clear sense of the negative effects of ranching on the environment, nevertheless reveals that, like the earlier range-war Westerns, they primarily argue in favor of free-range ranching despite research since the 1940s demonstrating its disastrous consequences for the environment.

RANGE WAR MOVIES:
THE CASE OF *TUMBLEWEEDS*

Since Frederick Jackson Turner's 1890 argument about the significance of the frontier in the formation of the American character, at a time when the US frontier seemed to no longer exist, conceptions of an open road—a space to conquer—seem to have changed. Yet the image of an existing frontier—while there are none left geographically—remains an important one to maintain in an American consciousness shaped by mythical frontier ideals like independence, self-reliance, and ingenuity. The American dream and identity depend on the transformation of the landscape—as they always have—whether it is the open space of the West or the closed space of the inner city. They are reinforced and valorized by most Westerns.

The cowboy representations in these films embody these American ideals. Cinematic images of the cowboy were a blend of frontier andVictorian values that even retained signs of chivalry. The isolated working conditions of these men also bred a tradition of self-dependence and individualism, with great value put on personal honesty, exemplified in their songs and poetry (an image perpetuated by the Westerns we viewed). According to E. Cotton Mather:

> The heroic figure in the great plains is the cowboy. This figure has been romanticized and embellished since the days of the epic cattle drives fromTexas northward along such routes as the Chisholm Trail. The Western novel, the Western movie, and the Western television show have brought the tale to reader and nonreader alike. Chapters in the legend include the westward building railroads, the rise of the cow towns of Abilene, Dodge City, and Ogalalla, the supplying of meat contracts to Indian agencies, the stocking of the ranges on the northern plains, the buffalo hunts, and the conflicts between cattleman and sheepman and between rancher and sodbuster. (251)

He later asserts, "The Great Plainsman views his cowboy as a transcendental figure. This idol is a complex of past and present, and of the biologic, economic, and symbolic realms" (254). Western movies further popularized the cowboy image and lifestyle but also created persistent stereotypes.

Icons like John Wayne, for example, exemplify the ideal cowboy, one who fights for freedom and justice and is brave and honest, with strong ethics and values. As James T. Campbell explains, Wayne is "an embodiment of authority, masculinity, love of country, and other allegedly endangered virtues," values that live on in the image of the cowboy, an isolated figure who thrived on individualism and self-reliance but paved the way for imperial visions of progress at any cost (466). Cowboys are part of this vision of progress that idealizes individuals who tame the wilderness, exploiting its resources for profit and vanquishing the savage to make way for civilization. The myth of the cowboy lives on in the films, but so does the environmental degradation left behind by the free-range ranching such characters advocate.

Research since the 1920s demonstrates that whether or not cattle ranching serves nature better than homestead farming and ranching depends on environmental conditions and ecological priorities. Yet filmic representations of the open range perpetuate myths about the West established before and after the range closed in the 1890s. The history depicted in these films primarily responds to ideals of the Wild West rather than current research from ecologists. An eco-centric postmodern lens unmasks a reality that counters these ideals. Cattlemen not only acquired lands illegally during the climax of the ranching industry but also stole water rights, a necessary resource for themselves and their cattle and an environmental commodity either hoarded or sold to homesteaders for immense profit.

Battles over ranching methods, especially, are highlighted in both research and the Westerns of the period that broach environmental arguments and examine them either explicitly or implicitly. As early as 1926, Forrest M. Larmer claimed in *Financing the Livestock Industry* that the successes of free-rangers "were due largely to the bounteousness of nature. . . . The cost of the herd or flock was small and expenses of operation almost negligible, except for the death toll that Nature exacted" (1). According to historian Nathan Sayre, "International investors simply did not notice, or much care, when the effects of their money overwhelmed the vegetation growth, soils, water, and climate that sustained local and regional ecosystems" (240).

Many films tackling the evolution of free-range ranching, however, seem to neglect the negative effect ranching had on the land, instead not only focusing on the changes homesteaders brought to the western economy and, as Osage Indian writer

John Joseph Mathews describes it in *Wah'Kon-Tah: The Osage and the White Man's Road,* the changes brought by a colonizing Euro-American culture but also suggesting that homestead farmers would destroy the land and the life it provided, all in the name of civilization. The cowboy way was held up as an ideal in these films, as wild and free as the land that was depicted as untouched before farmers plowed it.

Tumbleweeds, for example, valorizes the cowboy myth even as it illustrates the westward movement caused by the land rush of 1893. The film begins with a shot of a cowboy in a wild landscape and a title card that reads, "Man and beast, both blissfully unaware that their reign is over," and then demonstrates the interconnected relationship cowboys share with the natural environment through the actions of Don Carver (William S. Hart). A cowboy and hence a tumbleweed, Carver first spares a snake's life. Then after a card that reads, "The most fertile spot in a fertile land—their ranch," he adopts wolf pups, willing to raise them after poisoning their mother—"it's our turn to take care of them."

These images of nature appear between verses of a song idealizing the cowboy life as a "rollin' rambler, a tumblin' tumbleweed" and set off the revelation that "the Strip's been opened to homesteaders. . . . this here Cherokee Strip we're standin' on right now." Although Molly Lassiter (Barbara Bedford), a love interest, interferes with the cowboy's desire for freedom, the film highlights the sacrifices Carver and others must make to accommodate these new settlers. A title card explains a scene in which cowboys herd hundreds of cattle off the land: "Clearing all the cattle from the rich grazing land by government order." The cards even identify the cowboy roles during the herding: "The Pointer"; "The Wheeler." As the others watch, Carver exclaims, "Boys that's the last of the West."

A dichotomy between wild cowboys, whose ways tie them to the land and its creatures, and domesticating homesteaders bent on destroying both the cowboy and the land has been established here, but the film takes an ambivalent stance on the clashing lifestyles, advocating homestead farming but only in the context of the fertile ranch Carver seems to have left behind. "It's called the Box K Ranch and controls the waterways. There's a million in it, and I'm going to get it," he declares.

This control of water sets up a conflict between Carver and Molly's brother, Noll (J. Gordon Russell), but the real struggle here is between ranching and homesteading. Although Carver's sidekick, Bill Freel (Richard R. Neill), argues that it is "no disgrace to be a homesteader when a woman like her [Molly] is one," the film also shows ominous images of wagon trains on the horizon, bringing in hordes of homesteaders. The movie seems to rest on its claim, "Ain't nothin' like ownin' land, no sir." It also promotes ideals like honor and family that the homesteaders might bring to the country and combats corruption from land grabbers. But it also highlights the consequences of empire building on the frontier. A title card clarifies the purpose behind this rush for land on the Cherokee Strip and beyond: "100,000 empire builders racing across the great barriers of the last frontier," building a society that rests on land ownership and linear views of progress.

The film ends, however, with a more moderate view of landowning, one that disqualifies the corruption embodied by Noll, whose greed would lead to riches only by exploiting natural resources (water) for economic gain. Noll is defeated, and Carver gets Molly and the Box K Ranch. While reclaiming the ranch he had left behind, Carver merges ranching with homestead farming in both staking a claim and embracing Molly.

The last scene of *Tumbleweeds* is said to illustrate this marriage between two ways of life in the West. We see barbed wire with tumbleweed rolling into it as Carver and Molly embrace, seemingly signifying a union not only between a man and a woman but also between two ways of life—ranching and homestead farming. But the ending is bittersweet. The couple watch the tumbleweed together, but Carver still holds the reins of his horse. When Molly rejected him in an earlier scene, Carver had declared: "Women ain't reliable. Cows are—that's why I'm

headin' for South America where there's millions of them."
Juxtaposing these words with the final tumbleweed scene reinforces the film's ambivalent stance toward the end of the cowboy life. Despite Carver's turn to homesteading, it is his life as a
cowboy that is valorized. Although the movie mourns the demise
of the cowboy and the West he represents, implications for the
environment are addressed primarily with references to water
rights that make clear that this is dry land unfit for farming.

The environmental history revealed by the ecological research
from the 1940s and 1950s seems just as torn in relation to best
ranching methods as do Westerns from their inception to today.[1]
The Sea of Grass and *Shane* are two films from a similar post–
World War II period that illustrate such ambivalence. Juxtaposing *The Sea of Grass,* a film in favor of free-range ranching, with
Shane, a film that favors fenced ranching and vilifies free-rangers,
illustrates how cinematic representations of environmental consequences both respond to and mythologize historical and ecological memory of the period.

THE SEA OF GRASS AND THE FREE RANGE:
A VISUAL ARGUMENT AGAINST HOMESTEADING

In *The Sea of Grass,* Jim Brewton (Spencer Tracy) argues that
cattle grazing serves the land better than homestead farming, an
argument John H. Lenihan takes at face value when he claims
that the character "expresses genuine affection for the rich grasslands, which he correctly believes would be ruined by the homesteader's plow" (100). Lenihan compares *The Sea of Grass* to New
Deal documentaries with both a conservationist and communal
message. In stark contrast to Lenihan, *The Sea of Grass* actually
constructs Brewton as a "frontier empire-builder" rather than
an agent for community building, and so the film, and Lenihan's reading of it, begs questions. The connection between Pare
Lorentz, a major director of New Deal documentaries, and Elia
Kazan, the director of *The Sea of Grass,* seems to have influenced

Kazan's attempt at an environmental message, an attempt that falls flat in relation to Brewton's unlimited drive to conquer the plains and maintain his claim to the range.

Instead of taking Brewton's claims and the film's narrative structure at face value, these invite an eco-critical reading that demystifies the dichotomy on which they rest—that between cattle ranchers and homesteaders in the 1880s Southwest. The film asserts that free-range ranching maintains the plains in their original state, just as did the buffalo and the Indian, and demonstrates that homestead farming destroys the environment, turning it into a dustbowl on screen like that invoked in Lorentz's *The Plow that Broke the Plains* (1936). What is missing are the repercussions of unfettered grazing environmental historian Mont H. Saunderson warned about in 1949. Although Brewton sees a clear ecological dichotomy between free-range ranching and homesteading, the former benefiting grasslands and the latter destroying them, research even from the film's period suggests otherwise. Studies from the 1970s forward demonstrate that free-range ranching contributed more to the loss of ecology than any other farming method.

An opening title card provides a context for *The Sea of Grass* and its argument: "This story takes place for the most part against the background of the sea of grass—that vast grazing empire which covered the western part of North America from the Great Plains to the Rocky Mountains, and beyond." To empower its argument in favor of free-range ranching and empire building, the film establishes conflicts between West and East as parallels to those between free-ranging and homesteading. Brewton embodies the West. His bride from St. Louis, Lutie Cameron (Katherine Hepburn), and the legal advocate for homesteading in Salt Fork, Brice Chamberlain (Melvyn Douglas), represent the East and its determination to "settle" the West and fetter its "wild," free-range state.

Lutie's first encounter with both Brewton and Chamberlain illustrate this bifurcation. After arriving early for her wedding in

Salt Fork, New Mexico, she learns from Chamberlain that he is
Brewton's "natural enemy" and wants to "make history in Salt
Fork" by convicting Brewton's men for injuring Andrew Boggs
(Trevor Bardette) to drive him off his land. Although he loses the
case, Chamberlain argues in favor of homesteading by question-
ing Brewton's ownership of the range in open court:

> Is it true that of this vast amount of property you actually
> own only a few scattered water holes that are filed on
> either in your own name or those of your men? That by
> far the greater part of it still belongs to the government?
> . . . Is it true that a million or more acres still belonging
> to the government, the same land from which Andrew
> Boggs, who merely wanted 160 acres, was run off and
> severely wounded by parties unknown? . . . Boggs is
> only a single man, and the court has already disposed
> of him. But waiting at the edge of Salt Fork to hear the
> outcome of this trial are other settlers, families, who've
> driven their wagons more than a thousand miles across
> the plains and left their dead from the Mississippi to the
> Rio Grande—all with one purpose—to find homes for
> themselves in this great territory. I want to ask you in
> the names of these families if you won't let them settle
> undisturbed on a few acres of the millions or more gov-
> ernment land on your range.

But Brewton sees himself and other ranchers as the rightful
"owners" of the range and denigrates the homesteader who
does not build an empire with his own hands but on the backs
of those who came before him:

> Chamberlain, I have sympathy for the early pioneer who
> risked his life and his family among the Indians, and I
> hope I have a little charity for the nester who waited

until the land was safe and peaceable before he filed a homestead of someone else who fought for it. But when that nester picks land like my big Vega, a thousand feet above the sea which nature intended for grazing land and always will be grazing land, when he wants to plow it up to support his family when there isn't enough rain for the crops to grow, when he only kills the grass that will grow when his crops starve for water and he ends up killing my beef and becomes a man without respect for himself and a menace to the territory, then I have neither sympathy nor charity. . . . Boggs is only a sample of what will happen if others try it.

When Brewton, the film's protagonist, introduces his new wife, Lutie, to his large ranch, he reinforces his belief that free-range ranching best serves the land, again establishing himself as the superior pole in the binary between free-range and fenced ranching. Brewton looks at the land and states, "Well, first of all I guess I hear the buffalo," and when Lutie asks him what else he hears, he explains his arguments for free-ranging while looking down on the grasslands: "I can remember the first time I saw her. We'd come a long way. And nobody was telling us about any surprises. We just came over the hill and there she was, sort of lying there all alone. Nobody wanted her then, except the antelope, the buffalo, and the Indians, so we took her, and we set her up right for cow country. We fought for her. Our blood sunk in every mile. Indian blood, too. I'm not so proud of some of that. My brother's out there. It's kind of the way God made it and wants it to stay, and I've got a hunch that He wants me to keep it that way." He has defeated both the native range animal—the buffalo—and the region's indigenous peoples. Yet this rancher sees himself and his cattle as native rather than imported and hence as making no mark on the landscape, of which they are a natural part. He also designates himself as the land's protector, with a manifest destiny to "keep it that way."

Yet Brewton does not acknowledge the irony that he has acquired this range only after destroying its original inhabitants. Instead, he asserts that the land is the same for him and his cattle as it was for the buffalo and the Indians before him. The film reinforces Brewton's assertions about the dangers of homesteading, first by demonstrating that ranchers and homesteaders cannot coexist because their methods contradict one another, then by illustrating the dire consequences of homesteading—destroying the grass and contributing to long-term drought and dustbowl conditions.

The experience of Selina (Ruth Nelson) and Sam Hall (James Bell) as homesteaders striking a claim on Brewton's range illustrates how conflicting free-range and fenced methods can become. When during a harsh winter storm some of Brewton's cattle trample Hall's barbed-wire fence, the farmer takes out his gun to defend his wheat crop and kills a steer. Brewton's men retaliate by beating him. Brewton has lost one steer, but Sam nearly lost his entire crop, and his pregnant wife, witnessing the beating, loses her child. The Halls leave their homestead and break all ties with Brewton and his wife, exacerbating the conflict between these two competing forces.

Lutie and Selina had built a friendship, so she mourns the Halls's move. But Jim Brewton reinforces his earlier claims about homesteaders when she defends them over his rangeland: "This is tough country, Lutie. . . . The Halls don't count for much, Lutie. Neither do we. That out there does, and men like Chamberlain, they want to farm it. They want to dig it up and take the water out of its veins way down deep. It will curl up and die then, Lutie. It would die, and so would the whole country. It would never live again." In this speech Brewton again expresses his role as the keeper of the land charged to keep it as it is.

Although the incident motivates Lutie to separate from Brewton and have an affair with Chamberlain, its claims about homesteaders are reinforced by a drought that hits the regions and destroys both farm and ranch land. At first it seems the

homesteaders have proven themselves to the ranchers. In a letter from Doc Reid (Harry Carey) to Lutie, for example, Reid
tells her that crops are good. Scenes of a thriving community of
homesteaders in Salt Fork illustrate his claims. But a few years
later, newspaper headlines come onscreen exclaiming: "Rain-
fall less this year. Farming to suffer, predicted by agricultural
experts." Others read, "crops in peril," and, "Manmade ruin, say
cattlemen" with a subheading that begins, "Farm destruction is
blamed on removal of grass. Drought result."

These headlines are juxtaposed with shots of drought-ridden
crops, thin stalks of wheat and corn blown from the dust left by a
scorched land of little rain. The shots seem to come directly from
New Deal documentaries like *The Plow that Broke the Plains,*
but they reinforce a one-sided argument that blames ecological
disaster solely on homesteaders. Free-range ranchers like Brewton are absolved of all responsibility for the barren land despite
clear evidence that unfettered cattle ranching denigrated the
range. Only a few lines from Chamberlain after he admits, "It's
all drying up and blowing away," suggest that farming might
prove successful. He claims that "irrigation ditches and culverts"
would have protected the land and asserts, "some day we'll do
that." But the film valorizes Brewton's claims that free-range
practices preserve the grass, while sod busting by homesteaders
destroys it. Both Brewton's and Chamberlain's claims, however,
are only partially supported by research from the film's period
and countered by studies since the 1970s.

For example, responses to grasses and grazing are complicated
further once comparisons include not only cattle ranchers, who
choose either free range or fenced methods, but also homesteaders and sheep ranchers. Karen R. Merrill reveals some of the
mythology hidden by Westerns bifurcating cattle ranchers and
homesteaders, suggesting that "these [filmic] representations tell
us that the cowboy looked down from his horse upon the sorry
sodbuster on the plains and that the ranch owner cursed the

breaking up of his range" (436). Merrill contends that such an opposition is either imagined or exaggerated, resting her views on policies promoted by Theodore Roosevelt and his supporters from the late 1890s until World War I. But she also suggests that Roosevelt sought to inspire homestead farmers to settle and civilize the West while also maintaining cattle ranching, though within limits. In a 1910 speech to the Colorado Stock Growers' Association, Roosevelt stated, "it is the homestead man, the single settlers, the actual homemaker whose interests we do most to preserve" (Merrill 436).

The Sea of Grass both counters and supports the policies that Roosevelt advocated in his speech. Land that was "naturally built for grazing land," declares Brewton, is not a "natural choice" for homesteaders. Yet the film does depict families of homesteaders staking their claims in Salt Fork. It shows us that all the "water holes and land are owned by the government and can be homesteaded" and reminds us that there were "160 acres per person from the Mississippi to the Rio Grande." Homesteaders arrive and one by one build farms where "crops are good," with wheat and corn growing everywhere, until two years of drought cause what Brewton calls "man-made ruin."

The film seems to valorize free-range cattle ranching over homesteading, but at the same time it demonstrates how homesteaders reinforce ideal family values that are missing from Brewton's home. In fact, the rancher kicks his wife out when she missteps and rears their children himself. A spoiled son (Robert Walker) later goes wild like the open range. The movie ends on a note about needing to guard "against the time when nature would fail us," but its message regarding the debate between cattle ranchers and homesteaders is less transparent than it at first appears. Although Brewton seems to prove his theory that grazing is better for the land than farming, ranching is not necessarily heralded as better for the country than homesteading—a message echoing Roosevelt's 1910 speech.

SHANE AS A COUNTERPOINT
FOR *THE SEA OF GRASS*

There are many other Westerns that turn the tables on characters like Jim Brewton, Charley Waite, and Boss Spearman, arguing in favor of homesteading and against free-range ranching. *Shane* is an iconic case in point. The film favors raising cattle in fenced enclosures and argues for the rights of homesteaders like the Starretts (Jean Arthur, Van Heflin, and Brandon de Wilde)—small farmers—over those of Rufus Ryker (Emile Meyer) a corporate free-range rancher who has no family (that is depicted) and uses the same violent tactics that Denton Baxter and Brewton use in support of their economic philosophies. Here Shane (Alan Ladd) fights on the side of justice, just as Charley and Boss Spearman do, but in *Shane* the just side supports raising cattle behind fences rather than on open lands. Ryker, the corporate free-ranger, serves the same role as Baxter did in *Open Range,* and Shane (in support of the Starretts) represents a role similar to that of Charley. But they are fighting over more than the rights of the little guys (Charley and Spearman/Shane/the Starretts) over the big guys (Baxter/Ryker). Their battle primarily is an environmental conflict over differing views of how best to preserve the land, if only for economic gain.

As broached in the introduction, in *Shane* the conflict between homesteaders and ranchers is skewed against the open range and for raising cattle, grain, and vegetables in fenced-in farmlands because their method is represented as better for the cattle, the agriculture that sustains them, and the environment. Using an ecological argument that aligns with sustainable-development principles rather than fair use, Joe Starrett, the chief homesteader in the film, explains to Shane why his method is superior: "The old-timers can't see it yet, but runnin' cattle on an open range can't go on. It takes too much space for too little results. Those herds aren't any good, they're all horns and bone. Cattle that is

Raising beef in small-farm cattle enclosures in *Shane*

bred for meat and fenced in and fed right, that's the thing. You gotta pick your spot, get your land, your own land. A home-steader can't run but a few beef, but he can grow grain, and then with his garden and hogs and milk, he'll be all right." According to Starrett then, open-range ranching is inefficient and wasteful, destroying more land than necessary and producing marginal beef. Grain-fed cattle, in contrast, are fat and happy and cause lit-tle damage to the fields. For the homesteaders, as Starrett argues: "This is farming country, a place for people to bring up their families. Who's Ryker to run us away from our own homes? He only wants to grow beef, and we want to grow families, to grow them good and strong, the way they were meant to be grown. God didn't make all this country just for one man like Ryker." Starrett asserts that his method will sustain the environment for himself, his family, and his community. Free-range methods, however, are based on greed—fair use that exploits resources solely for economic gain.

The small family farm in *Shane*

Ryker, though, believes his style of ranching is better not only for him and his way of life but also for the environment. He foremost believes that he has earned his right to ranch an open landscape and resents how easily homesteaders usurp it: "When I came to this country, you weren't much older than your boy. We had rough times. Me and other men that are mostly dead now. I got a bad shoulder yet from a Cheyenne arrowhead. We made this country, we found it and we made it, with blood and empty bellies. Cattle we brought in were hazed off by Indians and rustlers. They don't bother you much any more because we handled 'em. We made a safe range out of this. Some of us died doing it, but we made it. Then people move in who never had to raw-hide it through the old days." These words parallel Brewton's assertions to Chamberlain in the courtroom and to Lutie after the Halls have left Salt Fork.

Ryker also resents the environmental consequences of the homesteaders' presence: "They fence off my range and fence me off from water. Some of them plough ditches, take out irrigation water. So the creek runs dry sometimes and I gotta move my stock because of it. And you say we have no right to the range. The men that did the work and ran the risks have no rights? I take you for a fair man, Starrett. I'm not belittling what you did, but you didn't find this country. There were trappers here and Indian traders before you. They tamed this country." He makes the same arguments as Brewton, asserting that homesteaders dry up the land, but Ryker is constructed as a corrupt villain who must be destroyed to make way for settlers like Starrett, who will turn the wilderness into a civilization. According to Starrett: "We can have a regular settlement. We can have a town, and churches, and a school. . . . Stay for something that means more than anything. Your families. Your wives and kids. Like you, Lewis, your girls . . . and Shipstead with his boys. They've got the right to stay here and grow up and be happy. It's up to you people to have nerve enough to not give it up."

Both Starrett and Ryker believe that they have the right to the land not only because they have earned it—either through hard work or rule of law—but also because their methods coincide best with the landscape and preserve the land as well as fatten the cattle. The film's rhetoric, however, comes out in favor of fenced ranching and farming as a way to preserve not only the family but also the land. Its presentation of this landscape, however, shows us a forbidding land unfit for either ranch or farm.

THE SEA OF GRASS AND SHANE: PUTTING THE 1940s AND 1950s IN CONTEXT

Research from the 1940s and 1950s shares that uncertainty about which ranching methods serve the environment best. J. E. Weaver and R. W. Darland's 1948 *Ecology* article, "Changes in Vegetation and Production of Forage Resulting from Grazing Lowland Prairie," supports Waite and Spearman's view in *Open Range* that free-range ranching represented the best use of the terrain, the same argument Brewton makes in *The Sea of Grass*.

The Sea of Grass seems to respond to Weaver and Darland's views of cattle grazing: For them, as for Brewton, free-range ranching works best. Weaver and Darland claim, "it is only when grazing animals are circumscribed in their range by fences and when too large a population is thus confined for too long a time that grazing and trampling become so excessive that the normal cover cannot be maintained. The prairie degenerates" (1). Their argument, of course, begs the question of the elimination of competition from the buffalo. Its conclusions also seem based on anecdotal observation rather than longitudinal empirical research.

Floyd Larson's "The Role of Bison in Maintaining the Short Grass Plains," from 1940, agrees with Weaver and Darland and argues that overgrazing is not and has never been an issue. Instead, the "short grass plains" that are seen as a result of overgrazing—and as a replacement for the "taller grasses" eliminated by overgrazing—are actually a natural occurrence, "a true plant climax" (113). He suggests that because bison once numbered up to 45 million (before their slaughter), they, like the cattle that replaced them, maintained short-grass plains as climax grasses through their grazing—not overgrazing that eliminates the "truer" tall grasses. For Larson, neither free-range nor fenced grazing should negatively affect the land.

Writing in 1949 from an economic rather than ecological perspective, however, Mont H. Saunderson takes a more measured approach to the range issue, despite his snipe at conservationists, who he says see "'bogey men' under bed and in dark closets" (985). He takes an economic view of vegetation changes and argues that "it doesn't pay to overgraze this range" (986) because "continued losses in western range resources will . . . be of real consequence to the western economy" (990). His assertions in "Western Range Land Use and Conservation Problems" move beyond the *Open Range* and *The Sea of Grass* arguments for free-range grazing and suggest that, "for the conservation and good use of the *privately-owned* range resources of the West, we need a good program of educational and extension work in range management" (993, emphasis Saunderson's), a position perhaps more closely attuned to that of *Shane.*

These three articles, then, reveal three differing and contradictory opinions. Whereas Weaver and Darland would argue for free-range ranching as the best protector of grasslands habitat, and Larson would suggest grazing in general has no negative effect on the environment, Saunderson would disagree, asserting that the grasslands have been overgrazed and must be conserved. Films produced during the 1940s and 1950s seem to respond with the same ambivalence toward the environmental consequences of ranching.

REPRESENTATIONS OF THE JOHNSON COUNTY WAR IN CONTEMPORARY WESTERNS

Much has been written about *Shane* as a classic Western responding only peripherally to the Johnson County War of 1892 and (more often) featuring the embodiment of the ideal Western hero. Because the film is a product of a period in which positions on ranching methods were ambivalent, its environmental message is limited by its cultural and historical context. Later Westerns addressing the Johnson County War and its consequences, however, were produced after issues surrounding the environmental effect of various ranching methods had been resolved. Westerns from *The Rare Breed* (1966) to *Tom Horn* (1980), *Heaven's Gate* (1980), and *Monty Walsh* (1970, 2003) begin to demonstrate another, perhaps more crucial, struggle underlying all of their battles—that between land use and environmental conservation and preservation; or ultimate destruction and hence failure. The battle between cattle ranchers and homestead farmers grows more complex once environmental and legal history are mined and reveal that ranchers gained more land from the Homestead Act than did family farmers.

The rise of cattle barons in the western United States coincides with the passage of the Homestead Act of 1862, which, along with the Preemptive Act of 1841, provided means for cattlemen to obtain vast acreages of land for little or no money. According to John Upton Terrell, cattle barons used relatives, employees, and even prostitutes to gain the land they wanted to support their free-ranging cattle—160 acres from each person they employed (210). Passage of the Timber Culture Act of 1873 provided them with another way to gain land, this time with the promise to grow trees on at least 40 of the additional 160 acres they gained at no cost (210–12). The Desert Land Act of 1877 helped ranchers secure 640 acres more from each of their proxy as long as they promised to irrigate at least part of it (212–13).

The legal system seemed to be behind ranchers, despite what look like attempts to secure land for poor homestead farmers, until the blizzards of 1886–87 destroyed the ranch economy. The weather's devastation might also have been a product of overgrazing. According to Harold E. Briggs, in the fall of 1886, the Little Missouri Stock Growers' Association "decided that the ranges were badly overstocked in that roundup district and that in the future ranch hands there should refuse to work with new outfits running either cattle or horses" (533). The blizzards came soon after, with storms so powerful and temperatures so low that 80–92 percent of all cattle died (535). These storms, interspersed with drought conditions that destroyed grasses by drying them up or burning them away, nearly eradicated both ranchers and farmers. This disaster is suggested in *The Sea of Grass* when Brewton contemplates stocking shelters with water and hay.

The Rare Breed (1966) highlights the consequences of these blizzards in the 1880s West in the context of the introduction of Hereford cattle as a crossbreed for longhorns. The film is loosely based on the life of rancher William Burgess, who was responsible for bringing the Herefords into the American West from

England. The opening sequence at the 1884 St. Louis Exposition (exhibited on a banner) establishes the context of the film. There, a Herefordshire bull owned by Englishwoman Martha Evans (Maureen O'Hara) takes center stage. A bulldogging cowboy, Sam Burnett (James Stewart), with some intrigue behind his decision, agrees to escort the bull to its new owner, Alexander Bowen (Brian Keith), in Texas, where Evans attempts to convince Bowen to crossbreed it with his Longhorns. After the Hereford is set free on the open range, a worse than usual winter hits. Blizzards destroy most of Bowen's herd, including the Hereford bull, but the crossbred calves survive and provide Burnett and Evans with the basis for a growing mixed-breed herd.

Following the crippling blizzards and droughts of the mid-1880s, the conflict between ranchers and farmers came to a head in the 1892 range war in Johnson County, Wyoming. On the surface, the "war" certainly looks like that between economic classes (with homesteaders on one side and cattle barons on the other), or as Richard Maxwell Brown argues, between those in favor of and those against incorporation. In an attempt to eradicate homestead farmers, the ranchers who had rebuilt their stocks and their association after the blizzards and droughts found a way to justify violent action against homesteaders by declaring them criminals.

With the help of a "literary bureau" (Terrell 256), the cattle association flooded newspapers and magazines with false claims that rustlers had run amok in Wyoming and had to be stopped using frontier justice since the local legal system was corrupt. Wyoming law was changed so a state militia would not interfere with the association's hired guns, whom they called "regulators." Eventually these regulators were defeated by a small army of homestead farmers, but Wyoming's governor Amos Barber intervened, sending false reports to President Benjamin Harrison and the US Senate, although newspaper accounts made clear that the cattle association's claims regarding rustlers were completely untrue and that homesteaders "had gathered to defend their lives against hired gunmen and cattlemen bent on destroying them" and had not incited war (Terrell 259, 261). The movie *Tom Horn* (1980) highlights gunman Tom Horn (Steve McQueen), who not only works for John Coble (Richard Farnsworth), the land baron behind the Johnson County War, but also destroys so many homesteaders that the rancher himself supports legal action against him.

One of the most notorious film versions of the incident, *Heaven's Gate* (1980), depicts the battle with some nods to historical accuracy that foreground the conflict between corporate ranchers and homesteaders as a class struggle against incorporation. Drawing on the war's history, the film puts actual figures at the forefront of the action: Marshal James Averill (Kris Kristofferson), Nathan D. Champion (Christopher Walken), and Ella Watson (Isabelle Huppert). It highlights key battle scenes shot on location with historically accurate costuming and epic-level casts of extras. But the film fails in its accuracy on two accounts: its depiction of homestead farmers as a mass of ignorant immigrants, and its depiction of the consequences of the fighting. In addition, the US Army threatens to arrest the homesteaders, but in the actual crisis, the cattlemen and their association bore the brunt of the military's interventions. Like the claims of the cattlemen who incited the war in the first place, the outcome in *Heaven's Gate* is inaccurate and misleading. And the environmental message it highlights—that ranching is better for the ecology than homestead farming—is based on grounds just as faulty.

The film opens with a graduation speech that seems to set up the cattlemen's argument that the land and its people should remain unchanged. The orator, William Irvine (John Hurt), tells a story about a student striving to write better than he can, to illustrate his argument that "we must endeavor to speak to the best of our ability, but we must speak according to our ability." Irvine's speech contrasts with the immigrant experience articulated by Marshal Averill, who encounters citizens who "steal . . . to keep [their] famil[ies] from starving." The film shows us immigrants seeking "claims verification," not knowing "what's waitin' for 'em" in "the asshole of creation." Their life is also contrasted with that of a "rich firm" that is part of the Stockholders' Association.

Heaven's Gate makes clear that the association is responsible for the hiring of "a big mob from all over the Northwest" to retaliate against what its members claim are unfair practices. The ranchers declare, "these immigrants only pretend to be farmers. But we know many of them to be thieves and anarchists, openly preying on our ranges. No jury in Johnson County will indict them, even in the face of evidence." The cattlemen cite a case in which an immigrant was only convicted of petty larceny for "stealing the hide and the bones" of a cow.

But the loss of land that the association believes better supports ranching than farming is the real reason behind the contest. The ranchers state that the immigrants are there only to "displace us and our capital." They further declare that the land is unfit for farming: "years must pass before the earth can be made to produce the same wealth in any other form." For the cattlemen, the immigrants are "an ignorant, degraded gang of paupers" whose "only stock in trade consists of having large numbers of ragged kids." So the association makes false reports in the film—as in the actual war—and buys "regulators" to kill off a list of unpopular immigrants. But *Heaven's Gate* not only fails because it overreaches with its attempts to take on epic proportions, it also fails because its conclusion is historically inaccurate and its claims about ranching being better for the environment than farming are unsubstantiated—and in the long run, environmentally (and economically) disastrous. The actual Johnson County War was the result of a series of illegal tactics—some that helped restore the range (using wire cutters on barbed-wire fences) and some that incited the violence (hiring gunfighters and issuing inaccurate press releases, for example). In this battle and those that came after it, the small homestead farmer would gain footing, with cattle associations losing most of their power by 1902 (Terrell 266). But the struggle was not only over land and property rights but also over the key idea of land use.

On the surface, cattle ranching seems like a natural choice for the desertlike grasslands of the nineteenth century. In fact, like the original film in 1970, a remake of *Monte Walsh* (2003) responds to the frontier's close after the 1892 range war and valorizes the cowboy mythology as much as did its 1970 original. The film opens in a turn-of-the-century present but then flashes back to Monte (Tom Selleck) and his last winter in a cattle camp. In a clear parallel to the blizzards prior to the Johnson County War, the winter wipes out most of the ranchers, and eastern corporations threaten to destroy the free-range lifestyle that is again depicted as more in harmony with the natural world than fenced ranching. The conflict between free-range ranchers and corporations is manifested by a cowboy's killing himself after stringing too much barbed wire. The film even ends with Monte and his horse jumping over an automobile stuck in the mud—a clear dramatization of the superiority of his more natural lifestyle and closer, environmentally conscious relationship with the natural world. Here it is not the war that is highlighted but the cowboy lifestyle lost after homestead farmers and corporations won the West—at least according to this film.

CONCLUSION: ECOLOGY AND FREE-RANGE RANCHING

The deserts and grasslands of the West were incapable of supporting the masses of livestock herded there. John Upton Terrell first argues against farming, stating that "treeless and barren, swept by searing winds in summer and terrible blizzards in winter, plagued by drought and fires and dust storms, they offered no home to a man with a plow," and these plains were "virtually worthless for farming with the methods and facilities of the nineteenth century" (185). Cattle seemingly survived these conditions and thrived on the grasses there, possibly justifying the existence of ranching and cattle barons while negating the onslaught of homestead farmers.

Walter Prescott Webb, however, goes further, saying that ranching as it was practiced destroyed the land and its potential for sustaining grass for grazing. As he defines it, ranching is "the practice of raising cattle on a large scale," which also includes the potential to overgraze a range. Before, as Nathan Sayre reiterates, "ranching" livestock were raised with an eye to an "ecologically symbiotic" relationship between humans and their livestock (3). Cattle numbers remained small enough that the ecology could easily sustain them: "Due to the Apaches and other factors, trade in cattle was sufficiently limited that increases in stock were primarily endogenous to the region. Rates of animal reproduction depended directly on cycles of plant reproduction" (4).

Environmental historians like Sayre demonstrate that not only homesteading but also free-range ranching were unsuited for the plains, "not sustainable in any environment and would have collapsed even in the lushest and mildest of settings" (241). He goes on to explain:

> four conditions made the cattle boom possible. First, . . . Cattle eating free grass, drinking readily available water and generally following their natural instincts produced more cattle, which were shipped to markets elsewhere; the result was, for a time, staggering profits. Second, this form of capital accumulation was more profitable on the open range of the recently pacified [natural geography of the] West than elsewhere, and it held out the possibility of greater profits than other forms of production and accumulation. . . . Third, means were available for the large-scale movement of capital (as money and as cattle) from one place to another, across this economic-geographical boundary. And fourth, a huge surplus of capital existed and was looking for a form and place

to undergo transformation and reproduction as finance capital. Its availability enabled ranchers to expand their herds immensely, while its demands compelled them to disregard ecological limits until it was too late. (270)

Sayre concludes that all of these elements worked in concert to bring the cattle boom to its inevitable collapse. The ecology of the rangelands was "stripped bare" then, not only because of the huge influx of cattle but also because of the prominence of railroads that made national and international trade possible and a Euro-American culture that supported free-range ranching. His argument also holds ranchers rather than homestead farmers responsible for the environmental degradation still being addressed today.

Once the American Indians and buffalo were annihilated and a post–Civil War economy and transportation system (in the form of the railroad) emerged, cattle ranching boomed and lands became overgrazed. According to historian Conrad J. Bahre, "hundreds of square miles of rangeland [were] denuded of cover; the grasses, even the sacaton in the bottomlands [were] grazed to the ground; the hills [were] covered with cattle trails; erosion [was] rampant; and the oaks and other trees [had] browse lines" (113, qtd. in Sayre 249). Cattle have so destroyed the landscape that even in current photographs by Mike Hudak, the devastation remains. Yet in many Westerns, free-range cattle ranching is depicted as better for the environment than farming, fenced ranching, or sheep ranching, all of which were also in competition for the historical range prior to the 1970s.

Cattle, however, are much more voracious eaters than are sheep or any other livestock or wildlife. According to one study, "domestic livestock consumed 88.8 percent of the available forage (cattle and domesticated horses, 82.3 percent; free-roaming horses, 5.8 percent; sheep, 0.7 percent), leaving 11.2 percent to wildlife species" (Kindschy et al.). Forage use by AUM (animal unit month)—the amount necessary to sustain a cow and calf for one month—indicates that cattle ingest more than any other animal, one animal per AUM. The forage use for sheep is five animals per AUM. Cattle, then, eat five times more forage than do sheep. Yet sheep ranching is denigrated as environmentally unsound in many Westerns.[2]

All of the films discussed above highlight the dangers of sheep ranching, at least north of the dead line, the line cattle ranchers established that sheep crossed at the risk of their lives. They also base their judgment on a belief that cattle and sheep can not coexist, since sheep are said to eat the roots and destroy the grasses on which cattle thrive. Hudak's work, however, makes clear that "between 85% and 90% of the riparian areas throughout the Western states are degraded, primarily from livestock grazing or from livestock related agriculture." In a photo essay highlighting damage that continued into 1999, Hudak shows cattle damage to creeks that affect trout spawning and tree growth. He explains, "damage by cattle . . . is evident, not only by the absence of riparian trees, but also by the down cutting of the banks which occurred by the late nineteenth century." His essay illustrates the negative effect livestock grazing has on forests as well. In a photograph from 2002, Hudak demonstrates how "cattle remove virtually all new vegetation" in the Sequoia National Forest.

Hudak's study also refutes claims by cattle ranchers that only sheep eat grass down to the roots. Instead, "Perennial grasses have extensive roots that stabilize soil against flowing water. Incessant cattle grazing reduces those roots thereby leading to increased erosion." In a study of the grasslands of Arizona, California, and New Mexico, Hudak reveals the damage sheep and cattle have done to the landscape. These "desert and semi-desert grasslands . . . have been grazed by sheep and cattle since the 1860s, and in some locations since the early 1600s. By the late nineteenth century many of the native, perennial grasses had succumbed to this intense grazing thereby opening the way for short-lived weeds to take their place. This conversion is readily apparent during dry seasons after the weeds have blown away." Other animal life too has been harmed by overgrazing, all because the grasslands that sustained them have been degraded. According to Hudak, "farming, livestock grazing, and water diversions have reduced Sacaton [grass] communities to only 5% of their former range." Iain J. Gordon and Herbert H. T. Prins agree, asserting, "Landscapes all over the world have been changing, and herbivores whether they are wild, feral or domestic, live and die at the hand of man" (16).

Despite this clear evidence, recent films like *Open Range,* the later *Monte Walsh,* and *Brokeback Mountain* (2005) rest on an ecological history that is decades out of date. *Monte Walsh* laments the loss of the open range and instead blames incorporation from eastern investors after 1892 and barbed-wire fencing for the loss of both the cowboy lifestyle and the closeness to nature it exults. *Open Range* foregrounds a battle between small open-range ranchers and townspeople against a land baron they defeat. *Brokeback Mountain,* however, highlights the freedom that even sheep herding might provide on an open range without explicitly addressing a range conflict. These films assert claims about ecological damage grounded in old science. Instead of taking a more accurate approach to the environmental costs of ranching, they perpetuate the American ideal of the savage frontier and the rugged individual—the tumbleweed cowboy—who can tame it but use it well.

So when Kevin Costner and Robert Duvall (in *Open Range*) ride peacefully across a bucolic landscape covered by cattle grazing in the distance, we need to recognize the mythology behind the scene. Whether cattle or sheep grazed on a free range or fed on grain in a fenced yard, they contributed to the destruction of the rangelands of the United States. Once the buffalo and American Indians had been destroyed and the railroad lines had been completed, a cattle boom and rush to the West sparked a sense of both populist and progressive versions of progress that are still part of the American mythology. They also ensured irreparable damage to an already vulnerable environment—the grasslands and deserts of the American West.

CHAPTER 2

Mining Westerns

Seeking Sustainable Development in
McCabe and Mrs. Miller

Conflicts in Westerns typically maintain binaries between "little guys" and "big guys," but the frontier in question varies from movie to movie. Although many films examine ranching methods and battles between homestead farmers and ranchers, others highlight the mining frontier. Mining Westerns too address similar conflicts between individuals and corporations, but as with those exploring free-range and fenced ranching, the environment also contributes to these conflicts.

Most Westerns with mining at their center examine dichotomies between corporate and smalltime miners or between miners and ranchers or farmers in traditional ways, with the individual miner usually defeating the corporate miner or rancher. The conflicts here continue the big guy versus little guy theme found in other Westerns, yet the mining on display, no matter how buried in the action-packed plotline, reveals environmental issues worth exploring—those associated with both extraction and the long-term environmental consequences of the techniques themselves. These issues and their consequences are especially evident in *McCabe and Mrs. Miller* (1971), which not only reveals the environmental history of mining but also proposes a more effective way to maintain the ecology of the West: sustainable development.

Binaries between miners and an "other" blur when viewed through a postmodern eco-critical lens that makes these environmental issues more transparent. *The Tall T* (1957), for example, foregrounds a conflict between a drifting ex–ranch foreman, Pat Brennan (Randolph Scott), and a stage robber named Frank Usher (Richard Boone) and his gang. Mining becomes an integral part of the plot, however, because Usher discovers that one of the stage passengers, Doretta Mims (Maureen O'Sullivan) has a rich father, the owner of a corporate mine. To save his skin, Doretta's new husband, Willard (John Hubbard), makes a deal with Usher, agreeing to bargain with Doretta's father and send back a ransom for her release. The father's mine, then, serves as the driving force behind the film's major conflict, one that Brennan wins, not only by saving Doretta but also by making a romantic connection with her after her deadbeat husband is killed. Mining is peripheral here in a film that highlights ecology only in the grim arid landscape typical of Budd Boetticher Westerns. Yet the film complicates binaries between ranchers and miners with the final connection between Brennan and Doretta. It also rests on a history of environmental conflicts associated with mining, especially corporate mining, a history that is manifested in Westerns in which mining takes center stage.

Mining Westerns, then, not only make binaries between corporate and smalltime miners or between miners and ranchers or farmers more complex, they also (both explicitly and implicitly) highlight an environmental legal history that placed economics at the fore and underline the real issues behind such conflicts: land use and ecology. In the mining Westerns viewed for this study, the conflict between corporate and individual miners also reveals two conflicting views of ecology: the fair-use methods of corporations and the sustainable-development aspirations of individuals wishing to maintain resources for future generations of a growing community.

McCabe and Mrs. Miller focuses on zinc mining and comments on the environmental consequences of mining techniques, responding to a history that highlights the dangers of unrestrained landownership. The film both perpetuates and blurs the dichotomy between two "classes" of miners while examining ecological issues in both obvious and opaque ways. The debate between miners and their methods of destroying or sustaining the land continues in the cinematic genre, whether in relation to a sampling of classic Anthony Mann Westerns, cult Westerns from Budd Boetticher, or revisionist Westerns from Sam Peckinpah, Robert Altman, or Nils Gaup. But mining Westerns like these grounded the conflicts they illustrate in an environmental history that has not as yet been resolved. *McCabe and Mrs. Miller,* especially, reveals that history and proposes a more effective way to sustain the ecology of mining. Like other mining Westerns, it responds to a mining history and culture that was a product of the General Mining Act of 1872, a federal law that authorizes and governs prospecting and mining for economic minerals, such as gold, platinum, and silver, on federal public lands: "All citizens of the United States of America 18 years or older have the right under the 1872 mining law to locate a lode (hard rock) or placer (gravel) mining claim on federal lands open to mineral entry. These claims may be located once a discovery of a locatable mineral is made. Locatable minerals include but are not limited to platinum, gold, silver, copper, lead, zinc, uranium and tungsten" (General Mining Law of 1872).

As mentioned earlier, some of this environmental history is reconstructed in Clint Eastwood's *Pale Rider.* Here hydraulic mining is placed at the forefront and then critiqued in relation to California legal history. *Pale Rider* not only problematizes corporate-mining techniques, suggesting that the corporation should be obliterated, but also provides a viable alternative to the consequences of hydraulic mining—individual tin panning

Preacher (Clint Eastwood) witnesses the destructive power of hydraulic mining in *Pale Rider.*

in a cooperative community seeking to plant roots and raise families, an alternative that is attainable with the help of eco-resistance. The movie offers a politically charged solution to the environmental destruction threatened by hydraulic-mining interests: eco-activism that leads to eco-resistance. Since Preacher (Clint Eastwood) and Hull Barret (Michael Moriarty) take a collaborative approach to an eco-resistance that destroys hydraulic-mining camps and offers a way to defend against environmental exploitation, they promote communal sustainable development rather than individual or even populist progress like that Richard Slotkin describes in *Gunfighter Nation.*

GOLD MINING WESTERNS AND
SUSTAINABLE DEVELOPMENT

Although not always discussed in film scholarship, Westerns with gold mining at their center illustrate some of the environmental consequences of a variety of mining techniques. Although the ecological repercussions of gold mining are sometimes a peripheral issue in Westerns, in films like *The Treasure of Sierra Madre* (1947), such environmental degradation is addressed more directly. In this movie, three miners in Mexico battle a desert ecology, in which water is so scarce it is "sometimes more precious than gold," in order to dig up a fortune they can divide equally. With an emotionally unstable American named Dobbs (Humphrey Bogart) at the helm, the men primarily battle greed and emotional unrest. But the film also carries a powerful environmental message that begins when Howard, the old-timer (Walter Huston), lets his companions know when they have taken "about all the gold this mountain has."

Dobbs and the third partner, Curtin (Tim Holt), agree to call it quits, pack up, and leave their mining sites after they have exploited the area. But Howard sees the mountain as the owner of the gold they are taking and feels the men should treat it like a living thing. He explains to them that it will "take another week to break down the mine and put the mountain back in shape . . . make her appear like she was before we came." The old-timer first feminizes the mountain, then further humanizes it when he explains the reasons behind his insistence that they should restore the area: "We wounded this mountain, and it's our duty to close the wounds," he explains. "It's the least we can do to show all our gratitude for all the wealth she's given us."

Dobbs notes how much Howard has both humanized and feminized the mountain and exclaims, "You talk about that mountain as if she were a real woman." The old-timer only agrees, saying that it has "been a lot better to me than any other woman I ever knew." Both Dobbs and Curtin agree to help Howard with his task, then before leaving, they all thank the mountain for the wealth it has provided them. Howard's insistence on restoration gains an ironic tone at the end of the movie after Dobbs is killed by bandits, since the Mexicans steal only his burros and hides, leaving the gold dust to blow in the wind because they think it is nothing more than sand. Howard bursts out laughing when he sees the gold blowing around him. For him it is the judgment of fate or nature since the "gold went back to where [they] found it," a consequence demonstrating how fully the film comes out on the side of nature, despite its more complex psychological themes.

Other gold-mining Westerns set in the nineteenth-century seem to respond to consequences highlighted in the evolution toward the 1872 act, consequences based on free access to mining lands. But the effect on the environment is most clearly generated by the extraction and refining of the gold ore itself, either from veins (primary formations) or placers (secondary formations) on public or private lands. According to Edward Sherwood Mcade's "The Production of Gold since 1850," written in 1897, when extracting veins of gold, "the ore must be mined, often at great depths. It must then be sorted, crushed, stamped, and amalgamated with mercury. Special processes are necessary to treat gold ores which contain sulphur, or certain other substances" (3).

Mcade delineates this process as a way to demonstrate the difficulty of extracting veins of gold ore, but his description also highlights environmental consequences that include the deep extraction as well as the amalgamation of the ore with a toxin—mercury. In the late nineteenth century, this amalgamation was "improved," according to Mcade, with the inclusion of "smelting, chlorination, and the cyanide process" (14), all of which result in toxic runoff that pollutes ground and surface waters and anything with which they come in contact.

He claims that the process is much simpler when extracting ore from placer formations since "the gold is almost entirely freed from foreign substances [because of running water], and it usually lies at no great depth. . . . The miner's work consists merely in the further application of running water to the gold-bearing sand and gravel" by use of pan, cradle, and sluice (4). These are the tools the miners in *The Treasure of Sierra Madre* used. This process acted more lightly on the land than that needed for obtaining vein-formation ore. Another more devastating tool, however, emerged a little later—hydraulic mining.

Hydraulic mining provided an effective way to extract ore from irregular drifts. According to Mcade, "in this process, water is thrown against the gravel banks in large volume and under high pressure, supplied from reservoirs high above the point where washing is done. The banks are shaken by powder blasts, and when the water is turned against them, the gravel is torn down in large quantities through a long line of sluices, and much of the gold is caught on the riffles of the sluice boxes" (12). Hydraulic mining and its effect on the landscape are addressed, as noted, in *Pale Rider* as well as in Warner Brothers cartoons like *Gold Rush Daze* (1939) and *Daffy Duck in Hollywood* (1938). Mcade notes in his article how problems with the equipment are resolved and how modifications to hydraulic elevators are made (12). What he fails to do, however, is discuss any of the environmental repercussions of these technological advances.

Herbert A. Sawin, however, in "One Hundred Years of California Placer Mining," discusses the consequences of hydraulic mining on water sources from the 1870s to 1949. He cites a bulletin from the California Division of Mines, written by Charles Scott Haley, that discusses the effect of immigrant farmers on hydraulic mining. The bulletin notes that with the arrival of these farmers, "land . . . steadily mounted in value," as did the value of the farmers usurping power once monopolized by mining corporations. The debris from hydraulic mining that accumulated in rivers caused "considerable damage to the farmers" (Haley, qtd. in Sawin 58). Haley argues: "As the strength of the agricultural interests grew, protests against the overloading of the rivers became more and more frequent and more powerful until the struggle culminated in the famous Sawyer decision on January 23, 1884. This decision . . . wiped out at one blow property values exceeding one hundred million dollars and indefinitely postponed the addition to the world's wealth of what has been roughly estimated at from five hundred million dollars upwards in the value of placer gold" (Haley, qtd. in Sawin 58). Battles like these culminated in the Caminetti Act of 1893, which restricted runoff and tailings from hydraulic mining.

Dredging, which came later in the nineteenth century, caused further damage to rivers and farmlands, multiplying amounts of debris accumulating in waterways and flooding farmlands. Yet according to Clark C. Spence, "There would be far less criticism of their impact than there had been of hydraulic mining, although 'hysterical devotees of aestheticism' and 'sycophantic black-mailers,' as die-hard mining men called them, did mount limited and ineffectual attacks" (409–10). To describe the effect of dredging, he notes John Gunther's description: "the kind of furrow that an enormous obscene un-housebroken worm might leave—an encrusted seam of broken earth, with mud and rocks lying across a winding trail like excrement" (Gunther qtd. in Spence 410). Spence expands on this description, stating, "Topsoil lay buried deep under stones and cobbles in conical piles, long windrowed hills or rough, irregular heaps with pools between" (410).

These testimonies make clear that just about any form of gold mining had catastrophic environmental results, yet most gold-mining Westerns provide only a cursory view of such destruction, highlighting environmental consequences only in oblique ways. Early mining Westerns like *Greed* (1924), *The Gold Rush* (1925), *The Trail of '98* (1928), and *Smoke Bellew* (1929) play off gold-rush history, focusing on the consequences humans suffer from gold fever. *Greed* foregrounds a miner, but a lottery serves as the source of the money that leads to death and destruction. *The Gold Rush* details the consequences of the Klondike "rush" for riches, drawing on Chaplin's Tramp character and his suffering and success. *The Trail of '98* illustrates the negative repercussions associated with striking it rich as a gold miner and demonstrates humans' subordination to nature. *Smoke Bellew* provides a more positive view of making money through gold mining, pairing it with community and love.

Yet some of John Wayne's early B Westerns peripherally illustrate the environmental consequences of gold mining, or at least they emphasize the technology necessary to excavate for it, typically in an early twentieth-century context, one that demonstrates how far-reaching the 1872 general mining law was (and still is, to a certain extent), in addition to memories of placer mining before the coming of hydraulic-mining corporations. All of these films focus on smalltime placer miners without the tools of technology to destroy the landscape as dramatically as they do in *Pale Rider*. One example is *Blue Steel* (1934), in which Wayne preserves "the richest gold trace run[ning] through the middle of all the ranches" after a lengthy fight that includes the usual horse chase and an explosion that "save the lives of everyone in town." The chase and explosion also save the ranchers' land and, in the process, preserve the region's "topsoil." Wayne's *The Lucky Texan* (1934) also highlights corrupt town businessmen attempting to steal both a ranch and a gold mine in an indirect reference to the 1872 act through the work of two assayers (Lloyd Whitlock and Yakima Canutt), who steal ounces of gold from Jerry Mason (John Wayne) and Jake Benson (George "Gabby" Hayes) as they weigh it. Another Wayne film, *The Trail Beyond* (1934), moves gold mining north to a contest between crooked French Canadian trappers and British Canadians and highlights the pristine nature broken by mining. And in Wayne's *Rainbow Valley* (1935), environmental issues are illustrated only through spectacular visualizations of the devastation of the landscape; the focus of the film is on mail theft and gold mining.

B Westerns featuring Randolph Scott take a similar approach toward gold mining, mentioning only peripherally its environmental history and consequences. *The Fighting Westerner* (1935) begins with gold at its center but ends with both a murder and the discovery of radium. Mining is marginal in the film, but the story briefly discusses two unusual environmental issues: radium mining and ranching on ancient lava beds. In *Virginia City* (1940), a Civil War gold shipment bound for the South must be protected from Northerners by Southerner Vance Irby (Randolph Scott). Gold already refined is the focus here, so we see little explicit connection with ecology in the film, except in relation to its ecological source. That same peripheral strategy is taken with the William Wellman directed *Westward the Women*

(1951), a film in which 100 women journey west to a California gold town to marry miners.

Later full-length mining Westerns addressed environmental issues stylistically as well as through their narratives. In Anthony Mann's *The Far Country* (1954), the landscape is both personified and vilified as an ominous opponent that deserves the destruction caused by miners in the Canadian Rockies during the gold rush. Jeff Webster (James Stewart) leads a cattle drive to Seattle, where he is accused of murdering two of his men. He takes a boat to Skagway, Alaska, where he is arrested for breaking up a hanging, loses his cattle to the sheriff (John McIntire), but is hired by Ronda Castle (Ruth Roman) to serve as point man for her and others heading to Canada for gold and a new dance-hall saloon.

Webster steals back his cattle and leaves Ronda and her followers until an avalanche hits them. His only friend, Ben Tatum (Walter Brennan), convinces Webster to help them, if only half-heartedly. But after Ben is killed, Webster seeks revenge and battles nature and the corrupt sheriff, who does what he can to steal the miners' claims. Lucia Bozzola states in her review, "the film intersperses backdrops and rear projection with location shots, emphasizing the disjunction between Stewart and his surroundings, as he lives by his constant urge to move on rather than integrate himself." Nature, then, is constructed as an antagonist, though also as Webster's ally since he blends in with his surroundings more than he does with a community, even one led by Ronda, his love interest.

The Badlanders (1958), a remake of *The Asphalt Jungle* (1950), replays the revenge plot in an 1898 western setting, highlighting violence to both human and nonhuman nature. Within this typical storyline, however, is a fully timbered underground mine from which Peter Van Hoek (Alan Ladd) and his gang plan their robbery. With the expertise of Vincente (Nehemiah Persoff), they plan to get the ore out of the mine by setting their dynamite to explode at the same time that miners employed by Cyril

Lounsberry (Kent Smith) blow up their tunnel. A deputy stops their plan, embracing community values, but shots of the inner tunnels and exploding dynamite bring home the ecological devastation necessary to bring out the gold.

In contrast, Sam Peckinpah's *Ride the High Country* (1962) establishes a bifurcation between nature and Euro-American culture that laments the loss of both the wilderness and the values embodied by the Wild West. The plot centers on two aging westerners, Steve Judd (Joel McCrea), an ex-lawman, and Gil Westrum (Randolph Scott), a Wild West performer riding along to escort a gold shipment from the mining town of Coarse Gold, which looks as rough as its name. Westrum comments ironically on its repulsively polluted appearance as soon as they enter the town: "Lovely place. A beauty spot of nature—a Garden of Eden for the sore in heart and short of cash." Judd, his partner, replies only, "We didn't come here to admire the scenery."

The scenery in the lifeless gold camp contrasts dramatically with the aging but still virile and untamed high-country landscape. Both Judd and Westrum seem connected with this untamed West, and like the high country, they too are waning. Judd's death at the end parallels the death of the landscape, but Westrum carries on the wild western values Judd embodies. This seems to suggest that even though the Wild West is dying, its ideals will live on, at least for a little while. The film, though, makes a powerful environmental statement about humans' effect on the natural world with the contrasts it emphasizes between the mountains and the town that destroys them—visually and through the brief dialogue between Westrum and Judd.

MacKenna's Gold (1969) makes the landscape not only look threatening (as it does in *The Far Country*) but also shows it transformed because of a violent earthquake the Apaches believe is caused by their "Great Spirit." By the end of the film, the earth seems to reclaim its gold through a series of earthquakes that collapse a pueblo and destroy treasure on the hills of a hidden valley. The plot is thin, but MacKenna (Gregory Peck) escapes with gold still left in his saddlebags. The rest is buried or scattered by the wind, just as it was in *The Treasure of Sierra Madre.*

Other mining films highlight silver, rather than gold, mining. But the four silver-mining Westerns viewed, *Nevada* (1944), *Under Nevada Skies* (1946), *Bells of San Angelo* (1947), and *Grand Canyon Trail* (1948), offer only a glimpse at the environmental history behind the silver and uranium mining they place at their center, a history that reflects devastating consequences to the environment. Additional films highlight other forms of mining—like tungsten in *The Painted Desert* (1931—but all mining Westerns draw on a legal history that provides pioneers with the legal right to mine lands in the American West. Even a brief silver-mining documentary, *Modern Marvels: Silver Mining,* suggests that the ecological damage caused is a thing of the past, a past that has been erased and rewritten. Just as the landscape has been re-vegetated even on top of cyanide pads, these films suggest that cinematic depictions of mining practices rest on a legal history still in effect.

MCCABE AND MRS. MILLER: WHEN STYLE BECOMES ENVIRONMENTALISM

McCabe and Mrs. Miller illustrates how that legal history works for and against community building and the sustainable-development ideals behind it. The film inspires an eco-centric postmodern reading for several reasons. First it rests on a naturalist philosophy and takes a connection between dying men and a dying landscape even further than *Ride the High Country,* since the hero, John McCabe (Warren Beatty), literally dies in the snow, his body buried in a blowing drift while the rest of the town of Presbyterian Church attempts to put out a fire that is burning down their house of worship.

The film also grapples with the same big guys versus little guys conflict found in other mining Westerns, catalyzing with an altercation between McCabe and a corporation from Bear Claw, the town down the mountain from Presbyterian Church, but in *McCabe and Mrs. Miller,* the community nearly fails and is either bought or destroyed by a mining company. The company wants to buy McCabe's holdings and take over the town, but McCabe holds out for too much money and is killed after a long shoot-out with the corporation's assassins. In *McCabe and Mrs. Miller,* eco-resistance destroys the corporate gunslingers, but the film illustrates the cost of that vigilante justice: the death of a hero and the community he attempts to build.

Much has been written about landscape in *McCabe and Mrs. Miller,* primarily by examining the film's setting in relation to plot and character and defining the setting as a character or source of conflict, though without interrogating its environmental implications. Robert MacLean's "The Big-Bang Hypothesis: Blowing up the Image," for example, suggests that the film "may be thought of as a film about snow" (2). Doris Borden and Eric Essman, however, assert that Robert Altman's post-Western "demythologizes both the landscape and the hero within it" because nature is no longer redemptive and the hero "would rather flee and avoid the fight" (38, 9). And Robert T. Self's *Robert Atman's* McCabe and Mrs. Miller: *Reframing the West* highlights the countercultural context of the 1960s and 1970s in which the film was produced and released. Connecting the movie to both late-nineteenth-century environmental history and legal history provides an eco-critical perspective on landscape and setting that is missing from these studies.

The plot centers on McCabe and a whorehouse madam, Mrs. Constance Miller (Julie Christie), who together build a prosperous town. But because both McCabe's community values and the law are usurped by the power of corporate miners and their paid gunmen, the town of Presbyterian Church falters, its previous social ideals visually burning down with the church, as McCabe freezes to death in the snow. Yet the rest of the community bands together and extinguishes the fire, demonstrating its development from McCabe and Mrs. Miller's gritty commune, resting on alcohol and prostitution, to a more traditional society based on more sustainable values. Ultimately, *McCabe and Mrs. Miller* illustrates the end of an era as it grapples with the environmental and human consequences of mechanization. This simple plotline is augmented by Altman's direction, Leonard Cohen's score, and Vilmos Zsigmond's cinematography, all of which set the tone for a film chronicling the death of the Old West and its emphasis on both the individual and community as well as the rise of invisibly powerful corporate interests.

The opening of *McCabe and Mrs. Miller* illustrates both the hopeless battle between humans and a fateful natural world and the drive toward community building. A lone rider climbs a muddy trail in the rain, his buffalo fur masking his face and body. He rides past lines of tree stumps and massive piles of lumber, signs of environmental exploitation. But he also rides past the skeleton of a church, complete with steeple, a sign of community. When the stranger dismounts and takes off his coat, the town's desolate condition becomes clearer. A sluice, more lumber, a bridge, and a saloon look gray in the wet gloom. This is a mountain town in the Pacific Northwest that sprang up for and because of mining.

That mining seems peripheral at first. Sheehan (Rene Auberjonois), the saloon owner, first broaches mining when he tells McCabe about the Chinese in the area: "The Chinese don't own no property. They're just poaching mines." But McCabe is more concerned with community building than mining and buys prostitutes for his new Presbyterian Church business, a brothel to serve the mining town. He rides past the same cut lumber there when he entered town and through ice-covered puddles beside a working steam engine. The conflict between the natural environment and technology enacted by the steam engine's entrance foreshadows the conflict between a pioneering "natural" McCabe and mechanized corporate-mining interests.

Even after Mrs. Miller brings in the "class girls" for a real brothel, mining still seems peripheral, the hidden source of income for the community. Instead, Mrs. Miller's role as businesswoman and partner to McCabe is seen as breaking gender and genre rules, according to Brittany R. Powell and Todd Kennedy. Powell and Kennedy assert that *McCabe and Mrs. Miller* "works with largely the same themes as *Brokeback [Mountain]*, namely those of sexuality, gender, violence, and capitalism, but in a manner that deconstructs the very Western genre within which [Altman] is careful to situate his film" (116). They argue that "this genre destruction, furthermore, becomes the driving conflict in Altman's film, and it does so in a way that makes the audience question and define sexuality instead of simply accepting it as a part of an even more fully defined mythic structure" (116).

It is the equal business partnership between McCabe and Mrs. Miller, rather than mining, that seems to center the film, so when his men seem lackadaisical about their work, McCabe tells them, "I'm paying you boys . . . after you've been in them mines all day, so you'll have something to do besides go home and play with Mary Five Fingers." Instead of focusing on individual mining, McCabe and Mrs. Miller together build a community in Presbyterian Church where men bathe before entering their brothel, listen to music on a music box, and celebrate a prostitute's birthday. Mrs. Miller even provides a home for a widowed mail-order bride (Shelley Duvall). Although Patrick McGee highlights the pair's capitalist tendencies, their drive for money rests on a yearning for community, if not in Presbyterian Church then in San Francisco.

That community is shattered, however, when Eugene Sears (Michael Murphy) and Ernie Hollander (Antony Holland) confront McCabe as representatives of the M. H. Harrison Shaughnessy Mining Company. Sears explains, "The truth of the matter is, Mr. McCabe, we're interested in the mining deposits up here." McCabe still sees mining as peripheral to his business, so after a drink, he responds: "There's nothing to misunderstand. You want to buy out the zinc. Go ahead. I don't own any goddamn zinc mines." But then he tells the story of a frog that "got ate by the eagle" and, in the punch line, seems to get away with his cleverness, like Brer Rabbit and the briar patch. Still in the eagle's stomach, the frog asks how high they're flying, and when the eagle says they are "up about a mile, two miles," the frog exclaims, "Well, you wouldn't shit me now, would you." Rather than laughing and joining McCabe in a drink, however, Sears gets right down to business. They do not wish to join the community McCabe and Mrs. Miller have built here. They would like to "buy out [McCabe's] holdings . . . in Presbyterian Church" for $5,500, a price McCabe turns down, thinking he is negotiating with reasonable businessmen.

Sears and Hollander reject McCabe and Mrs. Miller's community, even balking at free offers for women at the brothel. After McCabe turns down another offer—for $6,250—the men leave. McCabe still believes that he is negotiating with members of a community rather than representatives of a corporate business with no such ideals. When he discusses his deal with Mrs. Miller, however, she understands the contrast between them and Shaughnessy: "Zinc. I should have known. You turned down Harrison Shaughnessy. You know who they are? You just hope they come back. They'd soon put a bullet in your back as look at ya." When McCabe gives Sears his final "no," they too fail to comprehend his position since their corporate mentality rests only on profit at any cost. "You've done a wonderful job here. You've built up a beautiful business. And here we are, ready to give you a substantial gain in capital. An offer from one of the most solid companies in the United States, and you say, 'no.' Well, frankly, I don't understand." And Sears warns him about the possible outcome: "I don't have to tell you that our people are going to be quite concerned, if you know what I mean."

McCabe, though, still believes that he and the Shaughnessy men share a communal business relationship. He replies to Sears: "The way I feel about this is that you gentlemen come up here, and you want a man in my position to sell off his property. I think there's got to be a good reason," and he provides the men with a possible price for a buyout. McCabe still thinks they will negotiate, but Mrs. Miller realizes that they share a different ideology and attempts to persuade him to leave.

His misguided belief continues even after Sears and Hollander are replaced by a huge gunman named Butler (Hugh Millais) and his sidekicks, Breed (Jace Van Der Veen) and Kid (Manfred Schulz). Butler will not make a deal with McCabe, claiming he is bear hunting, but he does reveal much about the kind of mining Shaughnessy wants to implement in Presbyterian Church. This also highlights the environmental concerns related to the incorporation of mining—a movement from placer to vein-mining techniques that include hydraulic mining and dredging:

> Up in Canada now, they're blasting tunnel for under ten dollars a foot, all done with a pigtail. They've got some new explosives up there. Fantastic stuff. They give it to Johnny Chinaman, send him in, down comes forty-five, fifty tons of rock, and one dead Chinaman. But you sir, do you know what the fine is for killing a Chinaman? Fifty dollars maximum. The inspector's working for the company; four times out of five, it's an accident. You could do this here with your own zinc. All you've got to do is give the bugger a box of this stuff, put him down the hole, up to the rock face—crash—and there's your zinc. Sixty-five cents a foot.

Although we never see mining in the film, miners populate the town and support its saloons, whorehouses, and restaurants. The interruption made by the company's thugs portends the death of the frontier, a demise that literally destroys McCabe and ushers Mrs. Miller into a permanent opium dream. For us, references to dynamite and its power to blast tunnels and kill "Johnny Chinaman" most clearly highlight the environmental message hidden behind the narrative: With corporate mining (led by Shaughnessy) comes blasting that leaves no room to rebuild the mountain as the three prospectors do in *The Treasure of Sierra Madre*.

In *McCabe and Mrs. Miller*, even the law supports this unfettered vision of progress embraced by Shaughnessy and his men. Unlike *Pale Rider*, where the government outlaws hydraulic mining, a fair-use option that destroys rather than sustains the environment, *McCabe and Mrs. Miller* shows how powerless McCabe and even the law are against the power of corporations. When McCabe visits the Shaughnessy Mining Company and discovers that Sears and Hollander have left, he turns to a lawyer, Clement Samuels (William Devane), to save his own life through legal channels. Samuels agrees to represent him for free, as "a little guy," because he believes winning the case will help him become "the next senator from the state of Washington." He makes a powerful speech about McCabe's status as a pioneer, but it rests on his own belief in community rather than corporate exploitation:

> When a man goes into the wilderness and with his bare hands, gives birth to a small enterprise, nourishes it and tends it while it grows, I'm here to tell you that no sons of bitches are going to take it from him.... You take that company, Harrison Shaughnessy. They have stockholders. Do you think they want their stockholders and the public thinking their management isn't imbued with fair play and justice, the very values that make this country what it is today? Busting up these trusts and monopolies is at the very root of the problem of creating a just society. McCabe, I'm here to tell you that this free enterprise system of ours works. And working within it, we can protect the small businessman, and the big businessman, as well.

Samuels draws on community values in his argument, but McCabe is now convinced that Butler intends to kill him, so

a long court battle will not save him, even if it stops Shaughnessy. Samuels, however, asserts that McCabe's death could work
for the community: "Until people stop dying for freedom, they
aren't going to be free. I can see it now, on the front page of
The Washington Post, right next to a picture of William Jennings
Bryan: 'McCabe strikes a blow for the little guy.'"

McCabe is nearly convinced and returns to Presbyterian
Church and Mrs. Miller. But refusing her pleas to run away, he
confronts the real violence Butler and his men bring with them,
the violence that blasts mountains and kills an innocent cowboy
(Keith Carradine). As if fulfilling the lawyer's dream, McCabe sacrifices himself for the town. Once he has killed off his three pursuers one by one, a wounded McCabe tries to drag himself back
to town through the snow. With Mrs. Miller deep in an opium
dream, the residents join forces not to help McCabe but to save
the burning church, set on fire when Butler mistakenly shoots
the pastor, who had just forcibly evicted McCabe from the sanc-
tuary within, as if he were evicting him from the community.

McCabe and Mrs. Miller deconstructs the Western genre, blowing up the hero myth McCabe at first seemed to represent.
The film does not valorize violence or a Western hero. Instead,
McCabe hides in an open shed and shoots his pursuers stealthily
and out of fear. The community works together to put out the
church fire. McCabe fights alone. He eradicates the three faces
of the corporation so the community can rebuild itself on the
values of a church rather than the brothel both McCabe and
Mrs. Miller have left behind. But neither his death nor her departure are valorized. Instead, extreme close-ups show McCabe's
snow-covered body and ice-streaked face and Mrs. Miller's
oblivious opiate stare, two views that illustrate their powerless
state. McCabe and Mrs. Miller confront nature and build a business community, confront a mining corporation and seem to
succeed, even in the face of their own sacrifices. But they vanish
in the face of change and represent a dying frontier and the drive
toward a more traditional community like that in *Pale Rider.*

The death of John McCabe (Warren Beatty), alone in the snow in *McCabe and Mrs. Miller*

In *McCabe and Mrs. Miller* the community members will not quit. Instead, they will build homes, schools, churches, raise their families, and sink roots—just as the people did in *Pale Rider*. And those roots rest on zinc mining without the corporate interference that kills off towns and community ideals.

MINING HISTORY, THE GENERAL MINING LAW OF 1872, AND EMPIRE BUILDING

Destructive corporate mining on display in films such as *McCabe and Mrs. Miller* and *Pale Rider* responds to the General Mining Act of 1872 and coincides with mining history in California (where *Pale Rider* is set) as well as other western states. Hydraulic mining was discontinued in California in the 1950s, and Montana outlawed it in 1972. According to "Gold Fever!: Giant Gold Machines—Hydraulic Mining": "Hydraulic mining may indeed have been an efficient mining method, but at what cost to the environment? Hydraulic monitors blasted 1.5 billion cubic yards of soil and rocks from the Sierra hillsides . . . [and] it was washed through sluice boxes and dumped into the nearest creek or river canyon." According to a visitor to the remains of a hydraulic-mining site, "Nature here reminds one of a princess fallen into the hands of robbers who cut off her fingers for the jewels she wears" (qtd. in "Gold Fever!").

Despite legal victories for environmentalists, however, environmental problems associated with mining in the West continue. Jared Diamond's recent study of why some civilizations disappear or evolve, *Collapse: How Societies Choose to Fail or Succeed,* validates environmental legal history. The study begins with a look at a current example of a "society" on the brink of collapse: Bitterroot Valley of southwestern Montana. On the surface this valley community appears to be an environmental Mecca where the leisure classes can purchase and preserve large ranchlands or fly fish in what seem like pristine streams. Diamond's study, however, sees a different ecology, one in which "almost all of the dozen types of problems that have undermined pre-industrial societies in the past, or that now threaten societies elsewhere in the world," exist (35). According to Diamond, problems associated with "toxic wastes, forests, soils, water (and sometimes air), climate change, biodiversity losses, and introduced pests" threaten to destroy the current society of Bitterroot Valley (35).

Toxic waste stands out because its biggest culprit is mining—copper, silver, and gold mining in the western United States since the early nineteenth century. Mining itself certainly destroys the landscape. Hydraulic mining depicted in *Pale Rider* erodes soil as it tears down trees, pulling them out by the roots, and sweeps away rocks and topsoil. Strip mining, a process still practiced, also tears away trees, grasses, and soil to get to the minerals (typically coal) below. When hills and mountains are "topped" for coal, their tops are literally cut off, providing access to the ores below but leaving a desecrated landscape behind. As historian Ray Allen Billington asserts, "by 1886 the prospectors were drifting away, leaving scarred hills, slashed gullies, and ghost towns behind them" (543). The USDA Forest Service also reports that because timbering techniques like "the square-set" that were used in silver mines like the Comstock left "a tunnel of timber to house the mine, . . . [f]orests of the Sierra Nevada were depleted to obtain the estimated 600 million board feet of timber used in the mine from 1860 to 1880."

All of these processes, however, not only destroy the landscape and forests but also dig up excess waste rock and tailings containing toxic waste, much of which make their way to waterways and soil—usually deliberately through water-driven runoff systems. Diamond counts 20,000 abandoned mines where toxic waste may become an issue and cites examples from 1907 to the present that support his claims (35). In 1907 the Anaconda Copper Mining Company, for example, was sued by ranch owners who blamed the company's copper mine and smelter for killing their cattle by poisoning watering sources with their toxic runoff (Diamond 36).

The Anaconda Copper Mining Company was established in the 1880s in Butte, Montana, and quickly grew rich because of several productive mines in a few square miles (Richter 689). According to F. E. Richter, even these rich ores were milled "to lessen the work that has to be done by the furnaces" (690). The company also needed smelters, so "a site, named Anaconda, was chosen, 26 miles from Butte, where there was a plentiful water supply and where the operations would not inflict the inevitable smoke nuisance on the town of Butte (691). Otis E. Young Jr. asserts that these "obnoxious fumes caused by open-air heap roasting . . . made both Orange County and the Copper Basin almost intolerable to all but human life" (135). The environmental consequences of smelting is touched on here—heavy use of water resources and air pollution—but it is exacerbated during the refining process, when electrolysis is applied. Copper smelting and refining also produces sulfuric acid, "using the sulphur in the furnace fumes" (Richter 694).

This acid was used to leach metals at other mines and smelters. Mines in Arizona, including the Anaconda, "from the early eighteen-nineties on, leached copper from some of its low-grade ores, using acid made at its smelter" (Richter 704). According to Young, by 1871 "the western copper ore deposits which

Dr. James Douglas helped pioneer would slowly but certainly usurp the crown [of copper mining] which Michigan had seized from Appalachia," especially in southeast Arizona "at the camp of Bisbee" (137). This ore, then, made southeast Arizona "king" of copper, a title that moved westward from the Appalachian Mountains over the years. Douglas and "a young British-born physician, Edward Weston," were the first to "use electrolysis and redeposition in a solution of copper sulfate to win virtually pure copper from heavily contaminated matte anodes" (Young 135).

Such conflicts between cattle ranchers and copper-mining companies come up often in Westerns, highlighting the environmental message behind the ranchers' complaints either explicitly or implicitly. Three examples highlight the range of films in this category: *Back in the Saddle* (1941), a Gene Autry musical; *Copper Canyon* (1950), a Paramount B movie about copper smelting; and *Broken Lance* (1954), an Edward Dmytryk film starring Spencer Tracy that explicitly critiques copper runoff's negative effects on drinking water, especially for cattle. *Broken Lance* most powerfully articulates its environmental message and, like *Pale Rider,* suggests a better way. In *Broken Lance,* however, ranching is constructed as the most environmentally sound way to utilize resources in sustainable ways, a claim that is questionable even in 1954, the film's release date. What is clear, however, is that toxic waste from copper smelters in Westerns set in nineteenth-century Arizona and the rest of the Southwest and Pacific Northwest rests on a history of mining-waste runoff destroying water sources both by poisoning them and clogging them with sediment.

Mining in the West also rests on an American cultural history that legitimates a pioneer spirit meant to "tame" an uncivilized land by not only ranching and farming but also mining. Just as there were homestead acts that provided free land for ranchers and farmers, there was also the 1872 mining act, which stated: "All valuable mineral deposits in lands belonging to the United States, both surveyed and unsurveyed, are hereby declared to

Cattlemen destroy copper-mining office in *Broken Lance*

be free and open to exploration and purchase, and the lands in which they are found to occupation and purchase, by citizens of the United States and those who have declared their intention to become such." This law applied to all white men but not to American Indians or married women.

According to Robert McClure and Andrew Schneider in "The General Mining Act of 1872 Has Left a Legacy of Riches and Ruins," their story for the *Seattle Post-Intelligencer,* "public lands the size of Connecticut have been made private under the terms of the 1872 law." Although the law has its roots in an 1848 push by Col. R. B. Mason to obtain, as Mason put it, "rents for . . . land, and immediate steps . . . to collect them, for the longer it is delayed the more difficult it will become" (qtd. in McClure and Schneider), the mining law evolved into "an incentive to those [miners] willing to push West and settle the frontier" (McClure and Schneider), an incentive that has had dire effects on the environment.

Opening lands for mining meant increased deforestation and erosion of topsoil. It also resulted in the toxic runoff discussed in *Back in the Saddle* and *Broken Lance* since copper ore (like any other ore) is leached "by misting cyanide over a barrel or large vat filled with crushed ore" (McClure and Schneider). According to McClure and Schneider, "The ore is often high in sulfides, and water passing through the rock and soil creates sulfuric acid, which in turn leaches poisonous heavy metals into run-off water, with iron in the rock turning streams an orange-red." Their news report traces decades of environmental problems from 1872 to 2001, when the article was published. The 1872 law remains in effect and still allows private companies to open public lands for mining, and the repercussions of cyanide use still affect western environments. Today the largest liquid-waste pit in the United States is in Butte, Montana, and it has become a tourist attraction.

CONCLUSION: CONTINUING EFFECTS OF THE 1872 GENERAL MINING LAW

The ongoing debate regarding mining and toxic-waste removal in and around mines, sometimes from more than a hundred years ago, is reflected in recent films like *Eight Legged Freaks* (2002) and *Silver City* (2004), movies set in the polluted West, as well as current events. *Eight Legged Freaks,* a science fiction comedy, foregrounds toxic-waste disposal. Even though the waste does not come directly from mining practices, it is dumped into a pond and into an abandoned mine, enters the water system, and genetically alters various spiders. *Silver City* highlights corruption and environmental damage surrounding a governor's race in Colorado. Ironically, cyanide-waste disposal is at the film's center: Instead of cleaning up this material, corporate officials dump it into an abandoned silver mine, where it leaks into surface waters and kills both fish and people.

The continuing ramifications of the General Mining Act of 1872 and the repercussions of toxic-waste disposal make it clear that mining in the West still affects us and our ecology today. The Anaconda Mines cited in *Collapse* continue to cause ecological damage. On March 30, 2006, for example, the US Army Corps of Engineers "authorized a gold mining corporation to dump millions of tons of mine tailings into pristine Lower Slate Lake in Alaska" ("No to Dumping Toxic Mine Waste"). Mining

Westerns since the 1920s reflect an ecological and legal history resting on politics that are ecologically destructive. The Westerns viewed for this book reinforce this message, either implicitly or explicitly, all having ties to unsound environmental policies. So when Preacher and Hull Barret blow up hydraulic-mining tools, Matt Devereaux or a Gene Autry sidekick blast and tear down a copper smelter, or McCabe dies in the snow, early environmentalists are on display taking the law in their own hands to save the land. Environmental legal history like this seems to go hand in hand with eco-terrorism. Both are reflected in American Westerns.

CHAPTER 3

Is Water a Right?

The Ballad of Cable Hogue and Environmental Law

The "big guys" versus "little guys" dichotomy found in a variety of Westerns pertains not only to cattle ranching and mining, as in *Open Range* (2003) and *Pale Rider* (1976), but also may highlight a battle over water rights or flood control. Definitions of the Western as a genre tend to promote the transformation of the desert lands of the Southwest into a garden, pointing to water rights and irrigation as mechanisms of a prosperous land. So it comes as no surprise that many films foreground consequences of big guys controlling water use so that little guys must either pay exorbitant prices or suffer drought conditions and thirst. In John Wayne's *Riders of Destiny* (1933), for example, the antagonist in the film, James Kincaid (Forest Taylor), has one of the only sources of water in the area and is charging outrageous prices to use it. Small farmers and ranchers, then, are forced to sell their land because they cannot afford Kincaid's prices until a government agent (Wayne, as Singin' Sandy) ensures that area farmers have free access to water.

The Ballad of Cable Hogue (1970), however, most clearly illustrates the effects land-acquisition laws had on development and, ultimately, environmental damage in the West. This film demonstrates the negative consequences of progress, whether for the few (progressivist) or the many (populist). As a powerless individual, Cable constructs an empire for himself based on ownership of water, a commodity he sells for profit. The water sustains him but is doled out to travelers by the cup for a fee. Commerce underpins his use of resources and highlights the consequences of progress as empire building in the West: environmental degradation and loss of community.

TWO SIDES OF THE WATER-RIGHTS ISSUES: DROUGHT VERSUS FLOOD

Two powerful Gene Autry films, *Man of the Frontier* (1936; later re-released as *Red River Valley*) and *Rovin' Tumbleweeds* (1939), illustrate the environmental consequences of controlling water and water rights. In *Man of the Frontier,* Autry presents us with a clear solution to drought—a lack of water sometimes resulting from overuse of land and water. And *Rovin' Tumbleweeds* provides us with viable solutions to flooding—another consequence of failure to control water usage.

Both of these films provide environmentalist readings of water use in the West, blatantly asserting wise-use policies that hark back to New Deal programs and the documentaries that promoted them.[1] Yet they also highlight wise use and sustainable development over fair use as a viable model for developing the West, development that ultimately destroys the frontier and exploits the very resources the films claim to conserve. Despite their populist politics, water-rights films from Autry's *Man of the Frontier* and *Rovin' Tumbleweeds* to Sam Peckinpah's *The Ballad of Cable Hogue* foreground an environmental history that valorized both water and land as property—a fair-use model resting on conquest more than conservation.

Ronald Bailey promotes such a "fair use" model in articles for *Reason* and for the *National Interest*. In "The Law of Increasing Returns," for example, Bailey asserts: "As history has amply shown, technological progress makes possible the economic growth that allows future generations to meet their own needs. There is only one proven way to improve the lot of hundreds of millions of poor people, and that is democratic capitalism. It is in rich democratic capitalist countries that the air and water are becoming cleaner, forests are expanding, food is abundant, education is universal, and women's rights respected. Whatever slows down economic growth also slows down environmental improvement." Unfettered economic growth, then, promotes environmental conservation, according to Bailey, so resources should be used as needed to advance economic development and thus environmental consciousness. Wise use and sustainable policies, though, contradict Bailey's premise. As the World Commission on Environment and Development declares, sustainable development is "[d]evelopment that meets the needs of the present without compromising the ability of future generations to meet their own needs" ("Report"). Development, then, is restrained in order to sustain resources for the future.

These three water-rights films first foreground wise-use ideals like those valorized in New Deal documentaries. Autry's *Man of the Frontier* highlights the dustbowl issues emphasized in *The Plow that Broke the Plains* within the parameters of an action-packed Western narrative. *Man of the Frontier* opens with a prologue warning that introduces the environmental concerns of the film: "Drought: The grim enemy that devastated once prosperous farm and ranch lands. Men have learned that bitter lesson of unpreparedness. Throughout stricken areas today, they are rallying forces to fight back with their only weapon—water." Water is introduced as a weapon to combat drought, then the camera pans to images of a dam and the water it holds back, along with a sign reading, "Red River Land and Irrigation Company." A company formed by area ranchers have pooled their resources to build this dam and a canal to irrigate their lands. When Gate Five is blown up, a rancher exclaims that rivals will "not stop at murder to stop us from finishing the canal," establishing the conflict of the film. Steve Conway (Boothe Howard) and the town banker, Hartley Moore (Frank LaRue), scheme to thwart the ranchers so that they can take over the water rights for the reservoir and canal and make a profit from the thirsty ranchers. Gene Autry and his sidekick, Frog Millhouse (Smiley Burnette), intervene and save the dam and canal, but more importantly, they save the ranchers' drought-ridden land.

Autry enters *Man of the Frontier* as a rancher who volunteers to serve as a ditch-rider for the Red River Land and Irrigation Company and protect the canal and dam, since the previous ditch-rider has been killed when the gate is dynamited. While damage to the gate is repaired, the water is shut off, endangering a whole season's crops as ranchers exclaim, "That water is our lifeblood." Autry's ditch-riding might save the land and the crops and cattle it sustains.

The film intertwines mining with cattle ranching and sheep ranching to explain the presence of dynamite, so it comes as no surprise when the banker's thugs set up Gate Nine for destruction. Their plan is to kill Autry when the dynamite goes off so they can stop construction, but Autry notices the dynamite and shoots the fuse off with his gun. When he comes back to town, the banker's henchmen go back to retrieve any dynamite left at the site—evidence of their foul play—but Autry and Frog rope one of the men and knock the other into the water. They take them back to town, but the men are set free since there is no evidence to convict them.

At this point Autry does not know who is behind the sabotage, but he stands behind George Baxter (Sam Flint), who heads the dam project, and his daughter, Mary (Frances Grant). After a series of altercations, including one that ends with Autry dragging the banker's men back across a desert, he saves the dam and canal for the ranchers and the Red River Land and Irrigation Company by retrieving a stolen payroll from Moore and Conway's henchmen. They celebrate with a song—"Red

Gene Autry and Frog (Smiley Burnette), saving a dam from destruction in *Man of the Frontier (Red River Valley)*

River Valley"—but the film's parting words highlight its environmental message regarding water as a weapon: held back by a dam and maneuvered through a canal, water will "transform the Red River Valley into one of the richest of farm lands in the world."

As with the New Deal documentaries, drought and the parched, infertile farm and ranch lands it causes are represented as environmental problems that can be solved with engineering miracles like dams and irrigation canals. Although it seems that Autry has defeated the corporate big guys to protect the small ranchers he represents, these "miracles" were, according to Frederick Jackson Turner, a product of the New West, one he said required "expensive irrigation works, . . . cooperative activity, . . . capital beyond the reach of the small farmer," and vast paternal enterprises of federal reclamation (258). In other words, the environmental solutions on display in *Man of the Frontier* promote corporate conquest and development rather than preservation of individual pioneer values.

In this film and in *The Ballad of Cable Hogue,* ownership of water builds empires, preserving and expanding a town and its values in the Autry film and conquering a piece of desert for one man in Peckinpah's movie. Water as property inevitably ties the frontier to capitalist and ultimately corporate values, so much so that Cable Hogue is literally run over by a product of corporate mechanization, a motorcar. As Wells A. Hutchins has explained: "Water, as well as land, is property. And just as privileges of land use are rights of property, so privileges of water use are recognized as property rights entitled to protection under the due process clause of the federal constitution" (867).

Water rights, according to Hutchins, can be categorized in two ways. The first is "[t]he riparian doctrine, based upon ownership of land bordering a natural stream. Such a situation of the land entitles the owner to use water of the stream on his riparian land." The second category is "[t]he appropriation doctrine. This sanctions the taking of water from a stream for use on or in connection with land, which need not border the stream. The essential principle is that priority in time of beginning the diversion and beneficial use of water gives priority of right." Thus, "the riparian right of a private landowner is held in the West to have accrued when title to the land passed from public to private ownership." The appropriation doctrine, Hutchins explains, was adopted by groups from the Utah Mormons to the California gold miners, who "developed comparable systems of priority of rights to the use of water based solely upon priority in time of initiating the uses" (867).

Riparian rights seem most associated with private ownership, while appropriation connects most clearly with public-land acts, according to Hutchins. Individuals seem to have the right to appropriate water on public lands, but once land is secured as private property, the owner gains control of its use. This battle between public and private use of water underpins *Man of the Frontier, Rovin' Tumbleweeds,* and *The Ballad of Cable Hogue,* but the seeming victory of the "little guy" over corporate interests masks the empire building all three films validate.

Autry's *Man of the Frontier* draws on New Deal issues but in conjunction with water-right issues from the nineteenth century, when the Homestead Act and the Desert Land Act provided opportunities for individuals to stake a claim on lands that provided the only access to water in the region. According to Donald Worster, this "increase in federal authority over western water in collusion with corporate water aggrandizement has produced a tragedy of unparalleled proportions" (*Rivers of Empire* 19). Bankers and corporate ranchers in the film take advantage of this access, attempting to monopolize water rights for financial gain no matter whom or what they needed to blow up to control vital resources.

These two figures represent what Worster calls the "emergence and collusion of two groups that constitute the 'power elite'—agribusiness and government officials, especially those in the Bureau of Reclamation" (*Rivers of Empire* 19). The conflicts in the film, then, are a product of both a contemporary and old West context. Water as a weapon to combat drought and bring back fecundity to the land makes *Man of the Frontier* a blatant environmental Western. But fecundity serves civilization in the film—a developing West seeking the progress of a new empire—rather than a wilderness. Autry's community values seem to overpower the corporation and ensure that small ranchers and town folk gain access to the benefits irrigation provides, but the consequences of rerouting water to support cattle grazing are unexplored, and human development outweighs land conservation.

The film adds weight to Worster's claim that "[a] by-product of this collusion [between agribusiness and government] has been human social costs in evasions of reclamation law and exploitation of field workers, as well as massive environmental despoliation resulting from dams, reservoirs, aqueducts, and economic (especially agricultural) development made possible through modern technology" (qtd. in Hundley 15). The human costs are on display in *Man of the Frontier*, but the environmental despoliation is only addressed as a problem irrigation can solve. Once the town and its surrounding ranches are provided with water, the land will prosper, the film seems to suggest. *Man of the Frontier*, then, illustrates an ecology based in the belief that modern technology can conserve and rejuvenate the environment, an ideology not only proven false by contemporary environmental history but also partly to blame for the overdevelopment that visions of progress as empire building encourage.

Autry's *Rovin' Tumbleweeds* (1939) also places New Deal programs at the forefront, this time in relation to flooding like that combated in *The River* (1938), a documentary promoting Tennessee Valley Authority (TVA) projects to thwart flooding on the Mississippi River and its tributaries. *The River* makes it clear that overuse of the land has caused erosion and loss of topsoils that have contributed to the river's flooding. Pare Lorenz wrote and directed *The River* as a tool for the policies of the Roosevelt administration and the US Farm Security Administration, policies that might be seen both as socialist and as appropriate for eradicating some of the problems caused by the Great Depression. The film also promotes "the Tennessee Valley Authority (TVA) as the solution to problems of flooding, agricultural depletion, and electrification" (Bordwell and Thompson 58).

Lorentz's documentary claims that the best way to solve the problems humans have caused by their degradation of nature is to implement a technological project driven by culture and mankind: the TVA's construction of enormous dams like the Norris Dam, started in 1933 and finished on March 4, 1936, at the head of the Tennessee River. As the film's narrator argues: "The old river *can* be controlled. We had the power to take the Valley apart. We have the power to put it together again."

According to *The River,* the TVA's dams "will transform the old Tennessee into a link of fresh water pools locked and dammed, regulated and controlled."

Autry's *Rovin' Tumbleweeds* concentrates on flooding as a problem without discussing its cause. The film instead focuses on its solution—a flood-control bill facilitating programs like those promoted in *The River* but that the local congressman (Fuller; Gordon Hart) chooses not to support. Like *Man of the Frontier, Rovin' Tumbleweeds* opens with a message about the power of water. The first part of this message reads, "Water—Man's Greatest Friend," and then we hear a thunderclap and see thrashing storms, and the rest of the message appears: "but unleashed, man's greatest foe." A newspaper headline shows the repercussions of the storm when it declares, "Green River Bursts Banks."

The force of water has been established, but Autry states the cause in an interview with a radio reporter: "We wouldn't have had this storm—I just wanna tell ya—we wouldn't have suffered this loss of life and property if that cheap politician Congressman Fuller had put through that flood control bill." He blames politicians for the flooding without referencing a war against nature, though a radio interviewer proclaims, "It looks like nature has called a truce," when the storm ends. Unlike the announcer, Autry has a philosophy that lines up with that portrayed in *The River:* to save working farmers and ranchers and their land, the government should intervene.

The connection of *Rovin' Tumbleweeds* to New Deal programs rings through this community-minded film. After halting flooding, for example, Autry sings a song about flooding rivers with an image of New Deal proletariats in the background. Newspaper headlines that spring up throughout the film carry a similar message. When ranchers washed out by the flooding migrate to Rand County in search of work, headlines read: "Community Minded, Promised Land." And Congressman Fuller serves as a representative of the company keeping them out (the Randville

Development Corporation), offering a tangible entity for Autry and his fellow workers to oppose, even going to jail to fight for their right to work.

Autry facilitates the contest between working people and greedy corporations and politicians initially by singing on the radio and donating his earnings to the people, but his efforts are unsuccessful. Headlines read, "One man relief agency on behalf of all the migratory workers—unfortunately Gene's generous contributions have proved pitifully inadequate in the face of the ever increasing hordes pouring into Rand County." When he and Congressman Fuller meet at a railway station, however, Autry chooses to be "the man in office who'll do something" to stop the flooding—a long-term environmental solution that will help ranchers reclaim their lands. The conflict is heightened, then, since viewers discover that Stephen Halloway (Douglass Dumbrille) and Fuller are a team determined to buy up the land along the Green River before flood control goes through. Autry's efforts for the workers pay off: he saves the radio station and also saves a camp of migrants from a sheriff who wants to burn them out—and he wins the congressional election in a landslide.

After a series of failures in Washington, D.C., Autry seems on the brink of getting the flood-control bill through. But the film takes an odd turn at the end when another storm erupts and the Green River floods again. Autry convinces the Rand County migrants to help him sandbag the banks of the river, and Halloway has a change of heart, joining in with the migrants. On the radio an announcer says, "With courage and cooperation" they all "work side by side" on the sandbagging effort; in addition, flood control is passed. Halloway even gives his money to labor in an act that seems to draw on New Deal socialist inclinations. Environmental degradation is thwarted by community efforts that cross class lines. The film argues effectively for measures like dams and levies, just as do New Deal documentaries like *The River.*

But just as in *The River, Rovin' Tumbleweeds* postulates only one solution to flooding: government-controlled technology as flood control. David Bordwell and Kristin Thompson point out, "Here is a case where one solution [building large dams like those on the Tennessee], because it has been effective in dealing with the problem, is taken to be *the* solution" (61). Bordwell and Thompson describe several alternatives to the TVA project and its possible negative repercussions, but they do not point out the economic reasons behind the FDR-led project: The federal government could not tell people threatened by catastrophic years of flooding and impoverished by the Great Depression (and perhaps by their own abuse of the environment) to let their land lay fallow for at least fifty years and deny themselves the civilizing force that work on these projects and the electricity produced by the dams would bring them.

While *The River* accurately highlights the environmental problems of the Tennessee Valley and offers a definitive solution, it depends on recent historical memory for the force of its argument. The catastrophic floods of 1927, 1936, and 1937 were still fresh in the nation's memory. But this film only provides a generalized portrait of the human hardships before the TVA project and can only speculate about the future benefits the dams they would produce might create. *Rovin' Tumbleweeds* illustrates the hardships of migrant ranchers but fails to address the possible causes for flooding. Instead, the film mentions nature's wrath only briefly and concentrates primarily on government's inaction due to the greed of the Randville Development Corporation. Unlike *The River,* other possible causes for flooding, including degradation of grasslands by the cattle Autry works to save, are glossed over.

These two Gene Autry films from the 1930s set up two poles of the water-rights argument. While most Westerns addressing issues related to water discuss drought and how best to resolve it, others show what happens when flooding, not drought, becomes the enemy. Two other Autry movies, *Rancho Grande* (1940) and *Sunset in Wyoming* (1941), illustrate the consequences of water running out of control, but each presents a different approach to controlling it. *Rancho Grande* concentrates on a dam and irrigation system as in other water Westerns, but the dam holds back "millions of gallons of water" rather than a shallow stream. *Sunset in Wyoming* shows the consequences of flooding—as does *Man of the Frontier*—but it also reveals the human cause behind the destructive waters.

In *Rancho Grande,* Gene Autry serves as guardian for his deceased boss's three grandchildren (June Story, Mary Lee, and Dick Hogan). In a recorded message, the grandfather explains that they must complete a dam and an irrigation project in order to renew the note on Rancho Grande and maintain the grandchildren's inheritance. As he puts it, they can put in an irrigation system and dam for the South as good as the North. And if the system is finished, "all that wasteland [behind the dam] will turn into orchards." The grandchildren are wild enough to run off horses in a plane and invite friends from the city to join them for all-night parties, but real problems arise when their lawyer, Emery Benson (Ferris Taylor), attempts to destroy the dam project and take over the ranch. With Autry and sidekick Frog (Smiley Burnette) helping them, the trio finish the project and indict Benson, but only after a series of mishaps, including a dynamite explosion meant to destroy piping in a train car. In *Rancho Grande,* waters are controlled by a dam and irrigation system that turns wastelands into gardens.

Sunset in Wyoming provides a clearer picture of the consequences of flooding. The film highlights the importance of forestation in the fight against erosion, which would lead to flooding. The film blatantly lays out its case, arguing first with a visual image of giant trees falling and piles of lumber rolling down a hill. A title then states, "With axes and saws the loggers of the Wentworth Lumber Company marched into the forests of Mount Warner and bared the land," and again, we see piles of lumber. Then another title appears that reads, "But Nature rebelled—and every inch of rain that fell on the thirstless hills became a threat of death—a tumult of destruction that swept the valleys below." To prove this point, a shot of flooding waters engulfing homes, bridges, fences, and cattle appears. These general notes and shots introduce the conflict, but the human influence becomes the main focus of the film. In *Sunset in Wyoming* the message is clear: humans' exploitation of nature's resources contributes to devastating results like flooding, another clear connection to *The River.*

The film places blame on one company and it owner, the Wentworth family, in order to illustrate the consequences of such misuse of resources: "The Wentworths have done enough. [They have] stripped the mountain, flooded farms. . . . It's no better than a slow death." In fact, the company's manager, Bull Wilson (Stanley Blystone), blames the weather for the flooding and rejects farmers' pleas to "plant something for everything they cut down." Instead Bull declares, "Reforestation is a government matter." After scuffles between Bull's men and local farmers, Gene Autry intervenes, stopping the fight with help from Jim Hayes (Monte Blue) and then heading to the city to talk to the Wentworths "about the other side of the story."

Governmental roles in environmental policy foreground these struggles between federal and local control of, in this case, reforestation. According to Somthawin Sungsuwan-Patanavanich's "Reforestation as a Carbon Sink: Toward Slowing Global Warming?":

> The ambiguity of forest laws and regulations has been an issue for some time. An important problem is the inadequate categorization of protected forests. A legal definition of a protected forest did not, until recently, differentiate between upper watershed forest, now facing destruction, and other protected forests. The definition of exactly what constitutes a forest area is not also clearly spelled out. According to the Forest Act of . . . 1941, "forest" is defined as "unowned" land and classified under the Land Act. This gives the false impression

that such "unowned" land, even though forested, can be cleared for settlement, thus leading to endless conflicts between settlers and government officials. (10)

This battle between individuals seeking control of forests (in this case for lumbering) and those seeking government action to reforest the land is highlighted in *Sunset in Wyoming.* Asa Wentworth (George Cleveland), however, has given over management of his lumber company to his granddaughter's boyfriend, Larry Drew (Robert Kent), so it seems that Autry and Frog's attempts to reforest the mountain and stop the flooding will fail.

But the pair draw on federal environmental law to make their case for preserving the mountain so trees can be planted to prevent flooding. They even attempt to convince Lt. Gov. Cornelius Peabody (Dick Elliot) and his wife Susanna Peabody (Sarah Edwards) to turn the mountain into an animal preserve and state park. Autry explains, "Some states have found it pays to save their forests, to protect their wild life and more important to control floods," and he convinces them to go to Mount Warner to ensure that it meets standards for a state park. When Mrs. Peabody arrives she exclaims, "can't you just smell the ozone?" Autry and Frog place "wildlife" on the mountain to impress the lieutenant governor and his wife. Their plan seems to be working at first. Deer and rabbits get the Peabodys' attention. But when Frog brings out strange animals like lions as proof that the region needs an animal preserve, all seems lost.

The situation changes, however, when a rainstorm comes through and floods the road so that the Wentworths and Peabodys cannot cross the wash. The film then shows images of people out sandbagging against the storm. Women and children move to high ground—to Autry's ranch. Then the Wentworths' car hydroplanes, and a mudslide stops them. The road is out. When Autry saves them and takes them to his home, he explains, "All these folks lost their homes tonight." This is enough to cause a transformation in Wentworth, who rejects his former prospective son-in-law's position and tells them he will replace the flood victims' losses and make their futures secure. "We could start the reconstruction right away," he says. Then a headline reads, "Dedicate Park at Mt. Warner Today," and we see a forest in the background as the credits roll.

In *Sunset in Wyoming* Autry not only shows us the consequences of flooding but also offers a solution that is based in the origin of the flooding—the Wentworths' baring the mountain and eroding topsoil needed to hold the waters. The film illustrates the merging of local and national interests as well, since Wentworth willingly transforms a timber-rich mountain into a "forest" that, with help from the federal government, can become a preserve for wildlife and a barrier for floodwaters.

Like *Man of the Frontier,* the film shows water as an enemy, but the ultimate enemies are the humans behind the clear-cutting that has bared the land to erosion. Here it interacts well with *The River,* since that documentary illustrates the consequences of clear-cutting and eroding the land in a variety of ways. The film, then, demonstrates the dangers of exploiting resources and argues for sustainable development. But the populist version of progress on display still results in empire building, even though a broader population is served by development. The few nature preserves are set aside to remind us of our wild frontiers, now transformed into "gardens" that exploit and deplete natural resources—for the many or the few.

WATER IN THE DESERT

The majority of Westerns, however, take place in the arid landscape of the Southwest, where irrigation and water rights provide life to cattle, to crops, and to settlers. *The Ballad of Cable Hogue* (1970) especially illustrates the influence land and water-rights issues had on the environment of the American Southwest.

Earlier films, however, demonstrate the variety of approaches Westerns take when illustrating how settlers overcome drought in the desert.

A battle over water fuels a feud in *The Painted Desert* (1931), though it also is discussed as a necessary resource in a dry land-scape—one that is more precious than food. The value of water rights allows Jeff and Cash's feud to continue for twenty years, until something even more precious—their adopted son and his discovery of tungsten—stops the dispute and, presumably, allows them all to share both water and wealth as a family. In *Under Western Skies* (1938), a Roy Rogers film, the big water-and-power company is thwarted by the federal government, and the community of Sageville gets its water and power. With water, cattle survive and ranchers make a living off the land. Water turns the dusty desert into a riparian oasis. But the argument in *Under Western Skies* is over the price of water—not whether or not it serves the environment best to use dams and canals to bring water to a dustbowl—and drought conditions are blamed not on overuse of land but on nature. The environmental bent of the film, then, is focused only on water as a necessary (and inherently free) resource.

In *Angel and the Badman* (1947), water serves as only one element in a romantic plot. Quirt Evans (John Wayne) pro-vides a Quaker family and other farmers with needed water now "owned" by a large farmer through dams and a reservoir, Frederick Carson (Paul Hurst). The film's arguments about water rights also parallel those in Wayne's earlier film, *Riders of Des-tiny* (1933), even nearly recreating the scenes between Wayne's Singin' Sandy and James Kincaid from the earlier film in those between Quirt and Carson. Ownership of water in *Angel and the Badman* has been shifted from an individual, Carson, to a collective that includes Quaker families with a more commu-nal view of nature. So this brief scene, juxtaposed with others that foreground community as a better goal than conflict and violent tyranny, demonstrates the power of water rights. When water rights become more equally distributed rather than an individually driven economic concern, farmers and their land are better served. Nature and humans here are shown as holding a reciprocal or even symbiotic relationship—the land and its people depend on water to sustain them. More water more widely distributed means more fertile land for farming and farmers.

Gene Autry's *Mule Train* (1950) highlights water rights in relation to both private ownership and government lands. Sheriff Gene Autry tells "Keg" Rollins (Gregg Barton) that he is "all through making [anyone] pay for water," an assertion Rollins contests. But Autry explains: "It's still government land and government water, and no one's going to charge for it. Water's free." Thus the conflict is established, all based on the question, can private companies own and control government lands and resources? But the opening scenes with Autry arguing for preservation of free water on public lands serve as the only clear reference to the positive consequences of discovering natural cement: better dams to store and distribute free water.

The Roy Rogers film *In Old Amarillo* (1951) provides a different answer to questions related to turning a desert into a garden—cloud seeding. Technology from a period concurrent with the film's production date ends up saving land from drought, but the conflict over water rights remains the same. As in *Angel and the Badman* and *Mule Train,* water is constructed as a right, a resource that should be available to all rather than a commodity to be either horded or withheld for profit. *In Old Amarillo* simply offers lack of water as a way to acquire lands for profit and for bringing in another source of riches—a cannery.

The Big Country (1958) presents an epic battle over water rights that is masked by a feud between two ranchers, Maj. Henry Terrill (Charles Bickford) and Rufus Hannassey (Burl Ives). When James McKay (Gregory Peck), a ship captain, comes to the West to marry the major's daughter, Pat (Carroll Baker), he brings with him a worldview like that of Singin' Sandy and the Quakers in *Angel and the Badman* and seeks to resolve conflict through negotiation rather than violence. More importantly, he buys the land that Terrill and Hannassey are fighting for, thus purchasing the water rights for the region. Unlike the Terrills and Hannasseys, however, McKay offers the water freely to both families. But only after a series of battles, at the end of which the two family patriarchs kill one another, is the feud, as well as the struggle over water, finally resolved.

Rufus Hannassey most eloquently defines the battle over water as a battle steeped in blood in his speech to Colonel Terrill:

> The next time you come a busting and blazing into my place scaring the kids and the women folks, when you invade my home, like you was the law or God Almighty . . . then I say to you, I've seen every kind of critter God ever made, and I ain't never seen a more meaner, lower, pitiful, yellow, stinking hypocrite than you! Now you can swallow up a lot of folks and make them like it, but you ain't swallowing me, I'm stuck in your craw, Major Terrill, and you can't spit me out! You hear me now! You've rode into my place and beat my men for the last time and I give ya warning, you step foot in Blanco Canyon once more and this country goin' to run red with blood until there ain't one of us left! Now I don't hold mine so precious, so if you want to start, here, start now!

McKay's purchase of the land owned by Julie Maragon (Jean Simmons), the woman McKay learns to love, helps halt the blood feud after the patriarchs' deaths and provides cooperative water rights for both ranches. Terrill and Hannassey's deaths not only symbolize a changing West but also reinforce the end of the feud and the return of free water.

THE BALLAD OF CABLE HOGUE:
MAKING ENVIRONMENTAL HISTORY
TRANSPARENT

The Ballad of Cable Hogue most clearly illustrates the effects land-acquisition acts had on development and, ultimately, environmental damage in the West. The film again takes a populist approach to progress and shows what happens in a desert like that depicted in *Waterhole #3* (1967), when there's "water enough for two, not three." Instead of arguing for communal use of free water, the film sympathizes with a lone hero, who profits off a waterhole found on land he claims for his own. The man has also been searching for gold in the desert but makes his profit from water. In a film immersed in the environmental history of the Old West, this lone hero battles a different corporation, a stagecoach company, as well as criminal gold-mining partners, and wins. But his victory comes at a cost.

In *The Ballad of Cable Hogue,* Cable (Jason Robards) is the "little guy" and illustrates populist views of progress as a working-class miner who uses water-rights policies to build himself a small empire. Even though the film promotes a broadened view of access to property and encourages "wise use" of water because its availability is limited by the price Cable charges, prosperity is built on exploitation of resources and signifies the movement into a modern, technological world. In fact, modern technology literally runs over Cable and appropriates his space in the western landscape.

This space appears inhospitable to settlers like Cable but is transformed, at least for a time, by the presence of water. The film highlights the arid setting beginning with its opening shots. This desert looks uninhabitable. In fact, the first scene opens on a desert lizard and Cable hissing at one another. Before Cable can shoot the lizard for food, however, his two partners steal his water and his gun and ride off on his mule.

Cable is left without water in this desert, so alone and vulnerable his death seems inevitable. His partners reinforce this impression, yelling, "It's all yours, Cable, 50,000 gallons of sand," as they ride off. The credits come up in a split image as he wanders around the desert muttering to God—"Ain't had no water since yesterday, Lord. Just thought I'd mention it." He yells at God each day. In an arid landscape, a sunburned Cable wanders through sand and dust storms, reinforcing his thirst. Finally he gives up: "Four days without water. You don't think I've put in my suffering. You oughta try being dry for a spell. . . . Careful now, you're apt to get my dander up. . . . Lord, you call it. I'm just plain done. Amen." But then, just as he is about to collapse for the last time, he finds water when his boots get muddy. "I told you I was going to live. This is Cable Hogue talking—me," he exclaims.

Cable has found water—a source of sustenance and of profit resting on the Desert Land Act. He collapses in the mud but wakes up in a water hole and thinks of ways from which to profit when he notices wagon tracks, signs of civilization. People in wagons, stagecoaches, and buckboards will need water in this desert land. According to Cable, there are "people going somewhere, and I'm on it, me and my water hole." He has found a way to serve travelers in the desert and plans to make a profit.

When a stage comes up, he asks if it would be "worth anything if I find water." The drivers tell him, "It would be a worth a damn sight more than gold," and after the passengers complain about the untimely stop, the drivers cut the ropes holding their luggage and leave it for Cable. Based on the drivers' claims, he builds a watering stop for the stage, profiting from the sale of his resource—water. Within the film's narrative, Cable also uses the watering stop to punish his partners for leaving him for dead in the desert, a landscape in which he has found water "where it wasn't."

That profit begins almost immediately when he charges a traveling preacher named Joshua (David Warner) ten cents for a drink of water. The preacher tells him that Cable has "builded an oasis out of his wilderness" and names it Cable Springs. More importantly, he explains to Cable that he must file a claim to keep the land, so he takes the preacher's horse and goes to town. A prostitute named Hildy (Stella Stevens) points him to the US Land Office, where the proprietor explains, "under The Desert Land act an individual can file for up to 320 acres for $1.25 per acre, plus proof of reclamation." He further points out that "land without water is not allowable" unless a claimant can substantiate either agricultural or horticultural development.

The film's explanation for the Desert Land Act is based in fact. On March 3, 1877, the Forty-Fourth Congress passed "An act to provide for the sale of desert lands in certain States and Territories." This measure asserts, "[t]hat it shall be lawful for any citizen of the United States, or any person of requisite age 'who may be entitled to become a citizen, and who has filed his declaration to become such' and upon payment of twenty five cents per acre—to file a declaration under oath with the register and the receiver of the lead district in which any desert land is situated, that he intends to reclaim a tract of desert land, not exceeding one section, by conducting water upon the same, within the period of three years thereafter."

Cable has enough money for two acres and files his claim, paying for both the initial fee and the dollar an acre required three years later, in the compacted context of the film. He takes the claim to the stagecoach office and pours water out of his boots to prove that he has water to sell on his land. When the office will not buy the claim for the thirty-five dollars Cable suggests, he tries the bank and asks for a thirty-five-dollar loan for "grub," with his homestead claim as collateral. The banker is reluctant until Cable tells him, "Well, I'm worth somethin', ain't I," and explains his situation. The banker gives him one hundred dollars, and his waterhole seems secure. Cable has staked his claim in response to the Desert Land Act, but the film glosses over the law's other requirements: reclamation and free access to water. Instead, Cable uses water for financial gain alone, reclaiming lands only by building a home and stage stop for himself. In

The grand opening of the water station in *The Ballad of Cable Hogue*

the context of *The Ballad of Cable Hogue,* water is property that cannot be appropriated and used by the public for irrigation, mining, or manufacturing purposes.

Cable befriends Hildy and builds a relationship with Preacher Joshua, but his relationship to water is most prominent in the film. The scenes surrounding the stagecoach line's response to Cable's claim begin to highlight the power of water. The company attempts to dig waterholes near his land but fails to find water. so it cuts a deal with Cable, and he places a US flag on his claim to show that his place is a stop on the stagecoach trail. After years of business, Cable builds a windmill and upgrades his home and the stop, but he will not sell his station and leave with Hildy until he has avenged his former partners' treatment of him. The former partners finally come to the waterhole and attempt to rob Cable, who then kills one (L. Q. Jones) in self-defense and almost sends the other, Sam (Strother Martin), out in the desert.

When Hildy drives up in a horseless carriage, Cable seems to have reached his apex: He has avenged his partners' mistreatment of him and now can sell his waterhole and leave with Hildy. But

Cable Hogue (Jason Robards) run over by the car of the future in *The Ballad of Cable Hogue*

when Cable tries to stop her car from rolling away, the vehicle rolls over him. It is not the desert—nature—but technology that kills him. On Cable's grave marker, Hildy and Preacher Joshua have written: "He found this water where it wasn't." Water remains the film's focus to its end.

Although the film's message differs from that of earlier Westerns focused on water rights, it is still immersed in historical memory, in references to environmental history that attempted to both settle the West and turn its deserts into gardens, an attempt that fails here because water serves only as a resource for financial gain. *The Ballad of Cable Hogue* demonstrates the negative effects that even a populist version of progress can have on individuals and their environment. Both populist and progressive visions of progress are represented by the changing road that passes by what was Cable's stagecoach stop. Cable both literally and figuratively "stands still" as stagecoaches and wagons are replaced by motorcars.

The Ballad of Cable Hogue seems to valorize Ronald Bailey's claim that economic growth facilitates environmental action, but it merely shows how a lone miner is able to exploit water resources for profit. No fecund valley emerges from Cable's discovery. His waterhole does not promote a garden in the desert. Cable uses water only for profit, not for community growth. Most telling, however, in the film is the use of technology as a signifier of progress. Indeed, progress literally runs over Cable, suggesting that unchecked technological advances may result in death not only for nature but also for ourselves.

CONCLUSION: WATER AND CULTURE

In films like *The Ballad of Cable Hogue,* the two views of progress Richard Slotkin postulates are in conflict: the "progressive" style, which "reads the history of savage warfare and westward expansion as a Social Darwinian parable, explaining the emergence of a new managerial ruling class and justifying its right to subordinate lesser classes to its purposes," and the "populist" style, which combines "the agrarian imagery of Jeffersonianism [with] the belief in economic individualism and mobility characteristic of pre–Civil War 'free labor' ideology" and views progress "by the degree to which the present state of society facilitates a broad diffusion of property, of the opportunity to 'rise in the world,' and of political power" (*Gunfighter Nation* 22).

The "big guys" take a "progressive" approach to westward expansion that stomps out individuals in favor of corporate control. The "little guys" approach progress from a "populist" perspective, seeking a "broad diffusion of property" and opportunity for the people. The films highlighted here valorize the populist approach to water rights and demonize progressive approaches, a position that seems fair and equitable. Missing from the conflict, however, is the environment, the water and land for which they fight. Ultimately, both progressive and populist views of progress rest on an empire-building model that exploits resources and desecrates the environment. Whether the empire sustains either the few or the many, the environment suffers since both "draw on a common myth," especially one that rests on "the vitality of 'democratic' politics and the relevance of something called 'The Frontier' as a way of explaining and rationalizing what is most distinctive and valuable in 'the American way'" (Slotkin, *Gunfighter Nation* 23–24).

All of these films address water rights in the West in relation to the historical, cultural, and regional contexts with which they interact. More importantly, the films all draw on both historical and environmental memory, one that reflects a context contemporary to the movies and to their settings. They also reflect a view that nature and culture are interconnected. Without natural resources, especially water, cultures fail. Donald Worster adds weight to this view when he states, "The idea that nature has had something to do with the shaping of cultures and history is an idea that is both obviously true and persistently neglected." His *Rivers of Empire* illustrates how integral water and its control have been in the construction of a history and culture of the West: "The American West is only the latest in a long series of experiments in building an irrigation society" (*Rivers of Empire* 19.)

Worster's work offers a purpose for examining not only the issue of water rights but also its portrayal in Westerns. The films explored here either explicitly or implicitly rest on "the idea that nature has had something to do with the shaping of cultures and history."Westerns highlighting water rights and control, either in relation to drought or flooding, build on this history, an ongoing history intertwined with nature and its resources. Drought in the Southwest and flooding on the coasts today only reinforce Worster's claims, which rest on environmental consequences, capital gains, and an ongoing contest over water.

That battle continues, and whether the big guys or the little guys win, nature loses. As Ralph A. Wurbs explains in "Water Rights in Texas," although "ground water is considered the property of the landowner," and "Texans are very sensitive to any governmental infringement on their personal-property rights, depleted ground water reserves are forcing the state to move slowly toward greater ground-water regulation." He asserts that "the development of permitting systems has been driven by increasing demands on limited resources. Relative to the severe droughts of the 1910s, 1930s, and 1950s, the state has had abundant precipitation during the last three decades. The water-management community is anticipating the occurrence of a future drought, with a severity comparable to the record 1950–1957 drought, to test and motivate further refinement of the water-rights system" (453).

Water-rights issues also continue to exploit less powerful populations as well. A study of desert ecosystems in relation to an attempt to build an eco-friendly city (Civano, Arizona) in the desert notes that "rights to water, which are key to development in the arid Southwest, have been taken from the Navajo and Hopi, on whose reservations Black Mesa [the source of huge aquifers] sits." Furthermore, the Navajo and Hopi sued the Peabody Western Coal Company, which leased those rights beginning in 1973, and by 2004 the results of the lawsuit were still pending. Yet the Navajo and Hopi "are frugal in their use of water. Water consumption of the Hopi Nation averages 28 gallons per capita per day (gpcpd). By contrast, the average use of water by neighboring non-Indian communities in Arizona was 160 gpcpd" (Jenkins et al. 292).

Both progressive and populist visions of progress result in such depletion, and at least according to Wurbs and Worster, water use must be limited and controlled to sustain future generations. Water-rights Westerns like *Man of the Frontier, Rovin' Tumbleweeds, Rancho Grande, Sunset in Wyoming,* and *The Ballad of Cable Hogue* valorize populist approaches to progress, but they bypass the fair use/wise use argument to concentrate on the little guy's triumph over the big guy. *Sunset in Wyoming* promotes sustainable practices, though only in the context of a nature preserve, not everyday lands developed for "empire's" sake. Instead, the West may need to look toward Worster's solution to the environmental consequences of the Desert Land Act. Worster claims that the manipulation of water in the American West

> has never been studied in the context of that larger world experience. As a result, the connections between aridity, human thirst, water control, and social power have not been obvious to the region or its historians. To remedy that failure . . . we must make a long, wide-ranging excursion . . . to the farthest points of the earth, wherever other people have also encountered dry places and tried to overcome their natural limits. . . . Then we may be able to say more precisely what the western manipulation of rivers has produced in social terms—what the flow of power in this region has been and is today. (*Rivers of Empire* 19)

When we connect ourselves and our use of water to power, just as the Hopi and Navajo do, we may come closer to sustaining rather than exploiting our resources in the American West and reveal that exploitation in Westerns.

CHAPTER 4

The Rush for Land,
the Rush for Oil,
the Rush for Progress

Spectacle in *Cimarron, Tulsa, Comes a Horseman,*
and *There Will Be Blood*

While exploring the new frontiers of homesteading and oil,
Westerns that focus on the "land rush" follow narrative patterns
that are similar to those found in ranching, mining, and water-
rights films. These oil-frontier movies equate land acquisition
with a sense of progress as a way to tame the frontier, no matter
what the consequences for native cultures or the land itself or
whether few (from a progressive perspective) or many (from a
populist point of view) gain access to its benefits. As with water-
rights Westerns, the focus on property and profit contributes to
the battle between "big guys" and "little guys" that inevitably
leads to overuse of land. The land rush of 1889 and 1892, especially, evolved from a desire for farm and ranch land to wildcatting, oil booms, busts, and ultimately the spectacular nature
of the force of oil gushers and oilfield fires in Oklahoma and
Indian Territories, Texas, and California. *Cimarron* (1931), *Tulsa*

(1949), *Comes a Horseman* (1978), and *There Will Be Blood* (2007) especially document the consequences of such visions of progress, yet only *Comes a Horseman* questions any environmental costs caused by such development, exploitation, and "rush" to riches.

Such environmental dislocations are the price of both progressive and populist forms of progress and the valorization of the modern mechanical world. They reach monumental levels in filmic representations of the opening of Oklahoma and Indian Territories, where oil provides the riches on which empires are built. From explicit depictions of the land rush itself to historical and contemporary visions of one of the results of the land rush, a booming oil industry that is both lauded and critiqued, these films illustrate the dire consequences of these policies. The hordes of settlers participating in a rush for land and all of the smoke and uncontrolled fire on display support assertions that these are eco-disaster films.

Such disasters, from a current point of view, seem to beg for an ecological reading. We have become committed to considering the consequences of uncontrolled oil-well fires and gushers, so from our current perspective, fire and smoke look destructive to humans and their environment. More than just spectacle, these burning oilfields, these obfuscating clouds of smoke, this general conflagration of the natural world, signify humans' rape of the landscape for personal gain—oil, whatever the price to the natural world.

Yet the environmental ramifications of the land rush and the oil frontier that followed are sometimes depicted either as "business as usual" or as a sign of progress. It is possible, then, to be caught in a conundrum with films like these, forced to struggle in uncertainty regarding the meaning of the extreme depictions of vibrant destruction. Is it meant to comment on our environment and our way of living, or merely show, with a certain casualness, the world as received? Whether examining depictions of the land rush in Oklahoma and Indian Territories, exploring filmic representations of the oil industry, analyzing visions of the oil frontier from a contemporary perspective, or highlighting critiques of the land rush and of the oil industry from both contemporary and historical perspectives, environmental consequences may be blurred by the exhibition on display, especially in relation to the historical and cultural contexts of both the film productions and their narrative settings.

TULSA: RANCHING AND OIL DRILLING AFTER THE LAND RUSH

Tulsa (1949), for example, embodies a variety of perspectives on the repercussions of land-rush policies, including a burgeoning oil industry, yet it nearly erases its environmental message with the incredible effects of oil-well fires on display. Although foregrounding a timeframe after the opening of Oklahoma—the 1920s to 1949, the film's production date—*Tulsa* shows how the land rush affected American Indians, especially after oil production soared. It demonstrates the spectacle of oil gushers and fires, and it critiques the environmental costs of rampant drilling, ultimately preaching conservation for the benefit of both human and nonhuman nature. As Peter C. Rollins asserts, "*Tulsa* reflects a national mind divided between enthusiastic approval of economic development and deep-seated anxieties [about] despoiling a Virgin land" (81). The film's stylistic choices reinforce this divide.

Westerns that foreground oil riches and progress as positive consequences of the land rush typically emphasize the impressive force of fire and gushing oil on display and minimize any environmental costs caused by the misuse of oil or land. *Tulsa* is no exception. As a post–World War II film about the Oklahoma oil boom of the 1920s, it seems at first to bypass spectacle and foreground the prosperity oil revenues can bring to a region (and the city of Tulsa) in response to the Oklahoma land rush. But after an initial opening that shows an aerial view of the bus-

Oilfield fire disaster in *Tulsa*

tling, prosperous city of Tulsa in 1949, the film backtracks to the 1920s conflict between ranchers and oil producers in Oklahoma, a conflict that results in a tremendous oil fire. The first 1920s scene highlights the pollution caused by oil exploitation when a stream polluted with oil kills cattle on a ranch owned by Nelse Lansing (Harry Shannon), the father of the film's protagonist, Cherokee Lansing (Susan Hayward).[1]

The scene also foreshadows the film's spectacular ending, when Lansing throws a match in the stream and ignites the oil floating on its top. And when in a fit of rage he "trespasses" on land owned by Bruce Tanner (Lloyd Gough), he is killed running from an oil gusher that blows up in a tornado of wood and metal. A brilliant display opens the film and seems to foreground pollution, but the main conflict is between cattle ranchers and oil producers, not environmentalists and land exploiters. Lansing attacks his rival not for the sake of the polluted stream alone, but because the fouled water kills his cattle. The oil fires and explosions here serve not only to move along the narrative but also to heighten the action with their impressive force. Both the stream fire and the exploding oil well are shot first in close-up and then from a distance to heighten their impression on the viewer—and portend an even greater and more monstrous spectacle to come.

The film's ending steals the show with a monstrous oil fire that, according to Hal Erickson, "must have cost as much as all the other Eagle-Lion releases of 1949 combined." Framing the 1920s burning stream opening, the film's "American Indian" lead, Jim Redbird (Pedro Armendáriz), sets another oil-laden stream on fire after a judge declares him incompetent so Cherokee and Tanner (now partners) can drill more wells on his land. With his cattle lying dead from drinking the poisoned water, Redbird throws a match in the stream and, it seems, waves it into flame with his jacket. The ensuing oilfield fire blasts up in red flames and black smoke that fill nearly half the frame. As in the opening sequence, erupting flames are shot first in close-up and then in a long shot that distances the viewer and adds force to the conflagration. Repeated shots of the heightening flames intensify the scene's force.

Although *Tulsa* resolves its conflicts in favor of both American Indians and conservation, it is the massive fire scene that sells the film. Its core foregrounds Cherokee and her rise to power as an oil queen, but it also tackles two conflicts: the first, between white oil moguls and American Indians, and the second, between greed and conservation, with an ending that resolves both. Jim Redbird chooses to destroy the oilfields that supplant cattle ranches, a choice that results in environmental destruction that is more massive than that caused by drilling wells too close together to accommodate cattle.

But the blasting fires Redbird ignites serve to awe viewers and raise suspense. The question becomes who will survive, not how

can the environment be saved? Spectacle overrides any sem-
blance of an environmental message in *Tulsa*. As in numerous
Westerns foregrounding the rush for land, here environmental
exploitation is on display but rarely discussed. The curious intersection of "western myth" and twentieth-century economic fact
run through many oil Westerns, with oil discoveries in Oklahoma, Indian Territory, and ultimately Texas propelling land rush
and progress to hyperbolic levels. Interrogating this intersection
will make transparent both the environmental degradation on
display and the attempts made by these films to critique such
eco-disaster. More importantly, contextualizing both the films
and their settings historically and culturally becomes a way to
reveal these roots in environmental history as both critique and
valorization of eco-disaster.

Land-rush Westerns from *'Neath Arizona Skies* (1934) to *Far and
Away* (1992) explore issues surrounding the land grab in similar
ways. Oil production and overuse of resources affect the environment and its human and nonhuman inhabitants in exploit-
ative ways, yet typically, ecological concerns are obscured in
these films by monumental mythologies of the American West
as a frontier meant to be conquered. A variety of Westerns foreground the land rush and what Carl Coke Rister calls the oil-
man's frontier, one conquered in the name of progress defined
by oil wealth. Films from the 1930s focus primarily on the land
rush, highlighting the oil-frontier myth in epic ways.[2] But progress continues to overshadow ecological concerns in films from
the 1940s and 1950s.[3] Only since the 1960s have these Westerns
explicitly critiqued the environmental consequences of actual
oil production.[4]

THE EFFECTS OF SPECTACLE

Cimarron, Tulsa, Comes a Horseman, and *There Will Be Blood* most
clearly illustrate the ongoing conflict between eco-disaster on
display and spectacle, a conflict between an explicit and implicit

environmental message and the "sensuous elaboration" that, as Susan Sontag argues, filmic representations provide (212). Whether the films respond to environmental history from the nineteenth century, the 1930s, 1940s, 1950s, 1960s, 1970s, or today, that conflict remains. Yet reading these images through an eco-centric postmodern lens based in environmental history can make the sometimes disastrous workings of the spectacular events transparent.

Oil-well fires and massive land runs play on what Nick Browne calls the "rhetoric of the spectacular." Browne asserts that "formally, the rhetorical parameters of the spectacular work by modulation of cinematic scale, repetition, and perspective." Here, filmed oil-well fires take on spectacular qualities when they assume the large-scale dimensions that such blazes produce, when they are shot repeatedly or for a long duration, and when they are shot from an angle that emphasizes the fires' force. According to Browne, the goal of spectacular effects in action films like the *Die Hard* and *Batman* series (1988–2007; 1989–2008) is to "recreate [an event] experientially, namely in a mode that displays the force, that is the physics of the event, but not its meaning."

Spectacle conflicts with the historically based environmental messages in these films, and what Browne calls the "big bang" overpowers any possible ecological leanings in *Tulsa, Cimarron, Comes a Horseman,* and *There Will Be Blood* especially and masks and deludes environmental concerns raised in later depictions of oil-well fires. Browne suggests that an "analysis of the spectacular explosion as an event and the movies which feature it pose a larger sociological question about entertainment's simulation of the war-like foundations of modern economies." He argues that when we watch such spectacular events, "we are meant to be aware of the expense and take pleasure in the simulation of destruction." Viewers are aware, generally, that there is expense to the environment when watching burning oil wells and black-clouded skies on the screen, but they also take pleasure in the events on display and do not pause to calculate the effects.

Resolving such a contradiction may require a negotiation. Geoff King argues that the spectacular features of a film do not necessarily erase "the kinds of underlying thematic oppositions and reconciliations associated with a broadly 'structuralist' analysis of narrative." He suggests that such events presented on film and the narratives that drive them can work together to illustrate and reinforce "the opposition between the 'frontier'—or its contemporary analogues—and a version of technological modernity" (25). King's reading reinforces the eco-critical reading on display here. His argument suggests that by making the workings of spectacle transparent, the underlying environmental issues on display in these oil-frontier Westerns can gain more force. Yet the conflict between the spectacular and the environmental degradation on display is not resolved, even from King's perspective; it is merely revealed. Knowing the conflict exists makes possible a double reading of the event both as spectacular and sublime splendor and as eco-disaster.

In fact, the filmic production of such events becomes part of this technological modernity on display. Browne even suggests that when it is turned into spectacle, at least in cinema, destruction can be evidence of a certain active social spirit. "Spectacular destruction," he writes, "is one of the opaque signs of life and types of pleasures evident under late, some would say, post-modern capitalism's commodification and marketing of the mass visual event, one whose investment sustains cinema as providing an experience of a certain scale and intensity in its struggle with television's miniaturization and sentimentalization of the contemporary world." Viewers cannot deny these spectacular events put on display precisely because they are so eye-catching, so undeniable; such spectacles are made more transparent, their causation more evident, through the structural and ahistorical lens cinematic drama provides. When placed within their cultural context, such events demonstrate the paradox that a highly industrial medium (film) provides a framework for unearthing possible environmental ideology. But can these environmental leanings, further revealed by historicized readings, also be explored when these seemingly contradictory approaches are applied together?

Eco-criticism, inherently interdisciplinary in nature, may work in tune with such readings to reveal the environmental ideology concealed by the spectacular. Here Browne's and King's arguments contradict one another. Browne argues that spectacle itself can provide the social action an eco-critical reading of the event behind it should reveal. King suggests that spectacles cannot erase or veil environmental issues behind them. Actually, spectacular events and the issues behind them are always already in conflict, so an eco-critical reading can only reveal the conflict itself, neither erasing nor valorizing either the spectacle or the message behind it. Contextualizing oil-frontier films can help make the underlying environmental consequences of oil production and industrialization more transparent, despite the brilliant effects gushers and well fires bring to the screen, especially in *Tulsa, Cimarron, Comes a Horseman,* and to a certain extent, *There Will Be Blood.*

LAND-RUSH ISSUES IN WESTERNS

Tumbleweeds (1925), the two versions of *Cimarron, 'Neath Arizona Skies,* and *In Old Oklahoma* demonstrate the consequences of land-rush politics in Oklahoma and Indian Territory and the continuing effects of the spectacular in Westerns. Whether or not that influence is revealed, however, depends on both the historical accuracy and the power of the spectacular effects on display in each film. As discussed in detail earlier, *Tumbleweeds* illustrates the Oklahoma land rush as a quest for a homestead, with "100,000 empire builders racing across the great barriers of the last frontier." The film rests on visions of progress that equate success with landownership, but the empire depicted is small, a ranch owned by one man and his prospective wife instead of the corporation Noll seeks, built on exploitation of water rights for economic gain. But the history behind the event is illustrated only by the land run itself and otherwise remains unaddressed in the film.

The 1931 *Cimarron* most clearly illustrates the land rush and its ramifications on the Oklahoma oil boom and its consequences. The film centers on a restless newspaperman, Yancey Cravat (Richard Dix), who wanders on farther west after marrying Sabra (Irene Dunne). It opens with spectacular footage of a land rush in 1890 in the Oklahoma Territory, beginning in Wichita, Texas, where newspapers promote Osage, Oklahoma, calling it a new empire with flowers and trees. The goal of the rush, as an intertitle announces, is to "[m]ake a model empire out of this

The grand land-rush sequence in *Cimarron* (1931)

new Oklahoma Territory Law of God and Government of these United States." The film even shows settlers who seek to establish a church (shown in deep focus) where Hebrews, Unitarians, Christians, and Indians are allowed, though no African Americans. Close-ups of notches on a gun, a water truck, and men laying pipe and digging pipe holes foreground the influence technology has had in Osage. Oil derricks quickly line streets and hillsides in the town, looking like a landscape of progress as empire building on the oil frontier.

But with women and marriage comes civilization, according to Yancey, a situation he wishes to avoid. After he sets up his newspaper in Osage, Yancey is ready to move on to another city. He serves as a representative of the oil frontier's lone pioneer, forced ever westward by civilizing forces, when he escapes Osage in 1893 and goes to Cherokee Land, where he establishes another newspaper.

That progress is documented by the film's narrative. Yancey leaves Sabra to take over as proprietor of the *Oklahoma Wigwam* when the Spanish-American War erupts, for example, and in Sabra's hands, this newspaper reports that Oklahoma becomes a state in 1907, with oil driving statehood: "Osage Indians Striking it Rich," reads a headline. The film takes a sympathetic look at the Osage Indians, however, and advocates miscegenation between Sabra's son, Cim (Don Dallaway), and Ruby Big Elk (Dolores Brown), who is part Osage, but it also highlights some of the corruption associated with white control of the former Indian Territory. These whites steal land and oil from the Osage without guilt. The Cravats' daughter, Donna (Judith Barrett), picks out the richest white man in town and marries him.

Near the end of the film, a spectacular oil-related effect reunites Sabra and Yancy when he saves a wildcatter from a gusher and prevents an explosion. But the impact of the gusher and his narrow escape from it end up killing Yancey. He dies in Sabra's arms, but the film's dramatic ending highlights the spectacular consequences oil wildcatting had on both human and nonhuman nature. The gush of black gold that signifies wealth and power destroys Yancey, the pioneer who, at least in the film's context, opened up the oil frontier in Oklahoma.

Cimarron shows the changes that come to Oklahoma Territory after oil is discovered, seemingly highlighting the advantages such progress brings to a region. Oklahoma gains statehood and a booming economy that allows for the technological advances associated with civilization, but the film also shows many of the consequences of conquering an oil frontier. The land is destroyed by drilling, gushers, and fires. Osage culture is destroyed by the land rush that brings whites to their lands after Oklahoma becomes a state, and Yancey is literally destroyed by an out-of-control gusher. Ultimately the film provides a cynical view of progress since it leaves Sabra alone and the oil frontier in physical shambles. Here the spectacle provided by the development of an oil frontier is nearly usurped by the history on display in the film, but the final gusher in the center of a booming city takes the show as both destructive and spectacular force. In *Cimarron,* as elsewhere, environmental degradation is revealed by a thorough examination of the environmental history illustrated by the film, but the spectacular effects overpower the message and romanticize the results of empire building, confining it to the love Yancy and Sabra still share. Two other land-rush films, *'Neath Arizona Skies* (1934) and *In Old Oklahoma* (1943), also critique whites' treatment of American Indians in oil-rich Indian Territory and include vivid documentary footage highlighting the vast forest of derricks an oil boom creates and the results of unchecked oil production and distribution. In one scene near the conclusion of *In Old Oklahoma,* for example, oil wagons explode into vertically shooting flames and black smoke.

A Brief History of the Oklahoma Land Rush

The films highlighted here either illustrate the rush for land in Oklahoma and Indian Territories or highlight its immediate repercussions. One firsthand account provides insight into the cultural context of the period that promulgated the rush. In a *Harper's Weekly* article dated May 18, 1889, William Williard Howard reveals the consequences of "The Rush to Oklahoma." According to John W. Reps, who reprinted the article, the account "is by a trained observer who was present on the day the territory was opened and who remained there for some time afterwards. . . . It documents the massive stupidity of federal policy with regard to the disposal of the public domain, but it scarcely more than hints at the tragic consequences to follow for the Indian tribes who had been forcibly relocated to Oklahoma under solemn promises that their land would be theirs forever." Howard recounts observations of illegal "sooners" crossing "the line before the appointed time" since much of the territory was unprotected by soldiers. He also notes corrupt practices by officials, saying, "The best lots in Oklahoma City, like the valuable locations in Guthrie, were seized by the deputy United States marshals." Howard ends his piece with some commentary about which of the settlers will most likely succeed on their homesteads, noting that money and fertile lands were necessary for success, so many without resources might lose their claims. But his narrative focuses entirely on the land rush of 1889, not on the usurpation of American Indian lands or on speculation about the future of oil and other mineral resources.[5]

After Oklahoma and Indian Territories were opened up for settlement, attempts were made to assimilate the native populations in Indian Territory, land set aside by the Indian Removal Act of 1830 that originally stretched from the Red River along the north border of Texas to the Platte and Missouri Rivers in Nebraska, but by this time only encompassing about the eastern third of modern Oklahoma. The US government wished not only to isolate American Indians on reservations but also sought to "civilize" them by encouraging adults to become settled farmers and by educating their children in religious schools run by white missionaries with white worldviews.[6]

The Dawes Act of 1887 was meant to facilitate this process (Wickett 51). The far-reaching land-allotment act was meant to break up tribes into nuclear families settled on homesteads of 160 acres that they then would farm. Not surprisingly, the measure "received the support of white land grabbers, traders, farmers, and lumbermen" because "their opportunity would be greater, either to obtain land from the Indian allottee or from the surplus after allotment" (Riegel 503). By 1898 even the Five Civilized Tribes were "forced into line" by the Curtis Act, which tied the Cherokee, Chickasaw, Choctaw, Creek, and Seminole tribes to allotments. By 1891, American Indians received "permission to lease" their lands, renting it for little money, and "in 1902 the Secretary of the Interior was permitted to shorten the trust period if he thought such action was wise, which meant that in many cases the Indian lost his land in less than the twenty-five years of the Dawes Act." Legislation in 1907 and 1908 allowed American Indians to sell off their own allotments, a decision Robert Riegel argues was "approved by the whites who were impatient to acquire Indian land" (502, 503). Films like *Cimarron* provide a visual history of the rush for land that followed this legislation.

In 1907 Oklahoma became a state, primarily because of the land rush. The territory had grown to a population of almost 260,000 in 1890, "enough for a congressional district, hence enough for statehood" (Ruth et al. 35). Oil had been discovered there, enticing pioneers to seek their fortunes in Oklahoma's oil-fields and help build Tulsa and Oklahoma City, the state's biggest cities. In becoming a state, Oklahoma Territory was combined with Indian Territory, forcing the tribes to give up their land and culture (through various legal and illegal means), at least until the late 1970s and early 1980s, when Oklahoma tribes like the Cherokee, Chickasaw, and Choctaw were again recognized as nations and adopted new constitutions (Conley 220, 221).

Also in 1907, however, geographers like G. E. Condra saw the Indian Territory—and all of Oklahoma—as a prime source of mineral resources. Condra called the territory "the Pennsylvania of the west," explaining that it contained "fair grades of stone, an abundance of material suited to the manufacture of brick and cement, [and] no less than eight distinct beds of coal and large storage of oil and gas" (333–34). In 1890 "small seepages of oil were discovered near Dewey and Chelsea," and the "first strong well" was drilled in Bartlesville soon after, in 1897 (337). Kristin L. Wells, in her "Discovering Indian Territory Oil," however, demonstrates that oil was discovered as early as 1859 by a Cherokee chief's brother, Lewis Ross, on the Grand River near Salina. His well "produced about ten barrels a day for nearly a year." Adopted members of the Osage and Delaware tribes discovered oil in Bartlesville in 1875 but could not pursue their find further until 1884, when the Cherokee Nation passed a law supporting the "[o]rganization of a company for the purpose of finding petroleum, or rock oil, and thus increasing the revenue of the Cherokee Nation" (Wells). The law opened up the territory, and by 1890 oil was discovered in Dewey and Chelsea.

George B. Keeler and William Johnstone's "first strong well" in 1897 ensured that Oklahoma would emerge as an oil frontier. This well also illustrated the consequences of drilling and "shooting" for oil. Named the Nellie Johnstone No. 1 well after a partner's six-year-old daughter, the well exploded when nitroglycerine was poured into a metal canister and lowered down the hole. According to Wells, "The explosion caused Nellie Johnstone No. 1 to blow in as a gusher, producing from 50 to 75 barrels of oil a day." Production was slow, however, until the railroad came to Bartlesville in 1899, after which the oil could be shipped to a Standard Oil Company refinery. In 1900 the Nellie Johnstone drew a profit and, Wells notes, "ushered in the oil era for Oklahoma Territory. It produced more than 100,000 barrels of oil in its lifetime."

In the ten years following the Nellie Johnstone discovery, "Oklahoma's oil production grew from 1,000 barrels to over 43 million barrels annually" (Wells). Daniel Yergin asserts that

Oklahoma oil production outpaced that of Texas until 1928. According to Yergin, "a string of Oklahoma oil discoveries, beginning in 1901, culminated in the great Glenn Pool, near Tulsa, in 1905. . . . Oklahoma, not Texas became the dominant producer in the area, with over half of the region's total production in 1906" (87). This kind of wealth prompted concerted efforts to exploit the resource and to eliminate American Indians from lands that contained it, a historical context also explored in oil-frontier films.

THE OIL INDUSTRY AND THE SPECTACULAR IN WESTERNS

Westerns examining the oil frontier or consequences of both the land rush and oil boom seem more engrossed with earlier "spectacular developments," like wildcatting successes and failures, rather than with technological improvements in the oil industry, perhaps because of the brilliant effects that land runs, gushers, and oil fires produce on the screen.

Black Gold (1936), for example, foregrounds the possibilities wildcat ventures can provide entrepreneurs on the oil frontier. It also includes a series of spectacular effects that nearly obscure the eco-disaster on display. *Black Gold* first relies heavily on documentary footage for its oilfield sequences, highlighting the real environmental devastation such exploitation of resources might cause. The film opens with shots of derricks and a refinery with a car driving up on a dock. Then we see a documentary montage sequence of derricks, oil tanks, and workers, shot and synthesized with a variety of editing techniques. All of these reveal the immensity of the oilfield and the total lack of a natural environment around it. The landscape is a constructed one, with derricks taking the place of trees. The film begins to take on the look of a Western when it moves from the documentary footage to rugged sets that focus on a roughneck hooked to a derrick fishtail, showing the danger in which even human life is placed during oil production. A teacher comes to get the roughneck, Clifford

O'Reilly (Frankie Darro), nicknamed "Fishtail" because of his preferred work. Fishtail's father, Dan O'Reilly (Frank Shannon), has worked in the oilfields for forty years and will stop "when he's dripping black gold, so he will be a gentleman."

The film provides a portrait of the dangers of corporate oil in the Southwest by centering on the O'Reillys' conflicts with the Anderson Producing and Refining Company, led by J. C. Anderson (Berton Churchill), who wishes to steal every oil lease in the area. Anderson sabotages the O'Reilly well so that Dan falls to his death. Because Anderson had financed the well, he will gain possession of it unless O'Reilly's son hits oil. With the help of geologist Hank Langford (LeRoy Mason), Fishtail keeps drilling. Another montage sequence reveals the number of days he drills. Anderson attempts to stop O'Reilly, first through manipulation and then by kidnapping Langford. But Fishtail keeps drilling. While Langford is restrained, Anderson comes to the O'Reilly site with some of his men and tries to destroy the derrick and drilling machinery. Eventually these tactics backfire on him.

Ultimately, however, this B Western foregrounds spectacle over exploitation of either human or nonhuman nature. Near the film's end, one of the henchmen throws some nitroglycerine toward the derrick, blowing it up with a loud explosion that knocks the oil free. A gusher erupts from the well, with a spectacular display of wealth and natural destruction. One of the men exclaims, "Cap that baby," and asks, "Why didn't we think of nitro?" Now Fishtail is an oil magnate but must attend military school to learn how to be a gentleman. The film ends with another montage, this time of the derrick and the gusher, memories Fishtail ponders as he marches with "eyes front." *Black Gold,* then, shows both human loss, when Fishtail loses his father, and environmental devastation caused by oil drilling, production, and refining. But it presents the gusher as a successful conclusion to Fishtail's efforts, a spectacular image of wealth and power that even distracts the young man at the military school, not a devastating consequence of exploitation of nature's resources.

Boom Town (1940) also foregrounds oil production in spectacular ways, even as it valorizes, at least nominally, conservation. To highlight oil production as both spectacle and a sign of progress, the film opens on a shot of wells and derricks, this time in a muddy Texas town in 1918. Jonathan "Square John" Sand (Spencer Tracy) teams up with Big John McMasters (Clark Gable) drilling thirty miles from town, where they light water on fire to show there is oil to find there. Montage sequences illustrate the extent of the environmental devastation oil speculating causes. The first shows Square John and Big John traveling to work on different sites, drilling, wildcatting, and earning money to buy equipment for their own well. Derricks are in the background in almost every scene, even when the partners romance their mutual love interest, Elizabeth Bartlett (Claudette Colbert). There is even an oil well under a church pulpit. Another montage shows a series of derricks going up, all emphasizing progress rather than devastation, all in recognizable Western "mining" settlements.

This sequence of shots builds to more spectacular effects when the wells begin producing more oil. One well gushes in and catches fire, and we see immense plumes of fire and smoke erupt from the gushing oil. Firefighters and firedogs battle the flames, shielding themselves with water to get close, eventually igniting nitroglycerine to halt the flow of oil. Spectacular fires are everywhere when another gusher erupts, but the firefighters put them out. A complex love triangle drives the plot, but for us, gushing wells and burning derricks highlight one important environmental consequence. If oil derricks are everywhere, no one and nothing can ever be clean: "You can't get clean when you're wildcatting," they explain.

The film also shows fires in oil tanks lit by bandits and the Oklahoma Land Company, through which Big John steals lands from the Indian Nations. It illustrates how vertical monopolies are built, with refining and distribution integrated with production. Tank cars on trains and pipelines are used to move the oil, and offices are set up in New York City to control it all, with Big John at the helm. Square John wins both battles in the film, getting Big John to divorce Elizabeth and using the Sherman Antitrust Act to control what he calls "the oil octopus" that a vertical monopoly allows. Yet the film ends with a shot mirroring the opening view of derricks in Texas. This time rigs cover the Kettleman Hills in California, showing how far west the oil frontier extends. With this scene synthesizing others like it in the film, viewers are left in awe of the spectacular effects of progress on the oil frontier rather than concern for the environment.

Conquest of Cheyenne (1946) also displays oil production as a sign of progress and, as in Black Gold, gushers and fires as signs of wealth. It includes two spectacular scenes: a fire that might have destroyed the derrick and chances of success and a gusher that makes everyone laugh. Although the film does advocate communal speculation, with shareholders determining the terms for oil production and profiting from their successful drilling, it, like other oil-frontier Westerns, foregrounds the spectacular as a sign of progress. The fire encourages everyone to join together and fight back. The gusher, which literally covers them all in oil, "black gold," means wealth and power, not exploitation of resources or environmental degradation, at least not in the context of Conquest of Cheyenne. Ultimately, however, that black gold translates into environmental exploitation, an eco-disaster sometimes obscured by the spectacular effects on the screen. As viewers, we respond differently than do the characters in Black Gold, Boom Town, and Conquest of Cheyenne. In all of these films, the goal is to stop gushers and oil-well fires, but the spectacular effects on display take center stage rather than communal efforts to halt an environmental and economic disaster.

OIL-FRONTIER WESTERNS, 1930s–1950s

Other films foregrounding the oil frontier look at the contemporary situation in the West, situating their stories in relation to oil production in the 1930s, 1940s and 1950s and to their respective production eras. These movies demonstrate what happens when oil production becomes tied to vertical monopolies in the Southwest. With Gene Autry as the lead, *Mexicali Rose* (1939), for example, shows how oil profits can help those in need, in a Depression-era musical Western centered on saving Mexican orphans in a Catholic mission. With the help of bandits led by Valdez (Noah Beery), Autry and the orphans save the mission with profits from the oil well and accompanying stock. The well, thought to be a dud, blows up in a gusher, with everyone just before yelling it is "about to pop!" This spectacular explosion of oil has a different meaning here. Instead of representing wealth and power, the gusher signifies a home and family for destitute orphans. Yet the environmental question remains: Is the destruction of nature and exploitation of resources worth the benefits the well provides the orphans?

South of the Border (1939), another pre–World War II film, again foregrounds Gene Autry and Frog (Smiley Burnette), this time as federal agents sent to Mexico to stop foreign powers from fomenting a revolution and gaining control of that nation's refineries. Oil plays only a peripheral role in this film. When they reach Palermo and ride to the Mendoza ranch, Autry and Frog see derricks and rigs all around them. Autry seeks to take a herd of cattle to the ship, revolutionaries fighting them until the army arrives. Here oil becomes a tool for war, with the allies gaining ground when Autry intervenes as a government agent. *South of the Border,* like *Mexicali Rose,* foregrounds more-positive uses for oil, with the resources supporting another orphan— Patsy—as well as a righteous war effort. Because of the film's historical context, oil is represented as a necessary component of the US victory during World War II, a resource that must be saved to assist the war effort.

A Roy Rogers vehicle, *Apache Rose* (1947) looks at oil production in Mexico not to support either an orphanage or a war effort but to make money. As a post–World War II film, *Apache*

Rose reacts to changes in relationships with Mexico, which had nationalized its oil industry in 1938. Historian Daniel Yergin asserts, however, that by 1947 both Britain's Mexican Eagle and America's Shell Oil Companies had settled with Mexico and eased relations (279). *Apache Rose* is situated in this political context. Oil exploration is documented by drilling equipment on display more than actual gushers or fires, so exploitation of resources is signified only by the positive financial consequences of drilling on Rancho Grande.

Susanna Pass (1949), in contrast, offers a more environmentally sound alternative to oil speculation beneath a fish hatchery—conservation. As expected, Roy Rogers, the hero, and his US Marine sidekick, Doc Parker (Dale Evans), thwart the villain Martin Masters (Robert Emmett Keane), stopping any attempts to close the hatchery and drill for oil, a twist from other Roy Rogers oil-frontier films. Instead, they preserve the hatchery and the game reserve on which it sits, taking time to talk about its positive effects for sportsmen, vacationing Americans driving away from urban sprawl to the "natural" world found in game reserves and parks. According to Rogers: "It doesn't just mean stocking lakes and streams. It means that sportsmen and the youth of America will have a chance to get away from crowded cities and their troubles." The film ends with a post–World War II argument about getting back to the land: "Go fishin' and enjoy the privileges our forefathers had," he tells Doc Parker, a conservation message embedded in the preservation culture of postwar America.

The period during and after World War II is commonly associated with a drive for technological advancement, from constructing needed military equipment during the war to building highways and freeways and entering the space race after it ended.[7] There were noteworthy inclinations toward conservation prior to this, like Teddy Roosevelt's creation of the National Park Service and Franklin Delano Roosevelt's New Deal programs, along with noteworthy exceptions after World War II like William Vogt's bestselling conservation book *Road to Survival* and Fairfield Osborn's *Our Plundered Planet,* which came out in 1948. Aldo Leopold's *Sand County Almanac* was published a year later and proved to be one of the most influential eco-works ever written. Leopold's work had a positive influence on both Supreme Court justice William O. Douglas and Secretary of the Interior Bruce Babbitt. Douglas afterward began protesting what he saw as exploitation of nature as early as 1954, when he successfully opposed the building of a proposed highway that would have destroyed the Chesapeake and Ohio Canal and its towpath. Babbitt, who served under President Clinton, remains a tireless advocate of environmental issues, but he traces the origin of his stances to Leopold's *Sand County Almanac* in the preface to the 2000 edition he wrote in memory of Leopold and in honor of his work for the conservation movement.

After World War II, Americans gained enough economic stability to not only purchase cars in record numbers but also use them for traveling on cross-country highways like Routes 40 and 66. Americans took to the road, towing trailers behind them, so they could experience some of the nature they had left behind when they moved to the cities and the concrete suburbs surrounding them. According to Hal Rothman, Americans increasingly vacationed in national parks and forests after 1945. And "as more of them vacationed, exemplified by record numbers of visitors at Grand Canyon National Park each month after August 1945, they had an impact on the natural world that soon caused them to take notice" (85–86). Rothman asserts that "what Americans found in many of their national parks and forests shocked them: decrepit and outdated campgrounds, garbage piled high, and a lack of facilities and staff to manage them" (86).

Vacationing Americans noticed the devastation in national parks and forests, but the Wilderness Act that served to protect and preserve them was not passed until 1964, almost twenty years after the end of the war. Alexander Wilson argues that Americans in the late 1940s and 1950s saw "the open road [as] a metaphor for progress in the U.S. and for the cultural taming of the American Wilderness." He even suggests, "What we saw out the window of a speeding car . . . was the future itself" (34). These views of nature through the window of a car—or even the window of a camper in a national park—skewed Americans' vision of the natural world. Such confusion between seeking pristine nature and embracing progress at any cost complicated ideological views of the environment and environmentalism. In "Conservation Esthetic," a section of his *Sand County Almanac,* Aldo Leopold describes the views of nature and wildlife recreation during the late 1940s as a destructive search for meaning in an altered "natural" world:

> The automobile . . . has made scarce in the hinterlands something once abundant on the back forty. But that something must nevertheless be found. Like ions shot from the sun, the week-enders radiate from every town, generating heat and friction as they go. . . . Advertisements on rock and rill confide to all and sundry the whereabouts of new retreats, landscapes, hunting-grounds, fishing-lakes just beyond those recently over-run. Bureaus build roads into new hinterlands, then buy more hinterlands to absorb the exodus accelerated by the roads. A gadget industry pads the bumps against nature-in-the-raw. . . . And now, to cap the pyramid of banalities, the trailer. To him who seeks in the woods and mountains only those things obtainable from travel or golf, the present situation is tolerable. But to him who seeks something more, recreation has become a self-destructive process of seeking but never quite finding, a major frustration of mechanized society. (165–66)

Spoilers of the Plains (1951) foregrounds the technological development that followed World War II. Set in contemporary times, the film centers on rockets, stolen oil, and a phony derrick during the heyday of the Cold War. Roy Rogers and Splinters (Gordon Jones) drill for oil and build a pipeline. But Gregory Camwell (Grant Withers) and his company build a derrick to hide a rocket they have found that houses an experimental guidance system. Camwell is a traitor attempting to steal the rocket and the government secrets it holds, presumably for the "Reds." The film includes spectacular effects, like Camwell falling off a derrick and cowboys nearly missing jumps during a final wagon chase, but overall this is a peculiar wedding of the cowboy hero and modern science and technology. Oil here is peripheral and associated with the heroes, Rogers and Splinters. Camwell uses merely the illusion of oil production to hide a traitorous attempt to steal government technology for an "unfriendly power." The film clearly highlights the effects of the Cold War—all with singing cowboys in an oil-frontier Western.

This cycle of contemporary oil-frontier films culminated in the sprawling *Giant* (1956), which documents the epic personal history of the Benedict family, from the marriage of Jordan (Rock Hudson) to Leslie (Elizabeth Taylor) to their children's marriages and racial conflicts, primarily because Jordan's son, Jordan III (Dennis Hopper), marries a Mexican, Juana Guerra (Elsa Cárdenas). But it also highlights the family's move from cattle ranching to oil production, beginning in the 1920s. The focus of the film is on the continuation of an aristocracy that may serve to perpetuate rather than dissolve hierarchies, and any discussion of the landscape reacts to change rather than environmental exploitation. *Giant,* then, serves as a portrait of the rise and fall of economic classes in West Texas that also illustrates the rise of the oil industry, leaving an opening for an eco-critical reading of the change from a cattle-ranching to oil frontier.

CRITIQUES OF THE LAND RUSH AND
OF THE OIL INDUSTRY

Anthony Mann's 1960 *Cimarron* responds to critiques of the oil
frontier and its consequences to a land and its people. The film
opens with a title card that establishes the land-rush setting and
sets the tone of progress for the story: "At high noon on April 22,
1889, a section of the last unsettled territories in America was to
be given free to the first people who claimed it. They came from
the north and they came from the south and they came from
across the sea. In just one day an entire territory would be settled. A new state would be born. They called it Oklahoma." The
title claims that a territory previously reserved for the American
Indian tribes removed from the eastern states is unsettled and
that homesteaders claiming lands there ensure its statehood, a
bending of history to fit an ideology of conquest.

Yancey Cravat (Glenn Ford), a lawyer who takes over a friend's
newspaper, joins the rush for land and progress, along with his
new wife, Sabra (Maria Schell). In this version, however, Yancey
resists some of the consequences of conquest and more explicitly assists American Indians, helping a family settle a homestead
in Oklahoma Territory, then after the father, Ben Red Feather
(Eddie Little Sky), is lynched, caring for his wife, Arita (Dawn
Little Sky), and daughter, Ruby. Yancey's support for the Indians
extends to the Osage tribe when they strike oil on their reservation and Tom Wyatt (Arthur O'Connell), a former dirt farmer,
steals the tribe's land and oil.

Two events stand out visually as reminders of the consequences of white settlement in Oklahoma: the rush itself and
the proliferations of oil derricks in the region a few years later.
The land-rush sequence, as in other such epic films, shows the
immensity of the push for free land. Various sources of transportation roll over the line when the cannon sounds. A bicycle races
toward better land. Wagons overturn. Horses fall and jump over
wagons. Tom Wyatt falls off a stagecoach. And a newspaperman,

Sam Pegler (Robert Keith), crashes his wagon, falls in front of racing horses and is killed by horses and a wagon rolling over him. The shots are impressive here and provide both a demonstration of the title card's claims about settlement and statehood and motivation for Yancey's choice to give up a farm to a past love, Dixie Lee (Anne Baxter), and take over Pegler's newspaper, the *Oklahoma Wigwam*.

Later in the film Tom strikes oil, and a montage sequence of gusher scenes illustrates the extent of oil production in the region. One gusher blows and a couple yells, "we're rich!" Another gusher blows the top off a derrick. Then the shots of gushers move more quickly and are interspersed with shots of gold pieces.

A spectacular series of shots shows how much the oil resources were exploited in Oklahoma and how much destruction is associated with its production. The montage also serves to bridge to another scene that foregrounds the film's revisionist view of American Indian relations. Sabra is attending a social event at Tom Wyatt's new mansion when Yancey arrives, announcing joyfully that the Osage Indians have discovered oil on their land. Tom, however, owns it all, and Yancey leaves in anger. He and a group of governmental officials attempt to control Yancey by making him territorial governor, but the newspaperman refuses because his appointment would come at a great cost to the Osage.

The rest of *Cimarron* centers on the twenty-fifth anniversary of the newspaper and the territory, with Sabra contemplating what to include in the anniversary issue. She receives a telegram telling her that Yancey has been killed in action during World War I, and the film ends, with one last look at Sabra's face and a montage sequence representing her fond memories of her husband. The film lacks accuracy, either in relation to Edna Ferber's novel or to history, but it does question the treatment of American Indians in Oklahoma. Yancey's attempts to help the Osage stand out as one way the movie critiques the environmental consequences of the Oklahoma land rush, yet that message is obscured by the spectacular effects on display. Spectacular land runs and flaming explosions inspire awe.

Other films from the period critique changes from ranching to oil in different ways. In *Hud* (1963) the battle between cattle and oil in the Texas Panhandle comes out as a critique of the effect oil speculation has on the land, even in a film where a cattle rancher, Homer Bannon (Melvyn Douglas), must sacrifice his herd because they are contaminated with hoof and mouth disease. The environmental point in *Hud* is subtle and peripheral to its modernist message embodied by Hud Bannon (Paul Newman), Homer's son, who wants to profit without investing any part of himself. But the film points to a conflict confronted by the oil frontier of the period: Can the West maintain its character when cowboys are replaced by wildcatters and corporate-oil men?

According to Roger M. Olien and Diana Davids Olien's *Oil in Texas: The Gusher Age, 1895–1945,* oil resources were utilized differently than agricultural resources like cattle. The Oliens argue that the oil-gusher age in Texas provided economic growth first for rich white men but then also for women and men of different races and lower economic classes:

> The scholarly argument advanced by some historians of the American West, Walter Prescott Webb an early leader among them, that the American West, including Texas, was an exploited province, in which Eastern capital plundered resources, leaving regions poorer and natural resources depleted. With respect to petroleum in Texas, this argument does not hold up. Rather, the reverse: by controlling politics, Texans were able to use outside capital on their own terms and to control the industry within the state. In fact, they exploited outside capitalists and ended up the richer for it. So much for the idea that the story of oil in Texas might be compared with one of colonization and exploitation by an outside power. (x)

At least in economic terms, oil production served a wide demo-
graphic of citizens in Texas. Although the Oliens fail to address
the ramifications of oil leases on American Indian populations,
they do demonstrate how the gusher period helped build the
Texas economy in the twentieth century.

The Oliens' assertions regarding the lack of exploitation associated with oil production in Texas, however, fall flat if environmental concerns become part of the equation. *Tulsa* points out
one of the ecological consequences of drilling: poisoned water
that kills cattle and interferes with cattle ranching, a consequence
perhaps shaping conflicts between cattle and oil in *Giant*. Even a
2005 article from a drilling-equipment company, M-I SWACO,
"Drilling Frenzy in West Texas District Draws Hodgepodge of
Operators, Service Companies," reveals some of the environmental consequences of drilling still affecting the landscape and
its resources: "Since the early days of drilling, so-called double
horseshoe reserve pits have peppered the landscape throughout
much of the Western U.S. and elsewhere in the world. . . . Besides
being eyesores, reserve waste pits carry a host of environmental
liabilities, not the least of which are the risks of contaminat-
ing the subsoil and underground water aquifers from breached
liners. All too often, nearby residents also treat pits as their private garbage dump, disposing of everything from paint to pesti-
cides." Oil drilling, according to this article, contaminates subsoil
and underground water aquifers, still potentially poisoning the
water for both human and nonhuman nature. M-I SWACO
offers an alternative approach to cut down on waste and meet
new government standards, but their information and ideas
are from 2005. During the periods in which these oil-frontier
Westerns were set and produced, none of these standards were
in place.

The effect of oil production on the environment, however, was seen as a concern even as early as 1920, at least in Los
Angeles. There, citizens and local officials fought to combat oil

pollution. Nancy Quam-Wickham writes in "Cities Sacrificed on the Altar of Oil":

> Pollution, overproduction, and profligate waste were the consequences of unchecked oil development in the Los Angeles basin, consequences that reached crisis proportions in the 1920s. . . . Local initiatives were remarkably successful in slowing the pace of oil development, consequently . . . lessen [ing] the devastating effects of oil pollution on their immediate environment signaled the emergence of working-class conservationism. This type of conservationism can be defined as the sustained efforts of working people to shape public policy to protect their communities from environmental destruction. (189)

And in a 1943 article in *The Journal of Land and Public Utility Economics,* R. D. Davidson and Kenneth Wernimont note how the oil industry has negatively affected agriculture in Oklahoma, stating that "in many of the older fields, exhaustion of the oil supply has left fields ruined by overflow of salt water and oil waste, communities of semi-stranded subsistence farmers and a burden of local government debt out of proportion to remaining income resources" (40).

The federal government, however, was more concerned with voluntary conservation of oil resources than with control of oil pollution or drilling waste. Kendrick A. Clements writes that Herbert Hoover, first as secretary of commerce and then as president, advocated conservation goals aligned with his "theories of interstate compacts and voluntary self-regulation" that would, with suggestions from Hoover and his advisors, limit drilling. But Clements argues: "Adapting the theory to the realities of the oilfields, however, proved difficult, and no progress was made until Hoover became President in 1929. Armed with a hairsplitting distinction between agreements to restrict drilling (putatively legal under the Sherman Act) and those to restrict production (supposedly illegal), in April the administration proposed an agreement," and oil-producing states agreed to set drilling quotas (78).

Clements asserts, however, that "discoveries of new fields in East Texas disrupted the compact, which many smaller companies had opposed in any case. As a result, overproduction worsened." Hoover's reliance on voluntary interstate compacts and oil industry self-regulation proved overly optimistic. According to Clements, Hoover is said to have told a friend: "You know ..., the only trouble with capitalism is capitalists; they're too damned greedy.'" Clements then comments, "But he still based his conservation policy on the expectation of altruistic behavior by businessmen," an expectation doomed to failure, as oil-frontier films from the 1960s to today demonstrate (78, 81).

CRITIQUE OF THE OIL FRONTIER AND THE SPECTACLE BEHIND IT IN *COMES A HORSEMAN*

Comes a Horseman (1978) grapples with questions regarding ranching and oil frontiers, pitting ranchowners Ella Connors (Jane Fonda) and Frank "Buck" Athearn (James Caan) against Jacob "J. W." Ewing (Jason Robards) and his oil-developing friend, Neil Atkinson (George Grizzard). The film is set in post–World War II Montana but illustrates the conflict between oil production and cattle ranching immediately. Atkinson is negotiating with Ewing to drill on his land and claims from the film's beginning that "oil and cattle are not incompatible."

Ewing, however, still sees his ranch as a heartland and looks toward a painting of buffalo racing across a prairie to reinforce his point. He wishes to own the ranchland in the valley, but it is unclear at this point whether he supports drilling over ranching. Ewing's henchmen kill off one new rancher and injure another, Frank, thinking they will scare him into selling Ewing his land. Frank pairs up with Ella when she takes him back to her ranch and nurses him. Together they defeat Ewing and Atkinson, saving their land from both Ewing and oil production.

The first challenge they encounter concerns whether Ella can earn enough money from her cattle to save her ranch once her husband is dead. With only Dodger (Richard Farnsworth) to help her round up her herd, she seems doomed to failure. But Frank talks her into becoming partners for the season, so they work together to round up both of their ranches' cattle. The second begins when a geologist comes to the ranch to test for oil. He checks with Ella about getting a seismic record and completing the tests, but she refuses. Here Frank again supports Ella, making clear that he too rejects drilling because it "means they're going to tear the earth apart." He has "seen places where they've drilled for oil" and knows the score.

But Ewing is under the thumb of a banker, Virgil Hoverton (Macon McCalman), and must agree to allow them to test for oil on his land. We hear blasts from one test, and as if to reinforce the consequences of blasting on the environment, Dodger is thrown from his horse and breaks his ribs. The conflict between Ewing and Ella accelerates because Ewing may lose his ranch if no oil is found there, and he also wants Ella.

Before leaving, the geologist leaves a report that says seismic shooting brings up no good test area on Ewing's ranch. Good drilling is only available on Ella's ranch, so they must drill diagonally from his land to hers in order to strike oil. But they will need Ella's permission in order to continue. Hoverton tries to foreclose on Ewing's ranch, but Ewing kills Atkinson, the oil-man, in a plane crash, then kills Hoverton at Ella's house. The battle then is between Ewing and Frank, with Ella as the prize. Ultimately Frank and Ella survive, though she has lost her house but has kept her land.

Comes a Horseman critiques oil drilling in several ways. It illustrates how oil exacerbates greed, when Hoverton attempts to undermine even the cattle baron Ewing. It also explains how drilling tears up the land because Frank has witnessed its effects and rejects it. Finally the film critiques oil testing and drilling in a more general and dramatic way by associating them with Dodger's

Oilfield workers attempt to snuff out a burning well in *There Will Be Blood*

fall from his horse. More importantly, though, it avoids the reliance on spectacle and the spectacular evident in most oil-frontier Westerns. The seismic tests and blasting are heard only at a distance, and the violent confrontations are resolved. In this context no notion of spectacle obscures or even erases ecological readings.

There Will Be Blood (2007) attests to the continuing power of spectacle in oil-frontier Westerns. Despite its attempts to critique unfettered capitalism and development in oilfields, it is spectacle that underpins both the aesthetics of the film and its melodramatic center. In his *Rolling Stone* review of the film, Peter Travers highlights the repercussions of Daniel Plainview's (Daniel Day-Lewis) greed as a critique of unfettered capitalism, asserting: "This is [Paul Thomas Anderson's] bloody and brilliant *Citizen Kane*. . . . Social history isn't his concern. He's out to show how violence of the flesh and the spirit is hard-wired into the American character. . . . He rapes and pillages in the name of progress. and winds up estranged from the human species he has long ago forgotten to call his own."

But Travers also notes the spectacle on display in the film that entices the eye: "if you want proof that cinematography can be an art form, behold the brute force of the images captured by Robert Elswit, a genius of camera and lighting who can make visual poetry out of black smoke and an oil well consumed by flame." He calls *There Will Be Blood* "a beautiful beast of a film," perhaps because it rests on spectacular images. Roger Ebert even claims, "Watching the movie is like viewing a natural disaster that you cannot turn away." From the first accident that kills a partner and gives Plainview a son, HW (Dillon Freasier), to the massive blast that takes HW's hearing, spectacular effects propel the film's narrative and facilitate its melodramatic center—Plainview's fight with church and country and his mourning for his now deaf (and thus less useful) son.

CONCLUSION

Although *Comes a Horseman* is set in Montana and *There Will Be Blood* is set primarily in California, the environmental degradation on display in these and earlier oil-frontier films resembles that described in research addressing the burgeoning oil frontier in Texas during the early twentieth century. Texas oil booms ensured that state led US production from 1928 until today. According to a 1966 article in *The Journal of Southern History,* Texas usurped Oklahoma's dominance in the industry after Standard Oil began piping oil from Glenn Pool's "flush production" near Tulsa to the Gulf field in Texas (Johnson 523). Historian Arthur Johnson asserts that the Gulf Pipe Line Company sent about 13,500 barrels of oil per day from Oklahoma to the Gulf's Port Arthur refinery. Pipeline construction began in Texas after oil was discovered there, providing the state's oil companies with the opportunity for a vertical monopoly that ensured dominance over not only oil there but also that of other states, including Oklahoma. But as Johnson makes clear, "The Gulf Coast field had given them their initial opportunity" (524, 528). Oil discoveries in Texas connected oil companies there with Oklahoma's boom and facilitated a new oil frontier.

To illustrate the immediate effect of oil discoveries, Daniel Yergin explains how powerful the Spindletop gusher, the first big strike in Texas, was for the economy of the state: "On January 10, [1900] the memorable happened: Mud began to bubble with great force from the well. . . . As they started to clean the mess away, mud began to erupt again from the well, first with the sound of a cannon shot and then with a continuing and deafening roar. Gas started to flow out; and then oil, green and heavy, shot up with ever-increasing force, sending rocks hundreds of feet into the air. It pushed up in an ever-more-powerful stream, twice the height of the derrick itself, before cresting and falling back to the earth" (84).Yergin's description of this discovery also highlights the environmental affects of oil production: bubbling mud, exploding derricks, and gushing oil falling to the earth.

Spindletop brought wealth to the region, but it also brought planned and unplanned environmental disaster. Carl Coke Rister reinforces Yergin's claims about the predominance of the Texas oil frontier, asserting that this gusher "launched our modern 'oil age'" in Texas, with production jumping from 836,000 barrels in 1900 to 28,136,000 barrels in 1905. Hundreds of companies sprung up around Spindletop as more oil was discovered. More gushers were discovered near Henrietta, Texas, when ranchers drilled for water (7, 8).

Because such massive production brought down prices, efforts were made to control prices by finding alternative uses for oil and by manufacturing gushers to decrease available oil. Large-scale production initially brought down prices to as low as five cents a barrel until oil was found to refine to a perfect fuel for automobiles, an industry that kept growing after 1915 (Barbour 146; Rister 9). With automobiles came roads made of asphalt, another petroleum product, and thus Texas oil boomed. To raise prices, however, companies facilitated even more environmental damage by allowing "gushers to gush . . . and gas, an oil field's self-producing force, was thoughtlessly vented to the air or burned at the well" (Rister 10). These gushers and well fires become spectacular environmental disaster in oil-frontier films from *Tulsa* to *There Will Be Blood*.

The hazardous situation in the oil industry did not improve until the 1930s. F. E. Rister argues that those improvements sprang from "state conservation and proration, supported by federal departmental activity and legislation; cooperative agreements negotiated by the Interstate Compact Commission; sound principles of secondary recovery and oil field maintenance, planned by petroleum engineers and geologists; and the promotion of trade journal and press educational programs" (11–12). George Barbour's "Texas Oil" affirms the evolution of less dangerous conditions through new processes in place at that time to "reduce the hazards of wild-catting to reasonable proportions" (146). His article includes descriptions and photographs of a blazing well in Ector County, Texas, and a gusher "brought in by shooting after removing rig." But its focus is on the progress that technology provides in an evolving oil industry with, as he calls them, "spectacular developments in recent years" (150,153). These spectacular developments are reflected in Westerns exploring both the land rush and its consequences, including the exploration for oil.

Despite their varied degrees of critique, all of the land-rush and oil-frontier films explored here rest on a history related to land use, oil leases, and land-rush outcomes, especially when oil became a commodity necessary for both the automobile and the war effort during the world wars. Although most of these films entertain through spectacular effects more than they emphasize environmental degradation or resource exploitation, they all, either implicitly or explicitly, illustrate some of the environmental consequences of the oil boom. They may show gushers and fires as spectacle and environmental disaster, foreground white men's mistreatment of American Indians and present narratives critiquing corrupt land deals and oil leases, or explicitly address the ramifications oil drilling has on water sources and prairie grasses, making cattle ranching more and more difficult as ranchlands become ruined. But they also illustrate the economic, sociological, and ecological repercussions of conquering the oil frontier, perhaps the last frontier in the modern age.

CHAPTER 5

Transcontinental Technologies

Telegraphs, Trains, and the Environment in *Union Pacific, Jesse James,* and *The Last Hunt*

Killing is the only thing that makes you feel alive.

The Last Hunt

Although oil drove the progress of technology, the most influential technological developments in the American West were railroads and the telegraph. The first transcontinental railroad, in particular, affected the western ecology and milieu most dramatically. It led to the establishment of standard time, shortened travel durations, and reduced transportation costs to levels even the lower classes could afford. The railroads brought massive numbers of settlers to the West and carried massive amounts of resources to the East. Because the North controlled much of the rail lines by 1861, this helped ensure a Union victory in the Civil War and contributed to Northern dominance over the South after it was won. And railroads prompted near-instantaneous development of settlements along the rails and rapid movement of people and materials. The tracks also facilitated transcontinental

The Golden Spike is put in place in *Union Pacific*

communication by providing avenues for telegraph lines, further connecting East with West and simplifying the economic process that settled the continent. When the Union Pacific and the Central Pacific met in Utah, marking the completion of the first transcontinental railroad, the gold spike served as a symbol for western expansion.

Such a view of progress came with environmental costs. The environmental consequences of mining, ranching, farming, and overdevelopment in the desert and range lands of the West were exacerbated by rails that could now carry millions of pounds of goods across more than a thousand miles in a matter of days, not months. The influx of settlers destroyed fragile ecosystems in multiple ways. The railroads brought land speculators, buffalo hunters, miners, homesteaders, and eventually, oil speculators, all of whom changed the western landscape significantly, causing permanent damage to both human (multiple American Indian tribes) and nonhuman (foliage and wildlife) nature.

Westerns reflect this history of environmental destruction. In these films railroads are represented as tools to hasten both progressive and populist versions of progress rather than change or eliminate them. Trains and the telegraphs that follow them speed up settlement, communication, economic growth, and inevitably, environmental destruction. All of these repercussions of the railroad are illustrated in Westerns. Samuel Bowles demonstrates how powerfully the transcontinental railroad changed "the American Republic" in his 1869 *The Pacific Railroad Open:* "Whatever we go out to see, whatever pleasures we enjoy, whatever disappointments suffer, this, at least, will be our gain,—a new conception of the magnitude, the variety and the wealth, in nature and resource, in realization and in promise, of the American Republic—and a new idea of what it is to be an American citizen" (116). Westerns highlighting railroads rest on such a view. The transcontinental railroad and its offshoots accelerated the influx of settlers into what they considered a vacant West. What is missing from this mythology of the West, however, is a vision of the ecology usurped by the railroad and all it represents.

These missing pieces of the story of the railroad and telegraph in the Western is seen by foregrounding environmental issues in relation to three themes and their representative films: epic visions of the transcontinental railroad signifying unfettered visions of progress, as reflected by *Union Pacific* (1939); mythic reactions and resistance to railroads as an unbeatable opponent in films foregrounding the Jesse James gang, illustrated by *Jesse James* (1939); and revisionist views of the railroad that demonstrate both its vulnerability and its destructive capabilities, as highlighted in *The Last Hunt* (1956).

THE CONTEXT FOR EPIC, MYTHIC, AND REVISIONIST RAILROAD FILMS

The transcontinental railroads changed the landscape and population of the American West in dramatic ways. Railroads benefited the nation, diversifying populations by importing workers from Europe, Asia, and Latin America; facilitating business opportunities like those of Fred Harvey and his Harvey Girls; and encouraging the development of art colonies in Taos and Santa Fe. Many Westerns reflect these benefits. *The Harvey Girls* (1946), for example, provides a musical version of the influx of the Harvey Restaurants and girls at train stops in the Wild West. The film's preface explains the goal of these establishments: "When Fred Harvey pushed his chain of restaurants farther and farther west along the lengthening tracks of the Santa Fe, he brought with him one of the first civilizing forces this land had known . . . the Harvey girls." The preface continues, claiming that the girls "conquered the west as surely as the Davy Crocketts and the Kit Carsons . . . not with powder horn and rifle, but with a beefsteak and a cup of coffee." The rest of the film demonstrates this civilizing effect, all in song and dance.

This new civilization produced detrimental environmental consequences. Railroads contributed to the destruction of great buffalo herds, decimated American Indian tribes, damaged desert and Great Plains ecology, and confiscated lands from impoverished farmers for their rights of way. Trains changed cattle ranching, shortening the duration of cattle drives and lessening losses of animals along the way, creating the national and international markets for American beef. The Westerns highlighted here examine the influence the railroad had on multiple populations and the landscape.

In *Red River* (1948), for example, the railroad transforms a cattle drive and symbolizes a changing West from that of the cattleman days of old Tom Dunson (John Wayne) to a more communal and railroad-driven view represented by Matthew "Matt" Garth (Montgomery Clift). Conflict in the film at first seems to be between Dunson and Garth, but the main altercation is between old and new views of progress and, ultimately, between romantic (rural) and modern (urban) values. The coming of the railroad altered the myth of the West, aligning it with technological development.

Most significantly, this change in American mythology accelerated settlement and civilization across the plains and deserts of the West, permanently damaging the landscape and the human and nonhuman nature it sustained (Worster, *Under Western Skies* 45). As Donald Worster puts it, "the wildlife reeled and died in the onslaught" (45). Railroads also harmed herds of cattle, bringing diseased animals to the East to infect other herds. In his 1874 text, *Historic Sketches of the Cattle Trade of the West and Southwest,* Joseph G. McCoy notes that the railroad helped speed up movement of diseased cattle from Texas to Illinois, and more eastern herds became infected with "Spanish Fever." He writes that, as a consequence, armed resistance to the cattle drives came from concerned farmers more than armed gangs of rustlers.

Ultimately, the railroad altered its environment both because it required that millions of acres of land be confiscated and because it connected the densely populated East with the sparsely populated West, bringing in hordes of settlers and driving a new ranching system that devastated the range. As *Red River* suggests, the cattle ranch "began to emerge as an institution in the southern part of Texas during the 1860s, and its story belongs completely to the post–Civil War era of the nation" (Worster, *Under Western Skies* 40). As Worster asserts, the cattle industry "was continental, growing as it did with the national railroad lines; then, following the invention of the refrigerated ship in 1879, it became transoceanic and global" (*Under Western Skies* 40).

The environmental effect of the ranch industry was destructive. By 1888, according to Worster, "much of the western ranching industry was lying in ruins, the victim of severe overgrazing and desperately cold winters. Many thousands of animals were lying dead all over the range, starved and frozen; the survivors were riding in boxcars to the stockyards for rapid liquidation by their owners" (*Under Western Skies* 41). Worster asserts that the railroad brought the ranch industry to the American West and, in the process, destroyed American Indian civilizations and annihilated the buffalo and other indigenous range animals (45). And, as Robin Doughty argues, "[e]fforts to introduce and establish novel, potentially valuable animals and plants [in Texas] . . . created an agricultural landscape that massively disrupted and restructured native fauna and flora" (23).

Few Westerns foregrounding the transcontinental railroad explicitly address any of the environmental consequences, yet all of these films rest on an environmental history that demonstrates the railroad's far-ranging and ongoing negative effect on human and nonhuman nature on and across the range. *Union Pacific, Jesse James,* and *The Last Hunt* illustrate some of the profound environmental consequences associated with building a transcontinental railroad, which ultimately decimated native cultures and the buffalo that sustained them while opening up the West for overwhelming empire building—the development on which both progressive and populist versions of progress are built.

UNION PACIFIC: A RAILROAD EPIC

Epic railroad Westerns show the sacrifices necessary to stretch the rails across the vast wilderness of the American West and the benefits resulting from the railroad's completion. *Union Pacific* (1939) illustrates the challenges met by brave (white) men seeking to conquer the West and link America's two shores. This epic, like *The Iron Horse* (1924) and *Western Union* (1941), follows a plotline that embraces the politics of unfettered progress and demonstrates the destruction necessary to complete the railroad, settle the West, and expand the power of the United States. What audiences are seeing in all three films is manufactured history, a history situated in a pre–World War II Hollywood vision of the West. From a contemporary eco-critical perspective, however, all of these films show that the transcontinental railroad was a vital part of both the development and the ecological destruction of the American West.

John P. Davis, writing in 1896, illustrates how significant a role railroads played in the conquest of the West. According to Davis, "the great expanse of public lands could hardly be sold to advantage by the government or settled by emigrants until railway lines had been built westward from the Mississippi." He asserts that these lines subjugated "hostile tribes of western Indians," thwarted a Mormon rebellion, fulfilled demand for communication with the East, and helped ensure a Northern victory during the Civil War (259–60). The passage of the Railroad Act on July 1, 1862, "to aid in the construction of a railroad and telegraph line from the Missouri River to the Pacific Ocean, and to seizure to the government the use of the same for postal, military, and other purposes," made construction of both the transcontinental railroad and additional telegraph lines inevitable (qtd. 261–62). As a railroad and technology epic, *Union Pacific* shows the important role the rails served in settling the American West—at any cost.

Union Pacific highlights this role in conquering the West and developing a United States built on "progressivist" politics. Directed by Cecil B. DeMille, the film foregrounds DeMille's philosophy he recorded in his 1939 autobiography: "History is not just a matter of names and dates—dry facts strung together. It is an endless, dramatic story, as alive as the news in the morning's papers. That's why I feel for the sake of lively dramatic construction, I am justified in making some contractions or compressions of historical detail, as long as I stick to the main facts" (qtd. in Smyth 115). *Union Pacific* approaches the history of the railroad from this dramatic perspective from its opening shot of train tracks viewed under the opening credits until its epic conclusion. A prologue title card onscreen reinforces this dramatic approach: "The legend of the Union Pacific is the drama of a nation, young, tough, prodigal and invincible, conquering with an iron highroad the endless reaches of the West. For the West is America's empire, and only yesterday Union Pacific was the West." According to J. E. Smyth, the film's producer, William LeBaron, told DeMille the foreword should emphasize the national importance of the Union Pacific Railroad, advice DeMille seems to take to heart with reference to the West as empire (131). To reinforce the context of the film's history, a narrator explains that the story takes place in 1865 and that a railroad is being built from Omaha to California. This railroad will provide access to resources in the West, providing a route "through which may go the gold and silver from the West to the coffers of the East." The Union Pacific will also bring cattle and grain on a shorter route from what the narrator calls "her Orient," binding East and West and opening up the western range to cattle ranchers and farmers.

The film centers on the challenges the Union Pacific faces from a banker, Asa M. Barrows (Henry Kolker), and his partner, Dick Allen (Robert Preston); and a gambler, Sid Campeau (Brian Donlevy), and his henchmen, including Duke Ring (Robert Barrat) and Jack Cordray (Anthony Quinn). These villains seek to sabotage the railroad for their own profit, but Jeff Butler (Joel McCrea), a hired regulator, fights for the railroad and against the banker and his men. The plot of *Union Pacific*, like most Westerns, includes a romantic conflict, with the "good guy," Butler, vying for the affections of an engineer's daughter, Mollie Monahan (Barbara Stanwyck), who is also courted by Dick Allen. But here the romance also serves as a plot point that further connects the two coasts. Butler, Monahan, and the Union Pacific overcome the banker and his men to unite East and West, but they also face a landscape and people constructed as savage—the dry Great Plains and the American Indians sustained by the buffalo who graze on its grasses.

American Indians and the buffalo they hunt highlight the environmental degradation on display in the film. In several shots, for example, we see the bleached bones of a dead buffalo juxtaposed with shots of live buffalo outside the train-car doors. White railroad workers and magnates even call the buffalo "overcoats on the hoof," demonstrating their view of these animals as a commodity rather than a source of food and lifestyle. Attacks on them in the film are attacks on Plains Indians and their way of life. Killing the buffalo means destroying these peoples' source of food, shelter, and clothing. We learn that the American Indians the whites attack are Sioux and see them fight back, as they do near the film's end, in a spectacular disaster in which Indians pull down a water tower onto the tracks, crashing the engine and crumpling the train. What we do not see explicitly is the reason for such wrath: whites deliberately slaughter whole herds of buffalo, using some of their meat to feed workers on the railroad but mostly taking on the hides as blankets to sell to easterners seeking a touch of the Wild West.

DeMille had a different view of American Indians' place in history. According to Smyth, at the time of the film's production, Reverend Shiuhushu of the Indian Association of America "condemned the *Union Pacific*'s 'rotten' portrayal of American Indians as a 'savage race,'" but DeMille insisted that their portrayal was based in history (133). The Indians in *Union Pacific* are used primarily for spectacular sequences. The Sioux exist in the film solely to create DeMille's famous epic moments. They attack the train, destroy the water tower, and burn bridges, all for spectacular effect. Whites in the film call them "red devils" but successfully challenge these attacks, demonstrating the superiority of both the whites and their technology.

The Sioux have no chance against the whites or their railroad. Even when they shoot a telegraph operator reporting about one of their raids, the whites receive the message and prevail. The conflict continues between the American Indians and the railroad and the cavalry that protect it. The Sioux even set fire to the track to burn down a bridge, but the train goes through it. Ultimately *Union Pacific* asserts that the railroad brought civilization and progress to the West, helping settle a vast empire and connect western resources to eastern cities.

Migrating American Indians confront the transcontinental railroad in *Union Pacific*

But the buffalo bones beside the tracks tell a different story. They signify the environmental costs of "progress," and especially of the transcontinental railroad. The bones not only show the literal loss of buffalo herds but also represent the dire effect the railroad and its riders will have on human and nonhuman nature. The Sioux cannot defeat the railroad or its telegraph. Instead, these technological advances encroach on both the people and their lands. According to Donald Worster's *Under Western Skies,* the buffalo were nearly exterminated by the influx of cattle and settlers into the Great Plains. Their numbers once ranged from Tom McHugh's estimation of "32 million . . . animals on the grasslands, with another two million living in wooded areas bordering the plains" (16–17), to Ernest Thompson Seton's figure of 75 million buffalo in North America (386). Now, Worster explains, only 1 percent of that original number remains (17).

The railroad exacerbated the extermination of the buffalo. Heather Cox Richardson asserts, "Buffalo hunters came to the plains with the railroad crews that began to cut through Kansas during the Civil War." "Buffalo Bill" Cody was among them and in 1867 "began hunting buffalo to feed the men building the Kansas Pacific Railroad, the first stage of the great rail line to the Pacific." Other buffalo hunters "sent the hides east on the railroads to become cheap leather for machine belts and straps." Richardson states that "the buffalo hunt peaked in 1872; in the next two years settlers and sportsmen would tag animals for food and sport while hide hunters would kill 4,374,000 buffalo and Indians about 1,215,000" (73, 127).

The connection between the Indian Wars and buffalo extermination is direct and deadly. By 1873 the buffalo were all but destroyed, and American Indian tribes had been "made desperate by the destruction of the animals that supported them" and began "skirmishing with whites on the plains" in retaliation (Richardson 160). Their efforts were ultimately futile, and thus, as *Union Pacific* demonstrates, the railroad completely changed the West. The buffalo were gone, clearing the way for more cattle. The American Indians, for the most part, were contained. White settlers streamed westward, conquering the plains, the desert lands, and the west coast, marking their territory with environmental damage yet to be calculated (Worster, *Under Western Skies* 45).

The telegraph lines built to accompany the rails also contributed to this environmental destruction. The first transcontinental telegraph line was completed in 1861 (valorized in depth by Fritz Lang's *Western Union*), less than a year after Congress passed "an act granting federal aid to an overland telegraph from Missouri to San Francisco" (Ambrose 67). But historian Stephen Ambrose argues that a more important transcontinental line was built "right alongside the tracks" of the Union Pacific Railroad. The work involved in stretching this telegraph required as many men and as much effort as building the railroad itself. For Ambrose the two main obstacles to the telegraph's effectiveness were buffalo, which had a way of "using the poles as scratching posts and would sometimes knock them down," and liquor sold at whiskey ranches, which would "interfere materially" with the workers' effectiveness. He concludes, "Together, the Transcontinental Railroad and the telegraph made modern America possible" (250, 257, 258, 370).

The environmental consequences of that modern America, however, were astronomical. More settlers moved west, destroying fragile ecosystems in the prairies and deserts, and more resources moved east from western mines, farms, and ranches. Like the railroad, the telegraph was a vital part of this conquest of the American West. This destruction is reflected in epic railroad Westerns like *Union Pacific*.

MYTHIC REACTIONS AND RESISTANCE TO THE RAILROAD: THE CASE OF *JESSE JAMES*

Many railroad Westerns also highlight mythic reactions and resistance to the railroad, a legacy that continues with the 2007 remake of *3:10 to Yuma*.[1] The most effective of these mythic films, however, draw on the legends surrounding Jesse James, a tradition continuing with *The Assassination of Jesse James by the Coward Robert Ford* (2007). These Westerns either exult or resist the myth of the railroad. In them settlers become either bandits who resist the rail companies and their usurping of the land and power, or civilizing forces who seek to perpetuate the rails. But *Jesse James* (1939) and later James Gang films most clearly illustrate the railroad's consequences for landowners.

Jesse James shows the resistance the railroad stimulated in farmers whose land was taken to accommodate the rails. It includes text superimpositions that state how ruthlessly the railroad grabbed lands in its path. For example, the film begins with title cards that blame the unscrupulous railroad for the James Gang's exploits, when juxtaposed with images of the James family's resistance: "After the tragic war between the states, America turned to the winning of the West. The symbol of this era was the building of the transcontinental railroad. The advance of the railroad was, in some cases, predatory and unscrupulous. Whole communities found themselves victimized by an ever-growing ogre—the Iron Horse." It then shows members of the James family resisting an armed gang that demands that farmers sign over their property deeds at the point of a gun. To more explicitly connect the railroad with their resistance, the narration blames the James Gang's outlaw status on "this uncertain and lawless age."

The film takes a sympathetic approach to the James brothers as a way to discredit the myth of the railroad, justify the gang's crimes, and mythologize Jesse and Frank James as heroes fighting an unbeatable opponent. To do this, it first constructs Jesse (Tyrone Power) and Frank (Henry Fonda) as hardworking farmers forced to defend their mother from an armed gang of railroad thugs who demand that she sign over the deed to her farm or face a violent death. The James boys' resistance leads to a fight and their escape. But their mother is killed by a bomb thrown into her home by the thugs, and the brothers first seek personal vengeance and then retribution against the railroad. These events build sympathy for Frank and Jesse and provide a valid reason for their revenge.

This view of the railroad and the James boys is shared by other upstanding citizens in the film. Everyone hates the railroad because of its greed for property, paying owners even less than 10 percent of what their land is worth. The minister (Spencer Charters) in the James family church reinforces this claim of hatred toward the company when he states: "Do you realize, boy, that I had a farm giving nine hundred bushels of corn . . . until the railroad had taken it from me? Why I'd given up preaching . . . and was making an honest living off of the land, until that dad-swinged railroad swindled me out of my own home. By golly, son, do you know I had a big house . . . two barns . . . three outhouses . . . until that gol-danged railroad hornswoggled me!" Jesse James and his gang react to the corrupt practices of the railroad, a giant corporation constructed, in their eyes, to steal their land and way of life. The film's representation of both the railroad and the James brothers legitimizes their reaction.

Both *The True Story of Jesse James* (1957) and *The Great North-field Minnesota Raid* (1972) also highlight the James–Younger Gang's conflict with the railroad and, consequently, the North. Instead of highlighting the railroad's injustice to the James family after the Civil War, however, both of these films are set in 1876, after the Missouri legislature has failed in its attempts to pardon the gang's members, who then continue their battle with the North. *The Great Northfield Minnesota Raid,* especially, emphasizes this context.

The gang's actions still rest on their resistance to the railroad's land-grabbing policies, but they also respond to continuing post–Civil War conflicts between North and South. The railroad was a product of the war, with the Pacific Railroad Act becoming law in 1862 because Southern legislators were missing from the vote, according to John Gladstone. He argues: "The American Civil War was the world's first railroad war. The North, already heavily industrialized, had a crucial advantage over the South" and easily won this "modern war" (7). The railroad ensured that the North would dominate the South for years afterward.

In such a context, it comes as no surprise that the James-Younger Gang becomes idealized as a valid combatant to northern dominance. *The Great Northfield Minnesota Raid* questions whether the gang members are heroes or outlaws, but it opens with information about the railroad companies stealing land. The railroad has hired Allen Pinkerton (Dana Elcar) and his detectives (including Herbert Nelson) to make examples of the James–Younger Gang. The legislature cannot make up for fifteen years of criminal activity, according to the companies. The only amnesty the James and Younger boys can get is in death, from the perspective of railroad magnates and Pinkerton detectives.

The first shootout between the gang and the Pinkertons occurs early in the film and reveals the reasoning behind the gang's criminal acts. Cole Younger (Cliff Robertson) has been hit. Granny (Madeleine Taylor Holmes) tries to heal him in a cave. Jesse James (Robert Duvall) then reveals the railroad's tyranny: they "came down here and stole the land, blew off my granny's arm, killed Jim Younger [Luke Askew], and now Cole Younger!" Cole survives and later, after Jesse and others have left for Minnesota, tells them about the legislature's decision to offer amnesty. The boys debate the amnesty, but because the railroad magnates and the Pinkerton agents they hired attack them, they continue their fight to steal all the money they can for their last raid, this time in Northfield, Minnesota.

The rest of the film foregrounds the Northfield raid and its aftermath. Jesse James is battling more than the railroad, the film asserts—he is battling modernity. The modernist setting James fights is effectively reinforced by the few remaining buffalo they pass on the way to Minnesota. The American centennial celebration going on in Northfield when they arrive emphasizes the conflict between rural and urban values associated with a move toward modernity. In Northfield we see a baseball game, a steam engine pulling lumber, and a Dutch bakery—signs of the time—and we hear about the Panic of 1873, after which people stopped trusting banks. A steam calliope outside the town bank further establishes the modern setting. Later in the film, dolls from the house of an old woman (Nellie Burt) and a telephone foreground the movement away from the pastoral and into the technological age.

After the battle in town and the relentless pursuit of the remaining gang members as they try to escape back to Missouri, the Pinkertons have nearly won, ushering in the railroad and all the technology and convenience it brings to the West. The conclusion shows that Bob Ford kills Jesse six years later and that Cole lives until 1916, surviving in the Stillwater Penitentiary for twenty-five years. Ultimately, though, this film provides a keen picture of the conflict between rural and urban values, between romantic and modern worldviews, with the urban, modern Yankee ideals usurping those of the rural, romantic South.

From an ecological viewpoint, however, the land issue provides insight into some of the environmental consequences of the railroad's push into the frontier. The North represents progress, technological development, and corrupt laissez-faire politics. The South signifies rural values that embrace both the communal and the pastoral. By stealing land to disturb this southern worldview, the railroad makes way for a wave of northern settlers who industrialize even rural activities like farming and ranching. Although the conflict depicted here rests more in mythology than reality, it ends in accelerated desecration of the land, an inevitable consequence of both populist and progressive progress.

More recent Westerns examining the myth of Jesse James and the James Gang foreground the conflict between the ideology of the North and South more than between landowners and the railroad, but they continue to critique urban values that disregard the value of pastoral land and ideals. *The Long Riders* (1980), for example, again highlights the battle between the James-Younger Gang and the Pinkertons as representatives of the railroad when the Union Pacific Railroad and the Pinkerton Company offer $5,000 for bringing in the gang members. The action ensues, with the agents ultimately either killing or capturing every member, but the conflict between North and South, and between urban (signified by the railroad and Pinkertons) and rural (signified by the James-Younger Gang's resistance) provides the environmental bent of the film. The fight is over land and over values, with a northern ideology that embraces progressivist progress usurping the southern rural worldview based in, the movie asserts, conservation of family and land. *The Assassination of Jesse James by the Coward Robert Ford* continues this saga of disputes between urban and rural, North and South, and "big guys" and "little guys" along railroad routes.

All of these films foreground a rebellion against the railroads based in an economic history that forced out landowners along proposed rail lines and provided land grants and bonds to

The James-Younger Gang rob a train in *The Long Riders*

the railroad companies. When the Pacific Railroad Bill passed in 1862, resistance by farmers, ranchers, and other landowners also became inevitable. According to Stephen Ambrose, the bill "called for the creation of a corporation, The Union Pacific . . . that would build west from the Missouri River, while the Central Pacific would build East from Sacramento." Most importantly for these landowners, however, was the land distribution for the railroads. Ambrose explains: "Capital stock of the UP was to be a hundred thousand shares at $1,000 each, or $100 million. Both roads would have a right of way of two hundred feet on both sides of the road over public lands and would be given five alternate sections (square miles) on each side per mile, or sixty-four hundred acres per mile." The bill provided other benefits to the corporations, including "financial aid in the form of governmental bonds of $16,000 per mile for flat land, $32,000 for foothills, and $48,000 per mile for mountainous terrain after they had built forty miles approved by government commissioners" (80–81).

Jack Beatty's *The Age of Betrayal* (2006) also documents how this land "give away" assured guaranteed profits for the corporations and the politicians they bribed. Free land, free resources, financial support, and attendant political corruption ensured that the railroads would be constructed. They also meant that land-owners in the "right of way" areas of both roads would lose their holdings. Even Ambrose admits that: "What the Ames brothers, the Big Four, and others thought should have been regarded as a splendid achievement was widely viewed as full of serious abuse. For example, the corruption that was rife in the building of the railroads was widespread. Further, the railroads enjoyed a monopoly that allowed them to charge what most users came to regard as inflated rates for freight and passenger traffic. There was a great deal of shoddy construction that had to be replaced." Leaders from both the Central Pacific and the Union Pacific also lied to governmental officials despite the massive land grants and bonds they received (376).

Most importantly, however, transcontinental railroads brought millions more settlers to the West and provided access to billions more dollars of its resources. According to a *Putnam's Magazine* article from October 1868, "without the railroads . . . the Mississippi Valley would have fewer than four million inhabitants instead of the twelve million already there with more coming" (qtd. in Ambrose 371). Ambrose tells us that the *Putnam* piece also shows that "in the past fifteen years . . . , the population of the United States had increased 90 percent, while production had jumped 230 percent" (371).

More settlers meant more farmers, ranchers, and others seeking homesteads, many of whom traveled on railroads for less than one-tenth the earlier costs of an overland journey. Ambrose asserts that before the end of the Civil War, "it took a person months and might cost more than $1000 to go from New York to San Francisco" (369). In 1869 it cost as little as $70 on the railroad, a price that dropped to $65 a year later (Ambrose 369). This massive influx of pioneers dramatically changed the West, turning buffalo grasslands into cattle ranches and Indian hunting grounds into farms. Despite the massive changes trains and their cargo brought to the West, only a few Westerns explicitly address the environmental consequences. Railroads contributed greatly to "progress" in the West for both the corporate giants of the companies, the banks that supported them, and the populous that rode the rails to a new life on the frontier. These progressive and populist views of progress also contributed to environmental destruction still felt today.

REVISIONIST VISIONS OF THE RAILROAD AND ITS REPERCUSSIONS: *THE LAST HUNT*

Other Westerns take a revisionist approach to the history underpinning the construction of transcontinental railroads and telegraphs. *The Last Hunt* (1956), *How the West was Won* (1962), and *The White Buffalo* (1977) explicitly address the destruction of the buffalo. *Once Upon a Time in the West* (1968), *The Wild Bunch* (1969), and *Blazing Saddles* (1974) critique the railroad as a corrupt corporation as do the James Gang films, but in these revisionist Westerns, the company falls, with community values overcoming corporate greed. The pastoral, then, supersedes modern technology, so nature and the natural are embraced, if in a domesticated form.

How the West Was Won offers a revisionist view of American Indians and their treatment by the railroad and critiques the railroad's violation of a treaty that would maintain the Indians' hunting grounds and control the influx of white populations into their territory. *The Outlaws Is Coming* (1965) addresses and blatantly critiques the buffalo extermination from a comic perspective. *Once Upon a Time in the West,* directed by Sergio Leone, foregrounds the technology of the railroad as paramount, overshadowing even Morton (Gabriele Ferzetti), the railroad baron, and his violent henchmen. *The Wild Bunch,* however, examines corrupt banks and railroads and their progressive politics at the turn of the century. Mel Brooks's *Blazing Saddles* spoofs the Western, with a focus on a transcontinental railroad and its effect on landowners, American Indians, African Americans, Chinese

Americans, and Irish immigrant workers. And in *The White Buffalo* (1977), the slaughter of buffalo caused by the railroad's construction is critiqued in mythic ways.

But *The Last Hunt* most explicitly addresses the annihilation of the buffalo in the American West, offering a powerful account of the ecologically devastating repercussions of transcontinental railroads. As Worster makes clear in *Under Western Skies,* "The chief exception to our general ignorance [of environmental degradation] is the fate of the bison, whose near extermination we have documented in some detail" (45–46). *The Last Hunt* illustrates the effect of such slaughter in the wake of railroads. John Gladstone connects this to the destruction of the American Indian and their worldview as well in "The Romance of the Iron Horse": "The real winning of the West belongs to the railroads: the iron horse signaled the end of open grazing, with land apportioned off to cattlemen, and the end of the American buffalo; and it destroyed the Indians' hopes of ever regaining their traditional hunting grounds, thus sealing their fate forever" (10). This piece also demonstrates how depictions of the railroad in decorative and propaganda art changed from the nineteenth through the twentieth centuries, providing us with a pictorial history of the railroad and its repercussions. But a wood engraving of a mass slaughter of bison from 1871 (*The Far West— Shooting Buffalo on the Kansas-Pacific*) harshly illustrates this most devastating environmental catastrophe.

This history of the buffalo's destruction is examined either implicitly or explicitly in iconic Westerns. A center point in *The Searchers* (1956), for example, is the letter from Martin Pawley (Jeffrey Hunter) to Laurie Jorgensen (Vera Miles), which describes in flashback a moment in which Ethan Edwards (John Wayne) shoots wildly at a herd of buffalo, screaming that they will not feed any more Comanches. Martin's confusion about this is shared by the audience. But the full explanation for the elimination of the buffalo is answered in Richard Brook's *The Last Hunt,* an MGM film from the same year. *The Searchers* is set in 1867–72, during the height of the Indian Wars. But *The Last Hunt* is set in 1883, at the end of the extermination of both the buffalo and the Plains Indians.

Both of these films, however, illustrate the negative effect slaughtering buffalo had not only on the environment but also on the life of Plains Indians. Andrew Isenberg reinforces this connection between buffalo and Indians in *The Destruction of the Bison,* asserting: "The eighteenth-century invasion [of Euro-Americans] had levered the mounted bison hunters to dominance in the western plains; the renewed incursion of the nineteenth century devastated both the nomads and the bison" (93). The strategy of destroying the buffalo herds to eliminate the plains tribes was well in place at the point of Ethan Edwards's cinematic slaughter, but the railroads became the main driver for expansion and the primary reason for the elimination of the herds. *The Last Hunt* shows the consequences of this after the railroads have nearly civilized the West and closed the frontier.

The Last Hunt reflects this history of environmental destruction. It has been overlooked despite its close ties to *The Searchers* and its own powerful critique of the extermination of both the American Indians and the buffalo, meant to make room for ranchers, railroads, and homesteaders in the West. Although the film received little attention at or after its release, *The Last Hunt* deserves a reevaluation, if for no other reason than it rests on a similar philosophical grounding as *The Searchers,* and it offers as strong an indictment of the conquest of the frontier. Both films illustrate the extermination of American Indians to make way for white settlers, but *The Last Hunt* depicts one of the brutal strategies used by whites: the slaughter of the buffalo.

The film addresses the consequences of removing American Indians to reservations. But it most powerfully indicts Euro-American conquest of the West by graphically demonstrating the massive slaughter of buffalo herds and explicitly discussing the primary reason for their destruction: the annihilation of the American Indian presence to make way for the railroads and the settlers they brought. Because *The Last Hunt* illustrates the annihilation of human and nonhuman nature in stark detail, it offers a powerful critique of the destruction of the original West in the name of progress.

Although no one would argue that *The Last Hunt* provides as strong an aesthetic experience as *The Searchers,* the films exhibit many similarities. Both foreground similar sadistic heroes, Ethan Edwards in *The Searchers* and Charlie Gilson (Robert Taylor) in *The Last Hunt.* Ethan seeks revenge on Chief Scar (Henry Brandon) of the Comanche because the Indians slaughtered his brother's family, including his brother's wife and Ethan's one true love, Martha (Dorothy Jordan). Charlie seeks revenge on American Indians and the buffalo that sustain them because, as he asserts over and over, he lives to kill. The consequences are the same. Both Ethan and Charlie use violence without remorse, reaching levels that drive Ethan to nearly kill his niece, Debbie (Natalie Wood), because she has been "tainted" by living with the Comanche and that drive Charlie to kill Woodfoot (Lloyd Nolan), his buffalo skinner. Charlie becomes so "spooked" that he hears buffalo charging in a thunderclap.

Robert Taylor and John Wayne, top box-office stars, were popular with the studio system because of their rightwing politics. Yet both actors played roles in these films clearly meant to critique rather than validate the slaughter of American Indians and buffalo. Taylor's powerful performance heightened this critique. *The Last Hunt* was a departure for Taylor also because it was written and directed by Richard Brooks, who was regarded as an independent writer–director early in his career.

The films also explicitly illustrate reactions to the Civil War, highlighted by the intermittent insertion of the period song "Lorena," written by Joseph Philbrick Webster in 1857. Ethan refuses to relinquish his ties to the South after the war, even when faced with arrest, entering and exiting the Texas setting alone and isolated. Charlie embraced the Civil War because it taught him that killing gave him power and made him a man.

Both films also react to one of the consequences of the war, the transcontinental railroads.

The philosophy grounding *The Last Hunt* nearly replicates that of *The Searchers.* Both films critique the extermination of American Indians and the buffalo through the actions of their vengeful heroes. In *The Searchers,* as in *The Last Hunt,* numerous scenes offer an indictment of unrestrained conquest of the West through Ethan Edwards and his foil, Chief Scar. Two stand out in particular. The first occurs early in the film, when Ethan and a group of Texas Rangers take off after some cattle stolen by what they think are Caddo or Kiowa Indians. After riding through majestic landscapes of Monument Valley, the posse finds the cattle forty miles from the ranches, deliberately killed with Comanche lances, slaughtered but not eaten for food. Another scene is the third flashback during Laurie's reading of Martin Pauley's one letter. In it Martin and Ethan approach a snow-covered area where buffalo are gathered. Ethan shoots one of the animals, causing the rest to stampede. He then goes into a passionate frenzy, shooting wildly into the herd, his apparently senseless slaughter of the buffalo intended to starve and deprive the Indians of food. Marty protests the deliberate killings, but Ethan does not listen: "At least they won't feed any Comanches this winter. Killing buffalo is like killing Indians." Ethan's proclamation parallels the earlier actions of Scar's band, which slaughters Ethan's family, when they kill the homesteaders' cattle. This parallel complicates any attempt to bifurcate American Indians from white settlers; it also offers a critique by reinforcing an anti-environmental message, seemingly shared by both cultures, that valorizes death and destruction not for food or survival, but for revenge.

The Last Hunt shows us the mass extermination of the buffalo by including exhaustive authentic footage of government sharpshooters killing buffalo to thin out a herd. In the film this graphic slaughter goes on for at least three minutes of screen time and makes a powerful impression. Adding Charlie's sadistic

Two scenes from *The Searchers:* (*above*) Discovery of dead cattle and hunting buffalo; (*below*) Comanches and whites slaughter their adversaries' chief food source.

attitude toward buffalo and the American Indians sustained by buffalo hunting adds force to the film's message, which blatantly condemns one of the worst environmental catastrophes brought on by the transcontinental railroads. That indictment continues through the end, when Sandy McKenzie (Stewart Granger) and the American Indian girl (Debra Paget) ride away from the hunt, and their retreat crosses both piles of buffalo bones and Charlie's frozen body.

The Last Hunt opens on a painting similar to an 1871 woodcut depicting American Indians lancing buffalo. Then a written prologue scrolls up explaining the image's contribution to the film's critique of the extermination of the herds: "In 1853 the American plains thundered with the sound of 60,000,000 buffaloes. Thirty years later, at the time of this story, the hunters and Indians had recklessly slaughtered these herds to a bare 3000 survivors." In these early scenes, buffalo calves run alongside adults, with dust flying as their flight becomes a stampede. They race toward a small herd of cattle, and Sandy McKenzie tries to drive them off. The buffalo run on, leaving a distraught rancher, who must shoot all his trampled cattle. Charlie Gilson is then introduced into the plot when he rides by and recognizes Sandy as a former hunter for the army engineers. Through their conversation, we learn that Sandy has lost his entire herd in the stampede, and with it four years of planning, all "gone in a minute."

This opening introduces the dilemma Sandy faces: he has lost his cattle to the buffalo he used to kill, now he must find a way to replenish his herd for "good grass . . . rich earth, plenty of water year round" on his property. These scenes also illustrate the ideological conflict between the two men. Sandy was done chasing buffalo, telling Charlie he needed to "get the stink out of his insides" because he is "fed up with killing." But Charlie disagrees, telling him: "There ain't nothing wrong with [killing]. Killing's natural. Killing, fighting, war—that's the natural state of things. The more you kill, the better man you was." They had both fought in the Civil War, but Sandy "wasn't in it for the killing." He changes his mind, though, when Charlie declares: "Buffalo won't let you live peacefully like you want to live. They've got to die. Their hides would pay for your new stock of cattle." Now the two agree to hunt buffalo for their own reasons and go to town to pick up supplies and skinners.

Charlie's violence toward the buffalo is connected to a hatred for American Indians early in the film. While in town buying supplies, he and Sandy pass a "half-breed" boy, Jimmy O'Brien (Russ Tamblyn), in the general store. Charlie pushes the boy as he passes him and pulls a gun on him when he sees the boy is holding a revolver he wishes to buy. Sandy stops Charlie from shooting, and Jimmy walks to the barbershop to cut his hair, as if he too finds his Indian blood offensive. When he returns, however, he passes an old American Indian man tied to a post like a dog and gives him some water. Others in the town hate Indians, the image tells us, which is extended to Jimmy again for providing the water. The boy is a "stinking Indian," one of the men growls as he punches him into the mud.

Hatred of American Indians extends further to buffalo when Charlie talks with Woodfoot (Lloyd Nolan), a drunken buffalo skinner who lost his leg during the Civil War. Charlie offers him sixty dollars per month to skin buffalo for them, but Woodfoot rambles on, explaining that he "skinned for the Santa Fe, the army, Wild Bill." To him "the only good buffalo hunter left is Sandy McKenzie." He connects buffalo hunting generally with the railroad in his ramblings and, in turn, infers that the hunt is associated with the extermination of American Indians to make way for the railroads and the settlers it brings.

Woodfoot's behavior after Charlie hires him foreshadows Charlie's irrational slaughter of the animals. Charlie, Sandy, Jimmy, and Woodfoot race off across the plains toward the buffalo. Woodfoot leads the way in his wagon, chasing buffalo and shooting to get the herd moving. He races toward the animals frantically, with Charlie hanging on in the back. Then the skinner crashes the wagon in a creek and comes out of the water laughing. Charlie further reveals his irrational, sadistic personality when he pulls a gun on Woodfoot because of the crash. Sandy calms him down, telling him to round up the mules while he scouts out a campsite, but Charlie nearly explodes, yelling as he walks away, "Who you telling what to do?" He also goes after "fresh meat," even though

Sandy tells him it is too windy. The buffalo smell Charlie and run away from him, so he comes back empty handed. Woodfoot tells him, "you figure everybody and everything's again' ya," when Charlie grows angry even over biting bugs. He is angry at the buffalo, at Woodfoot, and especially at "Injuns," even claiming that he learned about guns by "killin' Injuns."

Charlie equates killing with power and sees the buffalo hunt as a way to regain that force. He sees this hunt as an ongoing battle that will prove his manhood, claiming, "None of us'll live to see the end of the buffalo." But the stories Woodfoot and Sandy tell demonstrate the inaccuracy of his claims. Woodfoot talks about buffalo slaughters and whole herd "suicides." Sandy explains that after the slaughter he faced "just bones, millions of bones, carcasses split naked for the hides." He cannot escape "the stink of it, shame of it." But Charlie maintains his belief in the killing, connecting it even more explicitly to the destruction of the American Indian. He remembers General Sheridan's medal for buffalo hunting, featuring a dead buffalo on one side and a dead Indian on the other. Buffalo and Indians are explicitly connected here, even from Sandy's perspective. "Sure, during the Indian war," he says. "Every dead buffalo meant a starvin' Indian," explaining that General Sheridan "wanted to starve 'em back on the reservation."

Charlie's sadism reaches hyperbolic levels when two of their mules are stolen by an American Indian family. Sandy explains that it is "not a crime to Indians. They don't think like us." Nevertheless, Charlie races after them with guns loaded. When he reaches the family with his mules, he shoots them all in cold blood, even an Indian girl (Debra Paget). He kills all the men but only wounds the woman, who crawls after a baby and runs away. Charlie walks into their camp nonchalantly, eating their meat right off the fire. He looks at the dead men and shows no emotion until he hears a baby crying. Then he throws down the meat and runs after the sound, drawing his gun when he sees the woman and child.

The next morning the violence is further displayed when Sandy rides over a wide shot of carcasses and bones of slaughtered buffalo. The scene also further bifurcates Sandy's and Charlie's attitudes. Charlie sets up his rifle in front of a herd and starts shooting, killing buffalo one by one. We hear the banging of the rifle until all the ammunition has been used. Sandy, in contrast, puts his rifle on a stand but cannot shoot immediately. Charlie has reloaded and kills the remaining animals. At the end of his load, he gets up from his stand and walks toward the annihilated herd, shooting with each step, emptying even his revolver. He kills all the animals in about two minutes of screen time. The ground shot of slaughtered buffalo at Charlie's feet reveals the extent of the slaughter, but Charlie merely stoops down, panting and smiling from his labor and cradling his hot Winchester like a lover.

The sheer volume of slaughter serves as a powerful critique here. It is painful to watch the destruction of buffalo on the screen. Sandy too shoots buffalo, for at least a minute of screen time, and Woodfoot drives his wagon over the bones and around the carcasses to skin them one by one. Calves walk around the dead in search of their mothers. The horror on the screen is emphasized too by Jimmy and Sandy's reactions to it. Jimmy watches motionlessly; Sandy begins to sweat and closes his eyes against the pain.

An argument over a white buffalo hide amplifies the conflict between the two ideologies represented by Charlie and Sandy and their differing reactions to both buffalo and American Indians. When Sandy sees a white buffalo emerge from the herd, he stops shooting, his face awestruck. But Charlie rides up to the animal on his horse and shoots it. Sandy seems stunned. "Did you have to kill him?" Sandy asks him, remarking that the white buffalo is "big medicine for the Indians." But Charlie wants to sell its hide, which will bring him two thousand dollars, more than all the hides together, he argues. Charlie's actions here also reinforce his hatred of American Indians. Jimmy wants to return the sacred hide to his tribe, but Charlie refuses. Woodfoot connects this response to racism and self-hatred, observing to Jimmy and Sandy, "Charlie don't like himself, so he don't like the Injun no better." The issue of the white buffalo soon elevates that hatred to extremes. When the Indian woman sees the white skin, she exclaims, "you take away our food and now you kill our religion." For Charlie, however, "[k]illing is the only real proof you're alive." He, like Ethan Edwards in *The Searchers,* believes that "[o]ne less buffalo means one less Indian." In fact, when a Sioux, Spotted Hand (Ed Lonehill), passes by and sees the white buffalo skin and asks to trade his ponies for it, Charlie refuses but agrees to fight for the hides. When asked what he would get out of shooting the Sioux, Charlie says, "pleasure, boy. Just pure pleasure." And he guns down Spotted Hand with a smile.

Charlie's hatred of American Indians conflicts with Woodfoot's respect for them and their culture. Woodfoot even tells Charlie that their religion "is the same as ours, only they don't pass the hat after they're done." As Sandy nurses Spotted Hand's mortal wounds, Woodfoot asserts, "buffalo mean an awful lot to the Indians—meat, rope for winter time, tanned hides for clothes, teepees, . . . shields for war." They even use the skin of the leg for moccasins. They use "every ounce," he says: "They mean life for Indians, so they made a religion of 'em." When the Indian woman gives Jimmy the white hide to take back with Spotted Hand's body, no one stops him: Charlie is away, busy filling cartridges.

Sandy also serves as a contrast for Charlie's hatred. He befriends the Indian girl and boy. When he goes to town to sell hides, he washes off the buffalo smell, gets drunk, and starts a fight, yelling, "It's a crime against nature and the Indian to kill the buffalo." Sandy returns to camp only to free the Indian girl and the baby she saved. Charlie, however, continues to connect the slaughter of buffalo with power and loses reason when the herds disappear. He thinks Sandy will bring back the nearly eradicated buffalo, so when Sandy returns and a storm blows up, Charlie thinks that he hears one hundred thousand buffalo in the thunder. With Charlie acting so irrationally, Sandy can save the Indian girl and baby from his partner's wrath. Sandy and Woodfoot get him drunk, and when Charlie awakens, Sandy, the Indian girl, and the baby are gone.

Charlie's sadistic hatred and need for the power killing brings him reaches psychotic levels at this point. He chases after Sandy, taking Jimmy and Woodfoot with him. When Woodfoot chases off Charlie's horse, Charlie kills him. In contrast, Sandy and the two Indians go to a reservation, and when they discover that the people are starving, they give them their mules for meat and go back to town for supplies from the army.

The irrational chase ultimately kills Charlie and serves as a powerful reproach of the attitudes he represents. Back at a cave, where Sandy, Jimmy, and the Indian girl warm themselves at a fire, Charlie calls out Sandy, whom he now sees as his enemy, telling him to wait until morning when he can see to shoot him. According to a hide dealer Charlie encountered in town, the winds are blowing up, bringing in winter colds so low they freeze buffalo hides solid as boards. But Charlie refuses to enter the cave, kills a lone buffalo, and wraps himself in its skin while he waits. When Sandy finds him the next day, both Charlie and the robe are frozen stiff. "Froze to death," Sandy remarks, and he and the others ride away with the white buffalo hide in a tree at the center of the screen. Their ride over piles of buffalo bones, however, highlights the powerful message of the film.

As Charlie asserts, "[o]ne less buffalo means one less Indian," so the bone-covered plains reveal and condemn the annihilation of both the buffalo and the American Indians they sustained. *The Last Hunt* stands out as a strong denouncement of this extermination. Robert Taylor's portrayal of Charlie resonates powerfully and serves as the final claim in support of this critique, since Charlie dies wearing the skin of one of the many buffalo he destroys. In this film Taylor reverses his role as a Medal of Honor–winning Shoshone in Anthony Mann's *Devil's Doorway* (1950) and makes a more powerful statement against eco-extermination.

CONCLUSION: THE MISSING HISTORIES

The ecological message in these railroad Westerns is clear. The railroad and all it represents destroyed the natural world and deliberately annihilated the buffalo, a massacre that, at least according to *The Last Hunt,* cannot go unpunished. All of the films highlighted here suggest that progress has an environmental price. The transcontinental railroad brought the buffalo hunters, who killed buffalo both for railroad workers' meals and for sport. As a consequence, this also destroyed American Indians, sending those who remained farther west in search of new hunting grounds and prey. It transformed the cattle industry too, bringing in cattle that decimated the grazing lands. And it brought millions of new settlers, who built cities and transformed a vital set of ecosystems into both garden and wasteland. Despite these environmental costs, history reflected in these films still valorizes the railroads. As Stephen Ambrose concludes about the building of the transcontinental railroad: "Things happened as they happened. It is possible to imagine all kinds of different routes across the continent, or a better way for the government to help private industry, or maybe to have the government build and own it. But those things didn't happen, and what did take place is grand. So we admire those who did it—even if they were far from perfect—for what they were and what they accomplished and how much each of us owes them" (382). Even though he admits those who built the it were "far from perfect," Ambrose celebrates the railroad as an engineering accomplishment that helped build a western empire, disregarding the devastation railroads and telegraphs brought to the human and nonhuman nature of the West. Examining these railroad Westerns through an eco-centric postmodern lens helps reveal some of the environmental history missing in Ambrose's conclusion, especially those that not only facilitated overdevelopment of land but also annihilated American Indian cultures and the buffalo that sustained them.

CHAPTER 6

Smoke Signals and
American Indian Westerns

Narratives of Environmental Adaptation

Representations of American Indians gain further authenticity and serve as more powerful critiques of environmental degradation when they are constructed by American Indian filmmakers rather than Euro-Americans, even Richard Brooks. In a scene near the middle of Sherman Alexie's *Smoke Signals* (1998), for example, Victor Joseph (Adam Beach) exclaims, when his traveling companion, Thomas Builds-the-Fire (Evan Adams), begins telling him about his dream of a fertile Spokane River thriving with fish, "There ain't any salmon in that river no more!" Victor's exclamation not only stops Thomas's storytelling, however, but also opens up space for a solution to environmental degradation shown through Victor's own dream-telling, a nightmare about his own boyhood attempts to wake up his drunk parents, who are passed out after a party. In retaliation Victor smashes empty beer bottles against his father's truck, seemingly expressing his anger, but the action also empowers him, offering a solution to at least one of the causes of the disaster he sees around him on the Coeur d'Alene Reservation. In his dream, then, Victor is finding a way to turn the hell of his reservation household into a home. Even as a child he attempts to adapt his environment to make it more habitable, just as Thomas adapts a lifeless river into a thriving ecosystem through his dreams.

Westerns in which American Indian characters are highlighted rest on this idea of adapting horrific environments into homes, or narratives of environmental adaptation. Although such films do construct American Indians as either savage or noble "others," they also (and most importantly here) demonstrate how effectively Indians have adapted, and adapted to, what white settlers see as an environmental "hell" or something worse. As the Fort Lowell commander, Major Cartwright (Douglass Watson), puts it in *Ulzana's Raid* (1972): "You know what General Sheridan said of this country, lieutenant? . . . If he owned hell and Arizona, he'd live in hell and rent out Arizona."

In a move toward a more sustainable view of prairie and desert ecosystems, American Indians in a variety of Westerns adapt a seemingly lifeless area into a place they can call home. This narrative of environmental adaptation continues even into contemporary films set on and near reservation lands and gains particular force in *Smoke Signals*.

RELOCATING AMERICAN INDIANS ON AND OFF SCREEN: WHEN BARREN LAND BECOMES HOME

Much has been written about American Indians' removal to barren reservation lands. After more than a century of skirmishes with tribes from New England to Florida, Andrew Jackson encouraged Congress to pass the 1830 Indian Removal Act, claiming it would separate American Indians from the onslaught of settlers moving ever westward and help them evolve into what he saw as a civilized community. In 1832 Jackson insisted that American Indians be removed from prime farming land in the Southeast and moved to Indian Territory (in what is now Oklahoma) on what has become known as the Trail of Tears. Of the

15,000 Cherokees who began the journey, 4,000 died, and many more of the 70,000 members of all tribes who made it to Indian Territory also died along the way. The move inaugurated the reservation system, however, and after battles with whites in the 1860s and 1870s, Plains Indian tribes were also forcibly moved to reservations, this time in Indian Territory, Arizona, Utah, and other less productive and arable lands in the West.

From the beginning of the reservation system, life on "the Rez" was like hell on earth. On these reservations Indian agents attempted to force their charges to farm infertile lands, leaving them close to starvation since their allotment of cattle was small and sometimes stolen by corrupt government officials. According to Gary D. Sandefur, "The lands reserved for Indian use were generally regarded as the least desirable by whites and were almost always located far from major population centers, trails, and transportation routes that later became part of the modern system of metropolitan areas, highways, and railroads" (37).

People on reservations were isolated "in places with few natural resources, far from contact with the developing U.S. economy and society" (Sandefur 37). Breaking up these lands into allotments after the 1887 Dawes Act only had a further negative effect since the parceled land was unfit for farming or ranching, and the remaining land was purchased at low prices or stolen for white settlers to homestead.

Reservation life for the Coeur d'Alene, Sherman Alexie's tribe, has an equally brutal history, but as Alexie asserts, "No one winds up on the Spokane Indian Reservation by accident" (qtd. in Cornwall). The Coeur d'Alene band of the Upper and Middle Spokanes were late to the reservation system, entering an agreement with the United States in 1887 after the Dawes Act was signed. These people entered into a treaty more than six years after the Lower Spokanes had moved onto the Spokane Indian Reservation, resisting relocation in lower Spokane County primarily because it was less desirable for hunting and fishing than the middle and upper Spokane. To maintain their claim on aboriginal lands, they moved onto the Coeur d'Alene Reservation in Idaho and other reservations, including the Spokane, receiving monetary compensation for houses, cattle, seeds, and farm implements. By 1905, however, the reservations lost rights to water in the Spokane River to the Little Falls Power Plant, and by 1909 the Spokane Reservation was opened up for homesteading. Coeur d'Alene and other tribes on the reservation were now limited to allotments of from 80 to 160 acres on land too rocky for farming.

A year later minerals were found on their lands in Idaho. But this seemingly beneficial discovery has had catastrophic environmental results. Traditional tribal fishing became impossible. According to the Official Site of the Coeur d'Alene Tribe of Indians: "Over a 100 year period, the mining industry in Idaho's Silver Valley dumped 72 million tons of mine waste into the Coeur d'Alene watershed. As mining and smelting operations grew, they produced billions of dollars in silver, lead, and zinc. In the process, natural life in the Coeur d'Alene River was wiped out."

The Spokane Reservation suffered even worse repercussions from mining waste. In 1954, at the height of the Cold War, Jim and John LeBret, both tribal members, found uranium on the edge of the Spokane Reservation, and the Newmont Mining Company bought the rights to the Sherwood, Dawn, and Midnight Mines, all on reservation lands. The Midnight Mine remained active for twenty-seven years and became "an economic and social mainstay of the reservation," but it also had devastating environmental consequences (Cornwall). Sherman Alexie "felt threatened by the uranium mines near his home on the Spokane Indian Reservation" after his grandmother died from esophageal cancer in 1980, asserting, "I have very little doubt that I'm going to get cancer" (qtd. in Cornwall).

Although the Midnight Mine closed in 1981, its devastating legacy continues. When the mine closed, it abandoned "2.4 million tons of stockpiled ore (containing 2 million pounds of uranium oxide) and 33 million tons of waste rock" ("Midnight Mine"). The company never conducted reclamation work, leaving two giant pits like "festering wounds" and a small lake of toxic radioactive brew that has since "leached into groundwater, and into the sand and water of several small streams feeding Blue Creek, which runs through the reservation, and eventually into the Spokane River" (Cornwall). Years of work near and around the uranium mines has also devastated the health of tribal peoples, perhaps leaving them "three times more likely to get lung cancer and more than twice as likely to get other serious lung diseases" (Cornwall). The federal government is compensating those workers in and around the mines who contract lung diseases, but no money has come to the Spokane Reservation. Cleanup has been slow, especially with the recent turn toward expanding nuclear power, creating a revived interest in mining uranium.

Economic and environmental disasters continue on reservations, perhaps like countries in the developing world where infant mortality, alcoholism, and poverty rates are shockingly high. Approximately one-third of American Indians live on reservations, and 25 percent live below the poverty line. Yet as Sandefur asserts, numbers living on reservations have increased from 25 to 34 percent from 1980 to 2000 because the reservation also provides a cultural base where tribal language and culture can be maintained, a strong sense of family and community thrives, and a sovereign system run by a tribal council and the Bureau of Indian Affairs operates. The goal for American Indians living there is to adapt the "hell" of their reservations into a home.

As Jace Weaver's preface to *Defending Mother Earth: American Indian Perspectives on Environmental Justice* explains, Erik Erikson formulated his book on the eight stages of psychosocial development "based on his work among the Sioux and Yurok of northern California, which he chose because of the widely divergent environments in which they lived." Weaver explains: "In the Western Hemisphere, American Indians learned to live in various regions, which were controlled by climate, water, earth and the supernatural. . . . Living in these areas meant surviving under harsh conditions, testing the ability of the people to adapt to their environments" (29, 33–34).

A review of the book in *Midwest Book Review* highlights the connection between environmental adaptation and environmental justice. According to the review, *Defending Mother Earth* "document[s] a range of ecological disasters, including the devastating effects of mining, water pollution, nuclear power facilities, and toxic waste dumps. In an expression of 'environmental racism,' such hazards are commonly located on or near Indian lands." The reviewer goes on to write, "these struggles are intimately tied to the assertion of Indian sovereignty and the affirmation of Native culture: The Earth is, indeed, Mother to these nations. . . . The affirmation of Indian spiritual values, especially the attitude toward the Earth, may hold out a key to the survival of the planet and its peoples." By adopting a worldview that rests on environmental adaptation, Euro-Americans may negotiate a resolution to the conflict between their culture and nature and sustain both.

In *Chato's Land* (1972), the perspective of Pardon Chato (Charles Bronson) helps illustrate the parameters and repercussions of such environmental adaptation. The film highlights the Apache worldview from a white perspective but provides insight into how Chato, a half-Apache *mestizo,* survives in what seems like uninhabitable land. According to Capt. Quincey Whitmore (Jack Palance), when Chato runs from the captain because he has killed a US marshal in self-defense, he "picks his ground" carefully. Unlike white soldiers, Chato has adapted to this inhospitable land and can use it to his advantage in a fight. The captain explains the wisdom of Chato's choice to run through such terrain: "To you this is so much bad land—rock, scrub, desert, and then more rock, a hard land that the sun has sucked all the good out of. You can't farm it, and you can't carve it out and call it your own . . . so you damn it to hell. And it all looks the same.

Chato (Charles Bronson) becoming part of the desert in *Chato's Land*

That is our way. To the breed now, it's his land. He don't expect it to give him much, and he don't force it none. And to him it's almost human—a livin' active thing. And it will make him a good place to make his fight against us."

Other Westerns address the American Indian perspective on adapting to their land in less obvious ways. *The Scalphunters* (1968), for example, complicates received beliefs regarding both American Indians and Comancheros when a group of Indians exchanges animal hides from Trapper Joe (Burt Lancaster) for an escaped slave named Joseph (Ossie Davis). When Comancheros led by Jim Howie (Telly Savalas) raid the Indians, racial binaries begin to disintegrate, making room for accommodation and a collective view of human and nonhuman nature. And *The Outlaw Josey Wales* (1976) examines American Indian worldviews both peripherally and from a first-person perspective—through the eyes of Lone Watie (Chief Dan George), who becomes part of a family of castoffs, including Josey Wales (Clint Eastwood). The majority of Westerns, however, construct Indians as an "other" who must be destroyed or vanquished for civilization to prosper. But even films like *The Searchers* (1956) provide a more complex look at them when scrutinized through a narrative of environmental adaptation.

Although American Indians seem to be constructed as either savages or "innocents" in most Westerns, with less maturity than Euro-Americans, their view of landscape and land use is usually valorized, especially from the mid-1950s forward. In these films they represent a more environmentally conscious perspective than that of Euro-Americans and signify the possibility for a simpler and less cynical view of life. In *Dances with Wolves,* for example, Ten Bears (Floyd "Red Crow" Westerman), the chief of the Sioux tribe befriended by Union soldier John Dunbar (Kevin Costner), explains that his tribe's differing view of land-ownership when he shows Dunbar an old Spanish conquistador's helmet: "The white men who wore this came around the time of my grandfather's grandfather. Eventually we drove them out. Then the Mexicans came. But they do not come here any more. In my own time, the Texans. They have been like all the others. They take without asking. But I think you are right. I think they will keep coming. When I think of that, I look at this helmet. I don't know if we are ready for these people. Our country is all that we have, and we will fight to keep it."

Dunbar's voice, however, drives the film's narrative. Through the lens of his journal, he tells us that the Sioux "were a people so eager to laugh, so devoted to family, so dedicated to each other. The only word that comes to mind is harmony." For Dunbar, the Sioux he encounters represent a worldview that embraces nature and lives within it communally, without the individual greed that drives whites to "take without asking."

The American Indian constructed in films like *Dances with Wolves* fulfills Shepard Kreck's criteria for what he calls "the ecological Indian." According to him, the trope and "dominant image" of the ecological Indian found in literature and film is "the Indian in nature who understands the systematic conse-quences of his actions, feels deep sympathy with all living forms, and takes steps to conserve so that earth's harmonies are never imbalanced and resources never in doubt" (21). The ecological Indian valorizes nature at the expense of progress, and this "Noble Savage" shatters when confronted with a modern world and its technologies. The ecological Indian cannot assimilate into western culture and vanishes or faces extermination. The westward movement of tribes is highlighted in many Westerns and reinforces this image. These cinematic marches are usually viewed from a distance, with the destination hidden over the horizon, as in films like *She Wore a Yellow Ribbon* (1949) and *White Feather* (1955), a disappearing thread demonstrating that an "ecological Indian" must either vanish or face annihilation.

These narratives of environmental adaptation become most convincing, however, from about 1990, when American Indians begin telling their own stories both as filmmakers and actors. Written by a Spokane/Coeur d'Alene Indian, Sherman Alexie, and directed by a Cheyenne-Arapaho, Chris Eyre, *Smoke Signals* illustrates how Indians still transform hell into home, in a narrative of environmental adaptation centering on two fatherless young men exploring their heritage outside the reservation.

DEFINING NARRATIVES OF
ENVIRONMENTAL ADAPTATION

In *Smoke Signals,* the ecological Indian faces neither banishment nor annihilation because he adapts the hell of both the reservation and the wider Eurocentric world into a home. Alexie calls *Smoke Signals* "a very basic story, a road trip/buddy movie about a lost father." He says that the film combines two mythic structures, one focused on the self, and the other on both a buddy and a lost father: "You can find them in everything from the *Bible* to *The Iliad* and *The Odyssey.* What is revolutionary or groundbreaking about the film is that the characters in it are Indians, and they're fully realized human beings" (Alexie). Such an archetypal reading suggests *Smoke Signals* may also combine the same three perspectives on the American myth Robert Baird suggests underpin the making of *Dances with Wolves:* "Claude Levi-Strauss's notion that myths and narratives reconcile cultural contradictions and bring opposing forces and values [like nature and industry, hunting and agrarianism, innocence and decadence] together"; R. W. B. Lewis's claim in *The American Adam* that "the American continent triggered images of the Garden among European immigrants," one in which the American Indian "provided a ready-made adamic figure"; and Freud's family romance theory, "where he attempted to account for certain fantasies of young children who denied their literal parentage in favor of more noble imaginary mothers and fathers" (154–55, 156). Amanda J. Cobb, however, draws on Alexie's notion of Indians as fully realized human beings when she asserts that *Smoke Signals* is "a significant act of self-definition, an exercise of 'cultural sovereignty'"(207). Most of the scholarship addressing this film examines it in relation to American Indian identity and representation.[1]

Yet the narrative in *Smoke Signals* goes beyond modifying *The Odyssey* story and examining American Indian identity, representation, and sovereignty. It adds both a collaborative component and a search outside the self, in this case for a father's ashes as the key to his truth. More important, the narrative centers on transforming the protagonists' starting and ending point into a home. Characters do gain self-awareness, as they do in *The Odyssey,* but the awareness extends to both others and their own seemingly barren and hopeless setting, the Coeur d'Alene Reservation. By translating four of a series of disjointed and primarily bitter stories from *The Lone Ranger and Tonto Fistfight in Heaven* into a filmic collaborative journey with what he calls "integrity," Alexie has constructed a narrative of environmental adaptation with a clear and cohesive structure that follows an evolutionary pattern focused on place.

By following this evolutionary pattern, *Smoke Signals* adheres to a narrative that is embedded in the comic and communal

rather than tragic and individualized, notions of species preservation found in the tragic evolutionary narrative of *The Odyssey* and of "early Darwinism" that supports extermination and
warfare rather than accommodation (Meeker 164). According to
Joseph Meeker, humans typically embrace a tragic evolutionary
narrative as in *The Odyssey* that counters the climax communities of plants and animals, which are "extremely diverse and
complicated." But this position comes at a price and may cost
humanity its existence, he asserts: "We demand that one species,
our own, achieve unchallenged dominance where hundreds of
species lived in complex equilibrium before our arrival." This
attitude may not only lead to the destruction of other species
but also of humanity itself. Meeker believes that humanity has
"a growing need to learn from the more stable comic heroes of
nature, the animals" (162, 164).

The evolutionary narrative of the film explores what might
happen if humanity did learn from these more stable comic
heroes since, according to Meeker: "Evolution itself is a gigantic
comic drama, not the bloody tragic spectacle imagined by the
sentimental humanists of early Darwinism." He asserts: "Nature
is not 'red in tooth and claw' as the nineteenth-century English
poet Alfred, Lord Tennyson characterized it, for evolution does
not proceed through battles fought among animals to see who
is fit enough to survive and who is not. Rather, the evolutionary process is one of adaptation and accommodation, with the
various species exploring opportunistically their environments
in search of a means to maintain their existence. Like comedy,
evolution is a matter of muddling through." For Meeker, successful evolution encourages communal action to ensure survival: "Its ground rules for participants (including man) are those
which also govern literary comedy: organisms must adapt themselves to their circumstances in every possible way, must studi-
ously avoid all-or-nothing choices, must prefer any alternative
to death, must accept and encourage maximum diversity, must
accommodate themselves to the accidental limitations of birth

and environment, and must always prefer love to war—though if warfare is inevitable, it should be prosecuted so as to humble the enemy without destroying him" (164, 166).

SMOKE SIGNALS AND ENVIRONMENTAL ADAPTATION

Characters in *Smoke Signals* embrace a focus on "adapting themselves to their circumstances in every possible way" while the film adds the element of ecology. The director emphasizes this relation between human and nonhuman nature by successfully fulfilling the writer's goal to "let the landscape tell a lot of story," not only outside the bus window and along the paths Victor Joseph and Thomas Builds-the-Fire follow toward Mars, Arizona, where the father's ashes wait, but also within Victor and Thomas themselves. As Thomas explains: "You know there are some children who aren't really children at all, they're just pillars of flame that burn everything they touch. And there are children who are just pillars of ash, that fall apart when you touch them. . . .Victor and me, we were children of flame and ash."

To build this narrative, the film follows a three-act narrative grounded in ecology:

> Establishing the reservation as an inhospitable setting for human and nonhuman nature.
> Leaving the reservation on a journey of landscapes.
> Returning to the reservation able to transform hell into a home.

The Reservation as Hell on Earth

The reservation's ecology seems less than life sustaining during the film's first act. *Smoke Signals* opens in 1976 with an announcement from the reservation radio station, KREZ. It is White People's Independence Day, the DJ, Randy Peone (John Trudell), explains before switching to Lester Fallsapart (Chief Leonard George) on the broken-down KREZ van at the crossroads. "Big truck just went by . . . now it's gone," Fallsapart reports, reinforcing the empty world of the reservation. The broadcast bridges to a house party that joins the bleak physical environment with reservation social life while it begins the film's narrative: the party celebrates the Fourth of July, despite the bitter emptiness it leaves for American Indians less than independent on the Rez.

Social images of reservation life highlight some of the real economic, environmental, and social problems still prevalent for American Indians. In one scene, for example, we see a drunken Arnold Joseph (Gary Farmer), Victor's father, who stumbles out of his house, throwing firecrackers to prolong the celebration. Beer cans and fireworks cover the lawn. The party is over, but Arnold fires a roman candle into the house, and the curtains and living-room furniture burst into flames. Thomas's voice says that the "fire swallowed up my mother and father," but Arnold catches an infant thrown from an upper-story window, saving it from the raging fire. It is Thomas, and Arnold places him in the arms of the child's grandmother (Monique Mojica). When she thanks him, he says he "didn't mean to," a sign of the guilt he will carry, which he validates when he cuts his hair and, as Thomas states, "practiced vanishing." Thomas and Victor have almost literally been "born of flame and ash" on a reservation where the only hope seems to be survival.

Twenty-two years later the same DJ broadcasts, "It's a good day to be indigenous," but life on the reservation is still bleak and barren of hope, and the flat brown landscape reflects that desolation. He reports on the few passing cars and the story surrounding each driver, but the road is empty. The Coeur d'Alene Reservation isolates these American Indians, the scene suggests, leaving them on a desert-like island with few prospects for economic gain or environmental fecundity.

A scene in a school gym where three young men play basketball reinforces this image. Thomas, wearing a suit, tells stories from the gym stage. "When Indians go away, they don't come back," he says, with novels like *The Last of the Mohicans* to back up his claim. The story acts as a bridge to a phone call received by Victor's mother, Arlene (Tantoo Cardinal). Arnold Joseph has passed away in Mars, Arizona, and Victor must find a way to bring home his remains. But narrratively, the forthcoming trip also highlights the inevitable path of the American Indian, according to their history. They have been removed to reservations or annihilated, so their representation vanishes from the face of the American myth.

Efforts to facilitate Victor's journey are thwarted because of the hopeless state of both Victor and the reservation. In the reservation grocery store, Thomas, who has "heard it on the wind" and seen Arlene crying, offers to pay for the trip as long as he takes him along. But Victor thinks about his father driving him around on the reservation for the last time, showing off his magic while drinking beer out of a cooler next to him. The buildings father and son pass are dilapidated and sit on hard-packed dirt, accentuating the lifeless state of the reservation. Arnold tells Victor, "[I] wave my hand and white people are gone." Everything he waves at, he says, will disappear, "the reservations . . . , the drunks . . . , the Catholics . . . , the drunk Catholics. . . . I'm so good, I'll make myself disappear," which he does. Arnold has so internalized the hell of the reservation and the message it represents that he literally vanishes. Victor too has internalized the desolation around him and its manifestation in Arnold, empty despair.

A Journey of Landscapes

The opening act closes when Victor and Thomas consult with their mother figures and move closer to their journey. Although Victor bears his pain in isolation, Thomas helps his grandmother make fry bread, gaining confidence that Victor will agree to travel with him to Arizona. The scene also illustrates the communal strength on which environmental adaptation can be built. Victor associates fry bread with relationship building when he hugs his mom and compliments her on her bread, the best on the reservation. Arlene's story about fry bread helps Victor make his decision about taking Thomas: "I don't make it by myself," Arlene tells him. "I got the recipe from my grandmother and she got it from her grandmother, and I listened to people," she says, showing him how building a new and better life—or fry bread—requires a collective process. As if responding to this communal vision, Victor goes to Thomas's house to invite him on his journey, and the setting and tone begin to change.

For example, when Victor and Thomas walk toward the bus that will take them from Spokane to Phoenix, Arizona, a comic tone overcomes the isolation of act one. They meet Velma (Michelle St. John) and Lucy (Elaine Miles) driving in reverse because their car's transmission is broken. According to the *Cineaste* interview with Alexie, the two women and their car provide a "sense of time in the movie, when the past, present, and future are all the same, that circular sense of time which plays itself out in the seamless transitions from past to present." For Alexie, the car is a visual metaphor for the adage, "Sometimes to go forward you have to drive in reverse." The Velma and Lucy storyline pays homage to Thelma and Louise but without the hopeless suicide pact that ends that duo's filmic lives. Instead of driving off a cliff, the two young women flirt with Thomas and Victor, giving them a ride only after Thomas tells them a story that reveals something about Arnold and his work for the American Indian Movement (AIM): "Arnold got arrested, you know. But he got lucky. They charged him with attempted murder. Then they plea-bargained that down to assault with a deadly weapon. Then they plea-bargained that down to being an Indian in the twentieth century. Then he got two years in Walla-Walla." The story also provides a comic turn in the film, especially when Velma laughs, "I think it's a fine example of the oral tradition."

The young men's journey off the reservation begins when Victor and Thomas enter a bus, a modern stagecoach going south to Arizona instead of west. Lucy and Velma tell them that they are going "to a whole 'nother country," since to the young women the United States is "as foreign as it gets." Dramatic changes in the film's ecology reinforce these words, as the bus carries the friends across flat brown steppe-like landscapes to the red rock of the Southwest.

The beginning of the bus trip prompts two more stories about Victor's father, one in flashback from Victor's perspective, the other directly from Thomas. These demonstrate that Victor and Thomas and their environment are moving from a lifeless and hopeless state toward the promise of life. Victor's flashback seems like a dream that is broken by Thomas's story.

Victor's story centers on another house party, this time before the celebrants have passed out for the night. Arnold and Arlene, now both drunk, ask young Victor (Cody Lightning) about his favorite Indian, and he yells "nobody" repeatedly and runs away. Before this story ends, though, Thomas tells Victor another story about his father that reveals a more hopeful take both on Arnold and his environment. This time, Thomas sits on a bridge in Spokane watching salmon run. Arnold sees him and invites him to breakfast at Denny's. As Thomas says, "Sometimes it's a good day to die. Sometimes it's a good day to eat breakfast."

The Spokane River is clear and running wildly with fish in this story, but Victor exclaims, "There ain't any salmon in that river no more!" before flashing back to his own narrative. The party is over now in his dream, and Victor sees his parents passed out fully clothed on their bed. He runs from the room, and soon we hear banging noises. Victor is throwing beer bottles at Arnold's truck, breaking them one by one. The hopeless drugged state of the reservation is critiqued through these stories, but in the context both of one solution—getting rid of the alcohol—and a more natural alternative—a return to the life-filled river.

The return to the river is metaphorical, though it also signifies a return to life, following a narrative of environmental adaptation that facilitates transforming a lifeless area into a home. This metaphor is reinforced when Victor insists that Thomas take off his suit—complete with vest—and let down his hair to become a "real Indian," telling him, "You've got to look like you just came back from killing a buffalo." Thomas knows better and explains, "But we were fishermen." When the bus stops at a gas station, Thomas changes his clothes, returning seemingly transformed but wearing a shirt that reads "Frybread Power." Now they both can be "stoic," as Victor asserts, and survive in a white world.

They also adapt to the world of white popular culture when two cowboys steal their bus seat and refuse to move, telling them to "find somewhere else to have a powwow." Thomas notes their failure, but together they turn the potential conflict into a success. He begins by observing that the cowboys always win, and lists a few, from Tom Mix to John Wayne. Victor laughs, remembering, "In all those movies, you never saw John Wayne's teeth," and the two build a chant around John Wayne's teeth. Here the landscape, where red rocky hills line the road, tells their story through the windows of the bus, emphasizing the hardships that must be faced on their journey toward Phoenix.

The walk from Phoenix to Mars provides one of these challenges. They walk through desert grasslands that for Thomas signify American Indians' continuous movement west: "Columbus shows up, and we keep walking," he says, and then repeats the mantra for historical white figures from Custer to Harry Truman. Yet Thomas slips in humor again to counter the setting and the message, saying that Victor's dad "looks like Charles Bronson." Mars, Arizona, however, looks like a crater in the desert, with a few trailers breaking the gold loneliness of the valley. When the two arrive in the valley, Suzy Song (Irene Bedard) greets them and offers Victor his father's ashes. A Western is playing on Suzy's

Victor Joseph (Adam Beach) and Thomas Builds-the-Fire (Evan Adams) sing about John Wayne's teeth in *Smoke Signals*

television, and Thomas jokes, "The only thing more pathetic than Indians on TV is Indians watching Indians on TV."

Suzy's willingness to help them and her clear affinity for Victor's father serves as the opening of a story that brings the young men closer to hope and life. Thomas tells about Victor's mother feeding a hundred hungry American Indians with fifty pieces of fry bread, a clear reference to the loaves and fishes parable from the Sermon on the Mount. Thomas accentuates Arlene's struggle to determine how to feed so many people, ending with a practical solution, tearing the bread in half, so each person gets a portion. The story again reinforces the need to work collectively to adapt to a sometimes hostile environment. Victor learns more about his father from Suzy, reenacts his father's ritual hair cutting when collecting personal items from Arnold's trailer, and then leaves with Thomas in Arnold's truck without telling Suzy goodbye. To Thomas, the connection between human and nonhuman nature drives their departure: "Suzy and drought, mother and hunger, father and magic," all "heavy with illusion."

Transforming Hell into a Home

One last conflict moves Victor and Thomas toward environmental adaptation and serves as the entrance into the third act
of the film. While fighting over visions of Arnold, Victor and
Thomas crash the truck, avoiding a car parked in the middle
of the highway. They turn what could be a dangerous altercation with police "off the Rez" into a triumph, though, changing
Arnold's past crimes into communal solutions. Instead of leaving the scene and avoiding a confrontation with police, Victor
helps an injured girl from the accident, running all the way to
the town hospital for assistance. Even when questioned by the
police before leaving the hospital, Thomas and Victor transform
an expected altercation into a ride home. The driver of the car
responsible for the accident accuses Victor of assaulting him, but
before Victor can defend himself, the white police chief (Tom
Skerritt) lets them go, saying, "Mr. Johnson's wife Holly says he's,
and I quote, 'a complete asshole.'" In a rewriting of Arnold's
earlier arrest for participation in an AIM demonstration, the
police even drive them back to their truck. This transformation
of expectations coincides with Suzy's burning of Arnold's trailer
back in Mars, a purifying action that parallels the opening fire
and cleanses Arnold and Victor of their past.

The fire and ride in the police car help Victor bring life to the
reservation as he brings back his father to his mother and home.
Victor shares some of Arnold's ashes with Thomas after thanking
him for his help. Then in a reversal of Westerns' foregrounding
progress, the film shows Victor and Thomas's ritual strewing of
Arnold's ashes into the Spokane River. The ashes look like magic
dust as they float toward the water. Once the ashes reach the surface, they race downstream like salmon. The overhead tracking
shot shows the waters crashing over rocks around curves like
the highway cloverleaf in *How the West Was Won,* but there is no
concrete along this river. It is lined with green and shows how
fire and ashes can transform into life.

Victor (Adam Beach) shares his father's ashes with Thomas (Evan Adams) in *Smoke Signals*

In *Smoke Signals* Victor and Thomas turn a bleak Rez hell into a thriving ecology in a narrative of environmental adaptation that includes collective views of human and nonhuman nature and provides a living community. Victor adapts to his once-bleak environment and finds hope and life. According to Alexie, the movie is about "Victor, Thomas, and everybody else calling for help. It's also about the theme of fire. The smoke that originates from the first fire in the movie is what causes these events, and the smoke from the second fire brings about the beginning of resolution."

For Victor and Thomas, who have been born of ashes and fire, it is the water of the Spokane River that actually leads them to love and life, because it is the river that at least metaphorically turns Arnold into a fish, connecting him and the two young men who scatter his ashes with nature and each other. They have fulfilled, as Joseph Meeker explains, an effective evolutionary process, "one of adaptation and accommodation, with the various species exploring opportunistically their environments in search of a means to maintain their existence." As Meeker concludes, "The lesson of ecology is balance and equilibrium, the lesson of comedy is humility and endurance" (164,168).Victor and Thomas learn these lessons well.

CONCLUSION

This narrative of environmental adaptation has evolved in Westerns with American Indians at their center, from the early valorization of their worldviews, through the vilification of the savage Indian in the 1940s and 1950s, back to a more revisionist, if condescending, look at Indian perspectives from the 1950s and 1960s through the 1990s that makes way for the Native American–centered narratives that followed. A review of *Smoke Signals* in *Rolling Stone* asserts, "When it comes to American Indians, Hollywood either trades in Injun stereotypes or dances with Disney." Certainly none of the films highlighted here comes close to the central evolutionary narrative of *Smoke Signals,* but they all rest on a similar structure that reaches a resolution either by relocating or assimilating complacent American Indians and destroying those who resist.

American Indian histories depend on who tells the story and when it is told, but they chiefly focus on one tribe or region. Two histories by seventeenth-century Puritans, for example, dehumanize the Pequods, providing a space to demonize them and valorize their extermination. William Hubbard's *Narrative of the Indian Wars in New England,* for example, centers on this tribe, commenting that during an attack on the Pequods at Mystic, Connecticut, the Indians "were killed in the Swamp like sullen Dogs" (36). John Winthrop's *Journal* of the same period asserts that the colonial military "marched in the night to a fort of the Pequods at Mistick [*sic*], and, besetting the same about break of the day, after two hours' fight they took it, (by firing it,) and slew therein two chief sachems, and one hundred and fifty fighting men, and about one hundred and fifty old men, women, and children" (220). In contrast, a 2005 history of the Cherokee

Nation by Robert J. Conley, a member representing the nation itself, provides a Cherokee-centered history and highlights the thirty-five treaties or agreements between the Cherokee and the United States, all of which were violated one by one and limited their sovereignty incrementally (249–50).

Westerns, though, tend to focus on Plains Indian tribes, the nomadic peoples of the lands settlers crossed to reach the West, with little distinction between tribes. The films also respond to cinematic history, a history that coincides with the political and cultural history of both Hollywood and the United States as a whole. According to Scott Simmon, American Indians were at the center of many early silent Westerns, from *The Red Girl* (1908) to *Hiawatha* (1913). He comments, "Indians may well have entered American film for the reason they came into the European tradition as a whole: Searching for stories to set in the landscape, pioneer filmmakers stumbled upon 'Indians,' the presumed men of nature." Set in lush eastern forests instead of desert canyons or grassy plains, the narratives of these silents "are set entirely within tribal communities or feature a 'noble redskin' as guide or savior to the white hero." By 1914, however, American Indian actors and sympathetic narratives were no longer prominent in Westerns, at least partly because the "U.S. Army began planning, with some innocence, for America's entry into World War I by requisitioning horses." Simmon notes, "The subsequent history of Indian images in silent-era Hollywood becomes a story with two paths—one about war, the other about love—neither leading anywhere except Indian death" (4, 80, 81).

Despite Simmon's contention, at least a few Westerns highlighting American Indian characters and narratives present a more sympathetic view of a possible comic evolutionary narrative, one of environmental adaptation that reveals the ineffectiveness of a tragic evolutionary path and the intruder pioneers who seek destruction rather than adaptation. Although racially flawed, *The Vanishing American* (1925) and *The Miracle Rider*

(1935) serve as two Westerns prior to World War II that draw on this more sympathetic perspective. *The Vanishing American* traces a history of domination of American Indians by pioneering intruders, including Booker (Noah Beery) an Indian agent over-seeing a Navajo reservation where he mistreats the Indians and steals their horses. Nophaie (Richard Dix), an educated Navajo who fought in World War I, is torn between his people and his white teacher, Marion Warner (Lois Wilson), when he returns from the war, and ultimately is sacrificed as he fights against Booker to regain his people's dignity. Miscegenation is avoided because of Nophaie's death, but the film's prologue, especially, foregrounds a history of conquest, one that is lamented even if painted as inevitable in the film. *The Miracle Rider,* a Tom Mix serial, opens with a chapter that is also dedicated to the "Van-ishing Indian." The episode provides historical background that bifurcates American Indians willing to adapt to their environ-ment from their white opponents, demonstrating how a tragic evolutionary narrative destroys both Indians and their hunting grounds. These films both valorize a comic evolutionary narra-tive, one from a silent big-budget perspective, the other from a small-budget serial point of view, but they both also demonstrate the futility of such a valorization.

From *Drums Along the Mohawk* (1939) through *Cheyenne Autumn* (1964), John Ford defines the idea of the West in relation to populist views of progress, which seeks to dominate human and nonhuman nature and civilize the wilderness. Within this ideology, American Indians must either be exterminated or removed to make way for pioneers ready to turn the forest wil-derness into a garden. Although Ford's later Westerns seem to gain more sympathy for the Indians and their plight, the results are the same, exploitation of nature for the sake of progress. As Ken Nolley asserts, "all of Ford's plots, with the exception of *Cheyenne Autumn,* construct Indians as a savage presence set in opposition to the advance of American civilization, particularly as that civilization is embodied in white families" (80).[2]

That opposition also points to a battle with the natural world and a possible narrative of environmental adaptation.[3] No matter how noble a savage the American Indians might be, they cannot assimilate into western culture and must be removed to reservations or destroyed. They, like other human and nonhuman nature, must be exploited for gain or, if they limit the construction of civilization, annihilated. These films reinforce the destiny of forced environmental change and eradicate the possibility of an alternative—a narrative of environmental adaptation.[4]

In most Westerns from the 1940s and 1950s, American Indians' narratives of environmental adaptation are broken either by removal to inhospitable reservations and forced assimilation into white culture or violent extermination. Angela Aleiss asserts that any "theme of an interracial brotherhood" found in these films overlay "a suspicion toward Indian/white differences." During the post–World War II period, "Conformity became crucial as a strong feeling of national unity and the prevailing political mood guaranteed that only Anglo-American values were safe." According to Aleiss, in films soon after the war, "peaceful coexistence between Indians and whites was achieved only through the loss of Indian identity" (87, 90). The Westerns highlighted here illustrate this move.

Whether or not these films humanize their American Indian characters, they all rest on a similar ideology of progress. To make way for civilization, Indians must be removed or eliminated. Only rarely is an alternative for them presented, and that alternative typically requires assimilation and renunciation of their savage culture. As John E. O'Connor argues: "The view that the Indian impeded progress because he lacked the ambition and 'good sense' the whites used in developing the American landscape has prevailed throughout our history. Movies and television, the popular art forms of today, continue to present images of American Indians that speak more about the current interests of the dominant culture than they do about the Indians" (27–28). Yet even within Westerns foregrounding this view, an alternative narrative of environmental adaptation is revealed—it is merely obscured by the evolutionary narrative that dominates the films.[5]

Smoke Signals stands out in contrast to other films from the 1990s hailed as groundbreaking because of their sympathetic portrayal. *Dances with Wolves,* for example, follows a pattern similar to that found in *Jeremiah Johnson* (1972), where a white American goes native, embracing and in the process co-opting American Indian culture and attitudes toward environmental adaptation. Sherman Alexie calls this "cultural appropriation" a threat to sovereignty. In the context of *Dances with Wolves,* such cultural appropriation serves as a threat to the Sioux Indians' very survival. John Dunbar penetrates their homes, families, and culture as a brother, but he represents the military that will soon force their banishment westward. Before the film's end, however, the narrative of environmental adaptation follows an evolutionary pattern: Dunbar's rebellion against and rejection of US culture, movement west, discovering American Indians on the plains, gaining sympathy for Sioux culture and internalizing their ideology, and clashing with the dominant culture he left behind.

The narrative in *Dances with Wolves* harkens back to *Run of the Arrow* (1957), in which Private O'Meara (Rod Steiger) leaves the defeated Confederacy, joins the Sioux as an ex-soldier, and takes a Sioux wife. Both films reverse the narrative of environmental adaptation by inserting a sympathetic white soldier as protagonist. Yet this evolutionary narrative fails because white intruders either banish or exterminate the Sioux. Despite the two soldiers' initial sympathy for the American Indians that adopt them, intruding pioneers dominate the narrative. As Joseph Meeker argues: "No human has ever known what it means to live in a climax ecosystem [in which human and nonhuman nature thrive], at least not since the emergence of consciousness which has made us human. We have generally acted the role of the pioneer species, dedicating ourselves to survival through the destruction of all our competitors and to achieving effective dominance over other forms of life" (162). In *Run of the Arrow* and *Dances with Wolves,* however, the Sioux and the white men they adopt are constructed as thriving members of a climax ecosystem that dissolves only when the pioneers—the cavalry—intervene.

In *Run of the Arrow,* O'Meara refuses to return home after the Civil War and pledge his allegiance to the Union, against which he had been fighting as a Rebel. He rejects reunification and flees to the West, meeting a tribe of Sioux that adopts him. He marries Yellow Moccasin (Sara Montiel) and lives peacefully with the Sioux until the cavalry begins building a fort on their land. This invasion into the Sioux domain disturbs the evolutionary narrative O'Meara had been following. In the end the cavalry defeat the Indians in battle. O'Meara rejoins the white military and helps defeat his adopted "family."

John Dunbar of *Dances with Wolves* rejects the civilization of the eastern United States when he asks to be reassigned to a western fort. His major (Maury Chaykin) asks him, "You wish to see the frontier?" And Dunbar answers, "Yes, sir, before it's gone," a subtle critique of the destruction in the West and of its resources by white settlers. Some time after arriving at his new assignment, he encounters Sioux near his abandoned fort and records his observations in a journal, all reported in voiceover narration. With each meeting, Dunbar gains more sympathy for the tribe. In one early entry, he notes: "Nothing I have been told about these people is correct. They are not thieves or beggars. They are not the bogeyman they are made out to be. On the contrary, they are polite guests and I enjoy their humor."

Before the end of Dunbar's evolutionary narrative, he has adopted an American Indian worldview. As Kicking Bird (Graham Greene) asserts of Dunbar's transformation: "I was just thinking of all the trails in this life, there are some that matter most. It is the trail of a true human being. I think you are on this trail, and it is a good one." Ten Bears even affirms, when Dunbar expresses concern about the cavalry's hunt for him: "The white man the soldiers are looking for no longer exists. Now there is only a Sioux named Dances with Wolves." Ultimately, however, the narrative breaks down because whites, like intruding pioneers, threaten to wipe out the Sioux and take their land. The cavalry eventually finds Dunbar and arrest him for desertion, but he escapes and, like the Sioux, vanishes into the wilderness, taking Stands with a Fist (Mary McDonnell) with him. Unlike their adopted community, Dunbar and Stands with a Fist are white and could reintegrate easily into white culture. The Sioux, however, must contend with white men whose numbers are, as Dunbar explains, "like the stars."[6]

Only films like Sherman Alexie and Chris Eyre's *Smoke Signals* can transcend this cultural erasure. Although Alexie admits his writing is influenced by dominant popular culture, as an American Indian who grew up on a reservation, he is tied by his experience to that worldview, one written as a narrative of environmental adaptation. When American Indians control the script, the direction, and the production of a film, they control its narrative, making space for a comic evolutionary story that, as Alexie states in *Smoke Signals,* chooses life.

Annette Kolodny's parting words in her "Rethinking the Ecological Indian" may shed some light on the significance of this change. When reading Shepard Kreck's *The Ecological Indian* alongside both Joseph Nicolar's *The Life and Traditions of the Red Man* and the historical documents on which they both draw, she and her students discovered: "Together they argue for cultural traditions that self-consciously promote ecological sanity. Dams could still be built on rivers, but they would be opened periodically to accommodate seasonal spawning migrations. Hunting would not be eliminated, but it would be regulated so as to allow the game populations to survive for future generations. And rather than use up or pollute the earth's resources merely 'for comfort's sake,' the land's bounty would be husbanded 'for love's sake'" (18). When choosing life, perhaps Alexie chooses love as well.

CHAPTER 7

A West and a Western that Works?

Contemporary Traditional Westerns,
Riders of the Whistling Pines, and *Silver City*

Environmental issues [should be] litigated before federal agencies or federal courts in the name of the inanimate object about to be despoiled, defaced, or invaded by roads and bulldozers and where injury is the subject of public outrage. . . . [S]o it should be as respects valleys, alpine meadows, rivers, lakes, estuaries, beaches, ridges, groves of trees, swampland, or even air that feels the destructive pressures of modern technology and modern life.

William O. Douglas, "Sierra Club v. Morton," 1972

Sherman Alexie and Chris Eyre's *Smoke Signals* illustrates a different way to view the West—not as an empire, but as a partner, a goal that parallels Joni Adamson's vision of a "garden" and Dan Daggett's description of its gardeners. Most recent Westerns, however, hark back to traditional narratives that valorize transforming a savage wilderness or desert into a civilized "empire." Although these Westerns primarily draw on more traditional perspectives of the American West, at least a few highlight mainstream environmentalist approaches to the natural world. The best of these, however, move beyond the mainstream to valorize Joni Adamson's garden metaphor and a middle place.

Although they do attempt to address current political and cultural concerns, *The Assassination of Jesse James by the Coward Robert Ford* (2007), *3:10 to Yuma* (2007), *Appaloosa* (2008), and *There Will Be Blood* (2009) all embrace a traditional Western narrative, with little reference to the environmental history on which the West was constructed. As if it were anticipating the 2008 devastation of western pine forests caused at least partly by relying on one environmental strategy, *Riders of the Whistling Pines* (1949) foregrounds a mainstream environmentalist message that valorizes the perspective of forest rangers over community members and a lumber magnate.[1] Only films like *Smoke Signals* and *Silver City* fulfill Adamson's goal, reinforcing a "garden" as a metaphor for the values and concerns of multicultural groups that fall outside mainstream American environmentalism and placing multiple voices into discussions about human and nonhuman nature.

CONTEMPORARY TRADITIONAL WESTERNS

The conquest of the West in film and the mythology grounding it "has been seen as a national epic and it was held to have enshrined an experience whose effects . . . have made Americans different from other peoples" (Murdoch vii). David Murdoch continues, "that experience seemed to be regarded as defining uniquely American characteristics and values—traditionally individualism, self reliance, and an instinctive commitment to democracy" (viii). American Westerns concentrate on the last thirty years of that conquest and, he explains, traditionally "are about conflict: they consistently pit the lone hero, often as not on behalf of the community, against enemies who impede 'progress'—the land itself, Indians, criminals, and those who would abuse power. In other words, affirm the values of individualism, self-reliance, and the democratic impulse" (ix). Such films valorize the mythology of the American West reflected in literature and policy more than a century after Turner's claim that the frontier had closed.

Rick Altman takes this mythology further, asserting that there is an "unspoken assumption that the film genre known as the Western is a straightforward extension of the nineteenth-century treatment of the 'American West as Symbol and Myth,' as the subtitle to Henry Nash Smith's (1950) influential *Virgin Lands* puts it. What makes a Western a Western, this implicit theory holds, has nothing to do with cinema. The Western is not, as it were, cinema's biological offspring, but its adopted child" (34). He argues against this assumption, hypothesizing that "even when a genre already exists in other media, the film genre of the same name cannot simply be borrowed from non-film sources. It must be recreated" (35). Yet Altman does admit that examples of the genre share "surface characteristics deployed within other generic contexts perceived as dominant" (36). For him, the Western is the offspring of two divergent "parents": the mythology and symbolism of the American West and the cinema that transforms it.

Altman claims that definitions of the genre need to combine syntactic explanations constructed from the mythology of the American West with the semantic descriptions built on cinematic representations. Accordingly, "we can as a whole distinguish between generic definitions that depend on a list of common traits, attitudes, characters, shots, locations, sets and the like—thus stressing the semantic elements that make up the genre—and definitions that play up instead certain constitutive relationships between undesignated and variable placeholders— relationships that might be called the genre's fundamental syntax" (30). To illustrate his approach, Altman outlines a syntactic definition: "For [Jim] Kitses the western grows out of a dialectic between the West as garden and as desert (between culture and nature, community and individual, future and past). . . . John Cawelti attempts to systematize the western in a similar fashion: the western is always set on or near a frontier, where man encounters his uncivilized double. The western thus takes place on the border between two lands, between two eras, and with a hero who remains divided between two value systems (for he combines the town's morals with the outlaw's skills)" (31). Then he combines it with a semantic definition: "[Marc] Vernet outlines general atmosphere ('emphasis on basic elements, such as earth, dust, water, and leather'), stock characters ('the tough/ soft cowboy, the lonely sheriff, the faithful or treacherous Indian, and the strong but tender woman'), as well as technical elements ('use of fast tracking and crane shots')" (30, 31). Together these approaches define a traditional Western.

The Assassination of Jesse James by the Coward Robert Ford, 3:10 to Yuma, Appaloosa, and There Will Be Blood seem at first to revise the Western as Altman and others define it and, as Lester D. Friedman's American Cinema of the 1970s explains, demystify its mythology. According to Friedman, revisionist Westerns "demystified the frontier and debunked its legendary figures, distinctly siding with the Indians as noble savages robbed of their birthright by the white settlers," illustrating his definition with a reading of Mel Brooks's Blazing Saddles (128). Despite their updated politics, however, none of these contemporary films challenges bifurcations between civilization and a wilderness or desert. Nor do they critique either populist or progressive visions of progress.

These films, unlike many earlier Westerns, herald the West and its mythology without acknowledging its connections with ecology. The plot of the 2007 remake of 3:10 to Yuma, for example, seems at first to rest on water-rights issues. Dan Evans (Christian Bale) struggles with his family to survive on an Arizona farm because the local land baron, Glen Hollander (Lennie Loftin), wants the Evans's land. A new railroad line is coming through it, so Hollander attempts to force them out by damming the stream that goes by their farm, stopping it completely. With little rain in the past two years to replenish the lost water, Evans cannot make the profit from his crops necessary to pay his mortgage. In such a desperate position, when the railroad (not the stagecoach line, as in the original 1957 film) offers him two hundred dollars, Evans decides to accompany the desperado Ben Wade (Russell Crowe) to Contention, where they will wait for the 3:10 to Yuma.

In *The Assassination of Jesse James by the Coward Robert Ford,* the James–Younger Gang historically and mythically fights the railroad for lands confiscated by the federal government to serve the company. The gang's robberies were seen by many as retaliation for what southern farmers viewed as land grabbing. This current Western at least peripherally responds to environmental issues related to conflicts between northern industrial and southern agrarian visions of land use, worldviews resting on progressive and populist versions of progress, respectively. As a traditional Western, however, the debate is unexplored and hidden behind the epic study of a rebellious hero at the film's center.

Even though Roger Ebert claims there are homosexual undertones in *The Assassination of Jesse James by the Coward Robert Ford,* especially in relation to Robert Ford's (Casey Affleck) obsession with Jesse (Brad Pitt), he calls the film a "classic Western epic" partly because "it was photographed in the wide opens spaces of western Canada, where the land is so empty, it creates a vacuum demanding men to become legends." Rebellious heroes like Jesse James gain mythic stature because they at least seem to rob symbols of corrupt corporate power for a reason: In the case of Jesse, federally backed corporations stole his and other families' land for a railroad, which thus seems to run on greed in the name of progress, though one that serves only the few. According to Ebert, the director, Andrew Dominik, "portrays his hero at a time when most men were so powerless, they envied Jesse James even for imposing his will on such as they." In this film, Jesse serves a community by embracing a mythos that empowers the populous even when their lands and lives are threatened.

Unlike earlier sagas of the James Gang, however, the history behind Jesse's robberies and murders goes unmentioned and emerges only in the portrayal of the character. According to Ebert, "Brad Pitt embodies Jesse James' mythic stature as if long accustomed to it." And Peter Travers explains, "Brad Pitt totally nails it as Jesse James," in what he calls "this intimate epic." The only reference to Jesse's past comes through a voiceover at the film's opening that calls him a "Southern loyalist and a guerilla," implying that the war never ended for him. No mention is made to the loss of his family's land to the railroad, even as he and his gang rob another train near the film's opening.

Only the landscape itself points to the environmental history behind the robberies, a landscape that becomes a character that seems to conquer figures who are shot and left in grasses or frozen streams. A claim that the Jesse and his brother Frank are "[g]etting back at Union men for wrongs" merely nods to the narrator's opening words. Jesse James may have been a southern loyalist and a guerilla, but in the James myth, he is something more: a hero defending the land and agrarian values of a post–Civil War South. *The Assassination of Jesse James by the Coward Robert Ford* adheres so tightly to the classic epic Western that it buries even that environmental message.

Peter Travers calls the most recent *3:10 to Yuma* deconstructionist rather than revisionist, claiming, "Despite kicking up the violence quotient . . . and freighting Freud into the subtext . . . , [director James] Mangold digs in his spurs as Dan takes on Wade's gang." Taking an opposite stance, Roger Ebert claims that it "restores the wounded heart of the Western and rescues it from the morass of pointless violence." David Denby, however, calls the film "familiar," not because it remakes the 1957 original but because it embraces conventions of the traditional Western, though with a harder edge: "*3:10 to Yuma* is a remake of a 1957 Western directed by Delmer Daves, and this version—directed by James Mangold and written by Michael Brandt and Derek Haas, who amplified Elmore Leonard's 1953 story and Halsted Welles's script for the original—is faster, more cynical, and more brutal than the first." Despite its nods toward the Iraq War, Denby

is closest to the mark: the remake of *3:10 to Yuma* merely amplifies conventions of the traditional Western. The original focused
more intently on the dried-up land, famished cattle, and the rain
that finally comes.

The remake also nearly erases the environmental history
illustrated by the original. The 2007 version uses post–Civil War
politics and railroad corruption and land grabbing as a backdrop
for an exploration of the hyperviolence associated with the Iraq
War and the Abu Ghraib scandal. The 1957 version, in contrast,
places water rights and drought at the forefront. Although the
Daves film also maintains conventions of the traditional Western,
because it places water at its center, it more accurately highlights
the environmental effects of both progressive and populist versions of progress.

The Daves original foregrounds the desert conditions from
its opening shots of a trail crossing an arid land and a stagecoach
throwing dust up from its forward wheels. Although Ben Wade
(Glenn Ford) and his gang rob a stagecoach, the lack of rain and
its consequences for ranching takes precedence for the Evans
family members witnessing the crime. Dan Evans (Van Heflin)
laments three years of drought killing his cattle, and when his
wife, Alice (Leora Dana), notes that Al Parker has a stream that
will not run dry, Dan explains that six months of water rights
costs two hundred dollars. His only solution seems to be the
possibility of rain. He refuses to beg or borrow the money, as
Alice suggests. When he looks at the land, however, he does go
to town to borrow the money because it will get them through
six months, and, according to Dan, "by then it will rain. All this
will be green in six months. The cattle will be fat" and not be
tired all the time. They will be happy.

The drought affects every aspect of the plotline in the 1957
version. When Dan attempts to borrow money, the banker refuses
to loan it to him because of the dry conditions: "What with the
drought, nobody pays back," he says. Dan chooses to help the
sheriff capture Wade because of this drought as well, tricking the

desperado into staying longer at the bar to pay him for his and his boys' work—and for his "tired cattle." When the lawmen put Wade in handcuffs, Dan explains to him: "My cattle is dying. I've got to take care of them." And when Mr. Butterfield (Robert Emhardt) offers two hundred dollars to anyone who will take Wade to Contention to catch the train to the penitentiary, Dan volunteers.

While they wait in a Contention hotel room for the 3:10 train, Wade even uses the drought to convince Dan to set him free for a price. "Three years of drought don't seem so bad," he says, and talks about a rancher surviving ten years of drought because a "big enough outfit had plenty of water." With Wade's seven thousand dollars, Dan could build a big enough outfit to survive until the rains return. Dan of course refuses, but we hear thunder in the background when Alice rides into Contention wearing a white cape. We again hear the thunder as Dan and Wade walk out of the back of the hotel, and wind blows up along a fence line. After cattle roll by, Dan and Wade hide behind water barrels, another nod to the film's central theme. And after they jump onto the Yuma train and wave at Alice, waiting in her wagon, the rain begins, amplifying Dan's success. Both the two hundred dollars for water rights and the rain will bring back the grasslands, feed his cattle, and save his family.

The 2007 remake of *3:10 to Yuma,* however, mentions the drought only in reference to a debt Dan Evans (Christian Bale) owes for three months of water rights and medicine for his youngest son (Ben Petry). Instead, as Peter Travers explains, the film "kick[s] up the violence quotient (a gatling gun figures in a coach robbery) and freight[s] Freud into the subtext" while reinforcing the original film's "moral code." The remake weakens Dan's character as a way to update the film and connect it with the contemporary Iraqi situation, but it valorizes messages about civilizing the West similar to those in the original. Here environmental history is nearly erased to highlight a post–Civil War setting constructed as parallel to conditions and actions in Iraq.

Connections with the Iraq War are emphasized throughout the film. Dan lost a leg in the Civil War not as a Union volunteer but as a Massachusetts militiaman conscripted into the army, and he, like modern National Guard veterans, fights for his benefits. Ben Wade (Russell Crowe) is tortured with electric shocks outside a railroad tunnel when he is caught after escaping Dan and the rest of the posse, paralleling the torture endured by Abu Ghraib prisoners. The hyperviolence throughout the film connects the two wars as well, as does the references to the railroad, rather than drought, as the source of Dan's woes.

Another film, *There Will be Blood,* not only follows a traditional Western narrative based on binaries like those between civilization and savagery but also obscures environmental disaster with a series of spectacular shots of explosions, dramatic falls, oil-well fires and gushers, and rolling rivers and lakes of oil. The opening scenes set the tone for this hyperbolic epic, with a soundtrack rising in pitch and volume as Daniel Plainview (Daniel Day-Lewis) digs for silver, dynamites a mine shaft, and falls from a broken ladder into the mine. It is 1898, and this incredible sequence prepares viewers for other, more amazing spectacles to come.

The series of spectacular scenes all but erase any references to the environmental consequences of mining or drilling. Instead, sublime incidents merely move the plot forward and construct Plainview's character: A falling drill bit kills a partner and provides Plainview with an adopted son, HW (Dillon Freasier). He and his son walk nonchalantly through an oil river flowing from a derrick "forest," which foreshadows the prosperity at any cost that lay ahead for Plainview.

One last spectacular scene transforms relationships in the film and illustrates Plainview's priorities. While HW watches a drill from the derrick frame, the drill begins to shake and the well explodes, knocking the boy onto a roof. A gusher shoots through the derrick and over its top. Plainview rescues his son, but the explosion has deafened him. A fire then explodes up the derrick in a yellow smoking flame, and Plainview leaves HW to knock down the derrick and stop the runaway well. Oil is more important to him than his son. This scene is beautiful spectacle. Yellow fire and black smoke fill the frame and reflect on the figures in an orange glow. Smoke fills half the frame and hovers over Plainview and his manager, Fletcher (Ciarán Hinds). Eli Sunday (Paul Dano), the minister, watches. The derrick falls. Shadowed figures are overpowered visually by the flames, seemingly enveloped by a glowing orange oval resembling an eye. Plainview watches the oceans of oil below. Then workers dynamite the well with barrels of explosives and finally stop the uncontrolled fire. Only now does Plainview returns to HW. This mesmerizing scene demonstrates his greed and the power behind his obsession with oil, a power of such mythic quality that it turns Plainview into a monster so monomaniacal that, as *Baltimore Sun* reviewer Michael Sragow suggests, he "makes Standard Oil look sympathetic." The spectacle also obscures the eco-disaster on display.

Plainview seems to internalize the power of such spectacle. As Sragow writes: "Cinematographer Robert Elswit and production designer Jack Fisk deliver the best performances. . . . [T]hey create harsh, bracing landscapes, with buildings huddled together as if for warmth, and images of a derrick fire that are Hadean in their power." And that power is paralleled in the film's final scene when Plainview declares, "I'm finished." *There Will Be Blood* is reminiscent of earlier oil-frontier films like *Giant* because of both the spectacle and the maniacal greed Plainview embodies. But it amplifies both the beautiful poetry of an oil gusher and the crazed greed of a rebellious tycoon like *Giant*'s Jett Rink (James Dean). Instead of revising the Western, *There Will Be Blood* amps it up and disguises ecological disaster with spectacular effect.

Appaloosa too reinforces the traditional Western. According to *Rolling Stone* reviewer Peter Travers: "There is nothing abstract about [Ed] Harris' approach to *Appaloosa*. Every frame of the movie indicates his bone-deep respect for classic film Westerns,

notably 1946's *My Darling Clementine,* in which director John
Ford took a low-key, almost lyrical approach to the gunfight
at the OK Corral." Travers explains that Harris's Western "isn't
revisionist like Clint Eastwood's *Unforgiven* or deconstructionist
like last year's *3:10 to Yuma.* His film resonates with themes of
personal honor that don't age." Michael Sragow agrees, com-
paring *Appaloosa* to "that last defiantly traditional big-screen
Western, Fred Schepisi's *Barbarosa* (1982)." Instead of revising the
Western, *Appaloosa* honors its codes, maintaining a friendship
between Everett Hitch (Viggo Mortensen) and Virgil Cole (Ed
Harris) even when Allie French (Renee Zellweger) steals Cole's
heart and Randall Bragg (Jeremy Irons) nearly steals their town.
Personal honor is maintained for Hitch when he rides off only
after ensuring that Cole will keep both town and girl, at least
for a little while. Despite the lack of environmental references
in *Appaloosa,* the landscape of the American West grounds the
film. Bragg represents the savagery of the free-range ranch life,
while the town wrests civilization out of a New Mexico desert
wilderness.

Although the environmental message is obscured by the traditional codes of the genre, these current Westerns reflect the
ongoing debate about the environment of the West. Donald
Worster even suggests that "one of the surprises of our time is
that people have begun to acknowledge their continuing depen-
dency on nature wherever they live," including the American
West (*Under Western Skies* 252).

MAINSTREAM ENVIRONMENTAL WESTERNS:
RIDERS OF THE WHISTLING PINE

In what looks like an anticipation of a 2008 eco-disaster, a
lodgepole-pine-beetle infestation in the high country of New
Mexico and Colorado, *Riders of the Whistling Pines* comes close to
fulfilling Joni Adamson's environmental justice aim but is limited
by its reliance on solely mainstream environmentalist views. The

50,000 acres of prime pine stand under federal quarantine in *Riders of the Whistling Pines.*

film "discusses differently situated human practices and perspectives on nature" and arrives at a contingent and localized consensus on how best to protect forests (Adamson xv). In *Riders of the Whistling Pines,* Gene Autry illustrates earnest, but potentially deadly, attempts to save a forest by spraying it with DDT. The remedies applied seem effective until assessed, understood, and critiqued in relation to our current context, one that demonstrates that this use of chemicals serves as one of Daggett's "failed remedies," with long-term detrimental consequences for water, soil, and wildlife in the Pacific Northwest. With its mainstream environmentalist message, *Riders of the Whistling Pines* falls short because it valorizes only one view—that of the park rangers, who act as environmentalists working to save a forest despite possible detrimental consequences to both humans and their domesticated animals.

This same valorization of mainstream environmentalist views contributed to the 2008 pine-beetle eco-disaster in Colorado. According to Stephanie Simon, "The mountain pine beetle has killed tens of millions of trees in Colorado alone and has destroyed forests from New Mexico to Canada. Across the Rocky Mountain West, iconic postcard vistas are vanishing as sickly mountainsides turn first a sickly shade of rust, then a ghostly gray." She further reported: "The beetle is expected to kill virtually every mature lodgepole pine in Colorado, or five million of the state's 22 million forested acres." Such devastation is on par with an environmental disaster and will have dire long-term consequences, including fires and falling trees destroying power lines, roads, trails, campgrounds, and fencing (Simon). Solutions, from turning dead trees into fuel pellets for stoves to converting the timber into ethanol, have been proposed, but effective solutions will require policy changes by environmental groups. Although factors like climate change and drought contributed to the problem, according to Simons, "foresters pin much of the blame on management practices. Decades of fire suppression and logging restrictions left the forests densely packed with towering, century-old lodgepole pines, which happen to be the beetles' favorite food." To avoid future infestations, mainstream environmentalists must take the advice of scientists and public citizens to implement strategies that promote "the ideal forest," where "old-growth trees would stand 20 feet apart from one another," and as Todd Hartmann suggested, forests must "have a better mix of tree species, as well as more age diversity, making it unlikely the beetles will find as many suitable hosts as in the pure 80-plus year-old lodgepole stands it has favored."

An ideal forest would require thinning of trees through controlled fires and sustainable lumbering. In *Riders of the Whistling Pines,* such strategies are constructed as bad for the environment. Instead, the forests must be preserved no matter what the cost. The tussock moths infesting the trees must be destroyed, so a lumber company cannot steal the rotted timber for themselves. In the film forest ranger Gene Autry discovers that moths are destroying a large swath of forest on federal lands. Lumberman Henry Mitchell (Douglass Dumbrille) has made the same discovery and wants to see the infestation continue, so the land will be given to him to be harvested. But Autry's proposal to use DDT to kill the moths and save the trees will foil the businessman's land grab. When Mitchell overhears townspeople discussing the potential dangers of DDT, he hires someone to spray other powerful chemicals to kill animal life and frighten farmers into believing that DDT is the cause so they will stop the rangers from saving the forest.

After Mitchell discusses the livestock and wild-animal deaths during a camp meeting with concerned ranchers and blames them on DDT, Autry and another ranger find his stronger chemicals and ride to the airstrip to stop Mitchell and his gang. Ultimately the logger and his henchman are killed, and the rangers return to their mission to spray DDT, kill the moths, and save the trees. The lumberman has been defeated, and spraying can continue, so the forests will survive, according to the narrative. Yet the consequences of maintaining forest growth no matter the cost or of widespread spraying of DDT are not explored chiefly because, it would seem, the film was released in 1949, and DDT was still viewed as a wonder chemical.

In 1945, however, years before the publication of Rachel Carson's *Silent Spring,* the seminal work that warned about the dire consequences of widespread DDT and other pesticide use, the US government restricted the use of DDT, complicating Autry's position and perhaps valorizing Mitchell and the townspeople's concerns. According to Edmund P. Russell's "The Strange Career of DDT," the United States had "apprehensions about the insecticide's effect on wildlife and 'the balance of nature.'" Russell explains that the policy asserted that "while it may be necessary to ignore these considerations in other parts of the world, in the United States such considerations cannot be neglected."

Representatives from the Fish and Wildlife Service, the Public Health Service, and other federal agencies restricted the use of DDT to rare circumstances because it harmed wildlife, caused cancer in humans, and passed through mothers' milk to their infants (770).

At the same time, however, DDT was hailed as "the War's greatest contribution to the future health of the world" (Russell 770–71). Russell explains that after its "release to civilians in August 1945, public health officials, farmers, and homeowners snapped up the wonder chemical to kill insects that caused disease, attacked crops, or created a nuisance." According to Russell, "in 1948, DDT developer Paul Muller received the Nobel Prize in physiology or medicine." Russell attempts to reconcile these two views by exploring the history of the pesticide's usage during and after World War II, suggesting that it met certain needs during the war like quelling insect-borne diseases among the troops (771, 774). When control of DDT passed from military to civilian hands in August 1945, the federal policy no longer applied to its usage. According to Russell, free and widespread use of DDT continued until scientists like Rachel Carson joined with environmental groups and pressured the government to ban DDT. The prohibition occurred in 1972, two years after the first Earth Day and the establishment of the Environmental Protection Agency.

In 2008, more than thirty-five years after DDT's ban, Colorado state foresters suggested using insecticides to ward off a bark-beetle infestation only "on high-value trees, such as those that provide shade or ornamental value" (Hartman). But the problems in the Wyoming and Colorado forests were "fueled in part by uniformly older lodgepole forests" (Hartman), there because, according to Jim Robbins, "fires have been suppressed for so long." Attempts by environmentalists in Colorado and Wyoming to preserve forests failed because they relied on only one perspective—that of mainstream environmentalism. By foregrounding use of DDT as the only environmental solution and valorizing the preservation of all trees in a forest, *Riders of the Whistling Pines* also highlights strengths and weaknesses of mainstream environmental views and reinforces the need for a "middle place."

THE HYBRID: *SILVER CITY* AND THE GARDEN AS A SPACE WHERE ALL HAVE A VOICE

Silver City (2004) offers an alternative view that begins to embrace a vision of a "garden" that supports human and nonhuman nature without exploiting either one. As Adamson asserts about multicultural literatures, this film begins to explore "the large-scale economic, political, cultural, historical, ecological, and spiritual forces affecting both the places where people live and where they do not" to help determine a middle place where all voices can discuss the role humans may play in the natural world (184).

Ranchers in Dan Daggett's *Beyond the Rangeland Conflict: Toward a West that Works* address their connection with the natural world in similar ways. Daggett provides contemporary examples of real ranches who take community-based approaches to addressing complicated environmental problems. Many "functional relationships" now exist "between humans and rangeland ecosystems," including "riparian recovery, sustaining endangered species, restoring grasslands and watershed, and reviving extinct springs." His text begins from the standpoint that "our way of relating to the arid open lands of the West is a failure" and that "as much as this devastation [of the land] is the result of more than a century of grazing mismanagement, it is also the legacy of more than a hundred years of failed remedies" (vii, 2).

Daggett's text highlight better ways to interact with the western environment that create "functional relationships . . . between humans and rangeland ecosystems." *Smoke Signals* points us to a better way to approach Westerns—infuse filmmaking with multicultural voices, especially those that, as Adamson explains of American Indian writers, "confront and problematize the dichotomization of people and nature that pervades contemporary environmentalism and much of American nature writing." Adamson draws on Simon Ortiz's, Rudolfo Anaya's, and Leslie Marmon Silko's use of the metaphor of the garden as "a powerful symbol not only of nature but of livelihood or the right of humans to derive a living from the earth," but this garden does not destroy nature as it sustains an ever-growing human community (181).

Instead, the garden metaphor Adamson describes "is often a powerful symbol of political resistance," as in Patricia Preciado Martin's story, "The Journey," which fights against destruction of barrios in Tucson (181). In many of the works Adamson examines:

> The garden becomes a metaphor for the values and concerns of multicultural groups that fall outside mainstream American environmentalism. However, I do not think that multicultural writers are urging readers to shift their energies from one Landscape to another—from the wilderness to the garden. . . . Not all of nature is wilderness, but not all is garden either. The Sonoran Desert, which is the setting of Zepeda's poetry, for instance, is a continuum of landscapes, from the college campus to thoroughly humanized areas where people raise livestock and grow gardens, to exploited areas where people extract minerals, to barely humanized reaches of saguaro, ironwood, and desert poppy. (183)

Adamson differentiates the garden metaphor highlighted in the American Indian works she examines from the garden associated with western settlement. This Euro-American vision builds civilization out of the wilderness, developing lands and using resources to serve humankind alone. For Adamson, however:

> the garden metaphor calls our attention to the world as a middle place, a contested terrain in which dispute

arises from divergent cultural ideas on what nature is and should be, and on what the human role in nature is and should be. Like the garden where the gardener endeavors to understand how nature's large-scale patterns work in specific places, multicultural writers are inviting readers into an ever-widening discussion focusing on the large-scale economic, political, cultural, historical, ecological, and spiritual forces affecting both the places where people live and where they do not. (183–84)

Such a vision serves as a call to action, a lens through which we can critique texts and practices in which nature and cultures are bifurcated. As Adamson explains: "The garden metaphor calls us to an awareness that if we want to work toward the creation of a more livable world, we must assess, understand, and critique these forces; come together to discuss differently situated human practices and perspectives on nature; and arrive at some consensus (however contingent and based on local people, situations, and places) about what our role in nature will be" (184).

Adamson highlights American Indian writers who integrate and draw on such a metaphor. But such a discussion can apply not only to literary texts and cultural contexts but also to films in which environmental issues take center stage. Such an approach offers a new and more effective lens through which to examine the Western and to demonstrate how best to produce films about the American West. Like multicultural writers, some films and filmmakers "are inviting readers into an ever-widening discussion focusing on the large-scale economic, political, cultural, historical, ecological, and spiritual forces affecting both the places where people live and where they do not" as a way to highlight both human and nonhuman nature (184). Those that also help us "arrive at some consensus . . . about what our role in nature will [and should?] be" come closest to Adamson's "middle place," a place where films and filmmakers strive to be "like the garden where the gardener endeavors to understand how nature's large-scale patterns work in specific places." Although most Westerns from the 1990s forward either obscure environmental issues with a traditional narrative of populist or progressivist visions of progress or limit environmental choices to those valorized by the mainstream environmental movement, *Smoke Signals* and *Silver City* embrace a middle place where multiple voices build toward a consensus "about what our role [in] nature will be" (183, 184).

Although *Silver City* fails to illustrate a garden like that Adamson proposes, it begins a discussion in the "middle place" that leans toward a new environmentalism like that Daggett describes, especially in his *Gardeners of Eden: Rediscovering Our Importance to Nature*. In that book Daggett moves beyond illustrating effective ranching methods and suggests people become "more native and less alien and . . . reestablish . . . the same sort of connection with nature that the earlier Gardeners of Eden had" (133). Like Adamson, he asserts that we need to find a middle ground between leaving the natural environment alone and exploiting it. He also draws on the experiences of American Indians' interactions with the environment to highlight a way to build the kind of garden Adamson proposes, one that includes human and nonhuman nature, valorizes multicultural perspectives, and seeks to integrate environmental practices that work for all.

Donald Worster's exploration of the effects of public and private ownership of rangelands in *Under Western Skies* illustrates how difficult it can be to determine best practices for conserving human and nonhuman nature. His study recalls the debate between free-range and fenced ranching explored in so many Westerns, from *Sea of Grass* to *Open Range*. Worster asserts that the rangelands "offered a pasture of considerable potential for livestock, one covering several hundred million acres," not fertile farmland. But these lands also broached several questions, he suggests, most importantly, "Was there any safe, humane, permanent way to turn that grass and the poor, dumb, hoofed animals living on it into modern dreams of unlimited personal wealth?" For Worster, there are two competing answers to that question:

give or sell the land to "private interests" or keep it in the hands of the federal government (42). He outlines a history in which both of these options are applied and explored, so much so that the two hypotheses of best land use still compete with one another in the West.

Worster calls for a "new history of the West that will compare the condition of the range under private and public (or quasi-public) ownership, that will explore the impact of rangeland science on management, that will test the claims made by rival parties and help resolve the old debate." Not surprisingly, private ranching has "had a degrading effect on the environment of the American West." Yet "ranching under supervision by the federal government has often not mitigated that impact and, in some ways, has made it worse" (45). Worster's study of rangeland and wildlife degradation through the late nineteenth and early twentieth centuries reveals that during that period, both privately and publicly owned lands suffered massive environmental devastation.

According to his preliminary conclusions, then, Worster asserts that "the safest strategy over the long run appears to be one that opens decisions about using the range to as many people as possible" (51). Still, no uniform solutions to conserving rangelands and their wildlife have been proposed. Even those suggested by Daggett and the ranchers he highlights in *Beyond the Rangeland Conflict* work only at the local level, only on the individual ranches discussed in each chapter of that short book.

The debate between public versus private landownership continues and has grown more complex as science offers alternative solutions to environmental problems. In Daggett's epilogue, he asks ecological questions about the Colorado Plateau that point to similar ambiguities. "Can spare beauty survive animal impact? What if cows can get grass to grow on the plateau? In Southern Arizona they're growing it on mine tailings. What do we do? How do we decide?" (*Beyond the Rangeland Conflict* 100). When examining possible answers, he concludes the following about public and private groups: "Both sides have their own 'best science.' Parks and preserves typically determine the health of grasslands by measuring the amount of vegetative canopy (the amount of standing plant material). Range biologists associated with ranches, on the other hand, record live basal area (the total area occupied by living plants)" (100). Daggett asserts that both sides are based in valid science but become unreliable when they dismiss or ignore the other side when advocating for their own. The real solution for him seems to come when, as Aldo Leopold states, we mix "a degree of wildness with utility" (qtd. in Daggett 101).

But solutions come when we build on Worster's advice to "open decisions about using the range to as many people as possible" and add nature into the mix. Contemporary films like *Smoke Signals* and *Silver City* best reflect this "middle place" and highlight ways to build a "garden" without destroying the land. These films invite viewers to "come together to discuss differently situated human practices and perspectives on nature; and arrive at consensus . . . about what our role in nature will be" (Adamson 184). The attention *Smoke Signals* gives to multicultural voices is clear. But John Sayles's *Silver City* also provides a space for multiple voices, especially those of the illegal migrant workers exploited in the film. As David Rooney notes in a *Variety* review, "While the Mexican characters are less rounded than the Americans, Sayles maps the socioeconomic disparities of his chosen microcosm without belaboring his agenda the way the director sometimes has."

Silver City harks back to Sayles's *Lone Star,* in which the story of a man and a murder is told multiculturally, all from each character's own distinct perspectives, highlighting, according to Roger Ebert, "how people try to live together at this moment in America." *Silver City* again valorizes these multiple voices but adds nature to the mix by illustrating the continuing conflict between federal control and private ownership of lands and resources. In this movie a George W. Bush–like candidate for

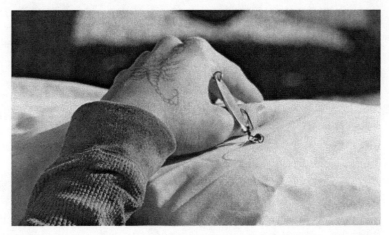

Fished corpse, caught by candidate Dickie Pilager (Chris Cooper), in *Silver City*

governor of Colorado, Dickie Pilager (Chris Cooper), advocates for small government and private ownership of public lands but unknowingly uncovers a murder and an environmental catastrophe. According to Ebert, "*Silver City* can be read as a social satire aimed at George Bush . . . but it takes wider aim on the entire political landscape we inhabit."

Silver City introduces its focus on environmental concerns, murder, and politics from its opening montage sequence of election-focused sound bites and out-of-focus images of flags and political speakers. Bands of white neon foreground the environmental message presented by Pilager's campaign with the title, "Richard Pilager cares about Colorado," and a commercial filming in front of a lake, "the bucolic fishing thing," Chuck Raven (Richard Dreyfuss), Pilager's campaign manager, explains.

During this sequence, however, the murder and its eco-disaster cause are introduced while Pilager voices his concern for the environment in a posed political advertisement and catches a human corpse instead of a fish. When the body smells of apricots, an environmental political message transforms into the site of a murder investigation and a possible environmental disaster. Through a covert murder investigation led by private detective Danny O'Brien (Danny Huston), *Silver City* not only foregrounds mainstream environmentalist concerns (toxic waste from silver-mining runoff) but also highlights environmental-justice concerns by placing multicultural voices at the center, the voices of migrant workers mistreated and misused almost as virulently as the land itself.

O'Brien begins his investigation in the web office of Mitch Paine (Tim Roth), his old newspaper editor, where the political machine behind Pilager is revealed. Paine's website also shows how privatization is (still) constructed as the best solution for western lands. The site illustrates the Pilager family's history of greed, questioning their claims that an ancestor was a lone-wolf prospector and explaining that the family had already diversified their interests after 1893, when the silver bubble burst. All of this is in relation to the Bentel Corporation, run by Wes Benteen (Kris Kristofferson), who wishes to own and control the public lands in Colorado.

To ensure that private control of public lands and their resources will be maintained, Benteen finances Pilager's guber-natorial race since he and Dickie's father, Sen. Judson Pilager (Michael Murphy), realize they can easily manipulate him. When Benteen and Dickie ride out on horses to see the land, for example, Benteen tells him this is a land where "[n]o Americans are allowed" because the bureaucrats own it all. "The Bureau of Land Management, the National Parks, the states" cannot see the big picture, which for Benteen means privatization. He asserts, "[t]he land was meant for the citizens, not the pencil pushers in Washington," claiming that they must "liberate those resources for the American people" and for men of vision like Benteen, who know how to use them. Through a patriotic speech fore-grounding private ownership, he convinces Dickie to work to privatize public lands.

The film also shows how this view of private ownership has dire environmental consequences. An ex–mining engineer leading a tour of the Silver City mines, Casey Lyle (Ralph Waite), one of Raven's suspects in the murder, reveals some of the eco-disasters perpetrated by Benteen and Pilager, owners of the mine: "You know, we think we can wound this planet. We think we can cut costs and stick the money in our pockets and just walk away with it. But some day the bill comes due." When O'Brien tells him that he is being watched, Lyle explains how he took on Benteen and the Silver City Mine, so he and his crew would clean up their ecosystem. He had found acres and acres of tailings piled up and measured nasty pH ratings from the water around the mine because Benteen and Pilager were using and unsafely disposing of cyanide so that it was getting in the water system. His plan to stop Benteen failed when he was fired for misuse of funds. But his story helps O'Brien begin solving the mystery of both the murder and the eco-disaster associated with it.

The trail of the murder victim, Lazaro Huerta (Donevon Martinez), however, leads O'Brien to another environmental disaster, one based on environmental injustice for illegal-immigrant workers. As Al Gedicks asserts, "Native peoples are under assault on every continent because their lands contain a wide variety of valuable resources needed for industrial and military production" (168). Benteen exploits Mexican migrant workers in two ways: He literally exploits their labor for little compensation and at great cost to their health and welfare. And he exploits what was once their land for unfettered profit.

Sayles adds these multicultural voices to the discussion when O'Brien hires Tony Guerra (Sal Lopez) to help him find the source of the victim's injuries and of the illegal migrant-worker industry. Guerra discovers that Vince Esparza (Luis Saguar) oversees illegal workers, including two, Fito (Aaron Vieyra) and Rafi (Hugo E Carbajal), who witnessed Huerta's death. Esparza nearly kills Guerra, but he survives to tell O'Brien about the two workers he had intended to meet. At the mine, Fito and Rafi tell him that Huerta was killed at the slaughterhouse, where they were forced to work as part of the cleaning crew after midnight, washing down the floors with water mixed with chloride. In a flashback we see Huerta fall to his death from a scaffold when an out-of-control waterhose hits him. According to Fito and Rafi, Esparza forced them to take the body to the mine and dump it in the shaft. When they returned three days later, the body was gone and the mine floor was full of water.

Now that the truth about Huerta's death is revealed, the truth about environmental degradation is also unearthed when O'Brien explores the mine to discover how the body floated to the lake where it was found. When the police arrive at the mine, Fito and Rafi run away while O'Brien grabs onto a timber near the shaft. When the beam breaks, he falls into the shaft and discovers why the body smelled of apricots. In the water around him are countless barrels labeled "toxic waste." By solving the murder case, then, O'Brien also reveals an eco-disaster and seeks environmental justice for the migrant workers and for the aquatic life in the nearby lake. Esparza and his employer, Benteen, chose not to clean up the toxic waste and just dumped it into the mineshaft. O'Brien secretly reports his discovery to Paine's office staff, knowing they will broadcast the news.

Toxic mine runoff leads to a climatic fish kill in *Silver City*

Even though the Pilagers and Benteens cover the entrance to the mine with concrete, and Paine and his reporters cannot uncover the waste containers, O'Brien addresses social injustices in the film. He sends Huerta's body home to Mexico and provides money for the family. At the film's conclusion, hundreds of dead fish appear on the lake where Dickie is giving another speech, with the patriotic song "America the Beautiful" ringing in the background, highlighting eco-disaster rather than land acquisition and upsetting the candidate's political ambitions.

Ultimately, the conflict between public and private ownership plays out against privatization in *Silver City*, even though the narrative seems to claim victory for Benteen. With public support from the governor's office, public lands seem to become private investments, but the evidence that privatization and eco-disaster go hand in hand is overwhelming. The film's parting scene of fish floating to the top of the poisoned lake provides hope because it makes the ecological nightmare transparent and inserts the environment into a discussion that includes a variety of perspectives. When all voices—including that of nature—are in conversation, a middle place may be possible.

Like Adamson, we have attempted here to highlight that middle place and demonstrate a viable alternative to mainstream environmentalism. The goal is to extend Adamson's "middle place" to readings of classic and contemporary Westerns. Films like *Smoke Signals* and *Silver City* best reflect this "middle place" and highlight ways to build a "garden" without destroying the land (Adamson 184).

As Donald Worster explains: "They say that we can live without the old fantasy of a pristine, inviolate, edenic wilderness—it was, after all, never adequate to the reality of the natural world as we found it. But we could never really turn all of nature into artifact. Nor could we live without nature. For all our ingenuity, we sense that we need that independent, self-organizing, resilient biophysical world to sustain it. If nature were ever truly at an end, then we would be finished. It is not however, and we are not" (253–54). Perhaps the continuing popularity of the Western as a genre rests on this same lesson. These films reflect the continuing debate about what is best for nature while they hark back to an American West in which life itself depended on our attachment to the natural environment—one that may be what those Western heroes were fighting about all along—a middle place where all are heard.

Notes

INTRODUCTION

1. Because the indigenous people of the United States currently prefer "American Indian" to "Native American," we also use that term throughout this book.

CHAPTER 1

1. See, for example, *Open Range* (2003) and *Brokeback Mountain* (2005).

2. See, for example, Roy Rogers's *Roll on Texas Moon* (1946), *The Sheep Man* (1958), and *The Ballad of Josie* (1968).

CHAPTER 3

1. See, for example, *The Plow that Broke the Plains* (1936) and *The River* (1937).

CHAPTER 4

1. Cherokee Lansing is one-quarter American Indian.

2. See, for example, *Cimarron* (1931), *'Neath Arizona Skies* (1934), *Black Gold* (1936), *Mexicali Rose* (1939), and *South of the Border* (1939).

3. See, for example, *Boom Town* (1940), *In Old Oklahoma* (1943), *Conquest of Cheyenne* (1946), *Apache Rose* (1947), *Riders of the Whistling Pines* (1949), *Tulsa* (1949), *Susanna Pass* (1949), *Spoilers of the Plains* (1951), *Giant* (1956), and *The Oklahoman* (1957).

4. See, for example, *Cimarron* (1960), *Hud* (1963), *Comes a Horseman* (1978), and *There Will Be Blood* (2007).

5. The term "sooner" had a derogatory connotation until the turn of the twentieth century, referring to settlers who laid claim to land before the official beginning of the territory. After 1908, however, the University of Oklahoma adopted "sooner" as their football team's name. Oklahoma has been known as the Sooner State ever since, and the term has become a badge of honor for many Oklahomans. The term "boomer," however, referred to those settlers who believed American Indian lands were public property and incited violence in order to remove the Indians from their lands.

6. See Debo, *And Still the Waters Run;* Wickett, *Contested Territory;* Conley, *Cherokee Nation;* Garrick Bailey and Roberta Glenn Bailey, "Indian Territory," in Hoxie, *Encyclopedia of North American Indians,* 271–73; and the Westerns that respond to this history.

7. See Rothman, *Saving the Planet;* and Shabecoff, *Fierce Green Fire.*

CHAPTER 5

1. See, for example, *Dodge City* (1939), *Jesse James* (1939), *When the Daltons Rode* (1940), *The Harvey Girls* (1946), *Fort Worth* (1951), *Night Passage* (1957), *The True Story of Jesse James* (1957), *The Great Northfield Minnesota Raid* (1972), and *The Long Riders* (1980).

CHAPTER 6

1. See, for example, Slethaug, "Hurricanes and Fires"; Hearne, "John Wayne's Teeth"; and Mihelich, "Smoke or Signals?"

2. Pekka Hamalainen revisits the history of Comanche power in *The Comanche Empire,* demonstrating the tribe's depth and breadth and its reliance on mediation more than a warrior-based conquest of other native territories. The Comanche, according to Hamalainen, also may have been responsible for US dominance over the Spanish in the Desert Southwest.

3. *Drums Along the Mohawk* (1939), *Fort Apache* (1948), *3 Godfathers* (1948), *She Wore a Yellow Ribbon* (1949), *Rio Grande* (1950), *Wagon Master*

(1950), *The Searchers* (1956), *Two Rode Together* (1961), and *Cheyenne Autumn* (1964) all assert the same argument.

4. *Under Nevada Skies* (1946), *Broken Arrow* (1950), *Colt .45* (1950), *Indian Territory* (1950), *North of the Great Divide* (1950), *Arrowhead* (1953), *Broken Lance* (1954), *Apache* (1954), *They Rode West* (1954), *White Feather* (1955), *The Indian Fighter* (1955), and *The Oregon Trail* (1959) also construct American Indians as savages and represent their worldview, no matter how connected to the environment, as inferior to that of whites and their focus on taming the frontier.

5. Westerns like *The Unforgiven* (1960), *The Canadians* (1961), *The Scalp-hunters* (1968), *A Man Called Horse* (1970), *Soldier Blue* (1970), *Little Big Man* (1970), *Chato's Land,* (1972) *Jeremiah Johnson* (1972), *Chino* (1973), *Prophecy* (1979), *The Outlaw Josey Wales* (1976), *Dances with Wolves* (1990), *Black Robe* (1991), *The Last of the Mohicans* (1992), *Thunderheart* (1992), *Geronimo* (1993), *Cheyenne Warrior* (1994), *North Star* (1996), *Grey Owl* (1999), *Shanghai Noon* (2000), and *The New World* (2005) illustrate, to differing degrees, the worth of the American Indian vision of environmental adaptation. Yet because, as Sherman Alexie asserts, they violate sovereignty by co-opting American Indian culture, they move toward tragic visions of progress similar to those in more traditional Westerns.

6. Other Westerns since 1990 revise perspectives on American Indians, humanizing them and representing their characters sympathetically. See, for example, *Black Robe* (1991), *The Last of the Mohicans* (1992), *Geronimo* (1993), *Cheyenne Warrior* (1994), *Pocahontas* (1995), *North Star* (1996), *Grey Owl* (1999), *Shanghai Noon* (2000), and *The New World* (2005). But these films all draw on similar ideologies of progress, even when they lament the loss of Indian cultures, which is constructed as a necessary sacrifice to promote "civilization" based in progress.

CHAPTER 7

1. *The Californians* (2005) also foregrounds mainstream environmentalist views as a way to combat real-estate overdevelopment.

Filmography

Angel and the Badman. Dir. James Edward Grant. Perfs. John Wayne and Gail Russell. Republic, 1947. DVD.

Apache. Dir. Robert Aldrich. Perfs. Burt Lancaster, Jean Peters. United Artists, 1954. DVD.

Apache Rose. Dir. William Witney. Perfs. Roy Rogers, Dale Evans. Republic, 1947. DVD.

Appaloosa. Dir. Ed Harris. Perfs. Viggo Mortensen, Ed Harris, Renee Zellweger. New Line Cinema, 2008. Film.

Arrowhead. Dir. Charles Marquis Warren. Perfs. Charlton Heston, Jack Palance, Katy Jurado. Paramount, 1953. DVD.

The Asphalt Jungle. Dir. John Huston. Perfs. Sterling Hayden, Louis Calhern. MGM, 1950. DVD.

The Assassination of Jesse James by the Coward Robert Ford. Dir. Andrew Dominik. Perfs. Brad Pitt, Mary-Louise Parker. Warner Brothers, 2007. Film.

Back in the Saddle. Dir. Lew Landers. Perfs. Gene Autry, Smiley Burnette. Republic, 1941. DVD.

The Badlanders. Dir. Delmer Daves. Perfs. Alan Ladd, Ernest Borgnine. MGM, 1958. DVD.

The Ballad of Cable Hogue. Dir. Sam Peckinpah. Perfs. Jason Robards, Stella Stevens. Warner Brothers, 1970. DVD.

The Ballad of Josie. Dir. Andrew V. McLaglen. Perfs. Doris Day, Peter Graves. Universal, 1968. DVD.

Barbed Wire. Dir. George Archainbaud. Perfs. Gene Autry, Pat Buttram. Columbia, 1952. DVD.

Bells of San Angelo. Dir. William Witney. Perfs. Roy Rogers, Dale Evans. Republic, 1947. DVD.

The Big Country. Dir. William Wyler. Perfs. Gregory Peck, Burl Ives, Jean Simmons, Charlton Heston. United Artists, 1958. DVD.

Billy the Kid's Range War. Dir. Sam Newfield. Perfs. Bob Steele, Joan Barclay. Producers Releasing Corporation, 1941. DVD.

Black Gold. Dir. Russell Hopton. Perfs. Frankie Darro, LeRoy Mason, Gloria Shea. Conn Pictures, 1936. DVD.

Black Robe. Dir. Bruce Beresford. Perfs. Lothaire Bluteau, Aden Young. MGM, 1991. DVD.

Blazing Saddles. Dir. Mel Brooks. Perfs. Cleavon Little, Gene Wilder. Warner Brothers, 1974. DVD.

Blue Steel. Dir. Robert North Bradbury. Perfs. John Wayne, Eleanor Hunt, George Hayes, Yakima Canutt. Monogram, 1934. DVD.

Boom Town. Dir. John Conway. Perfs. Clark Gable, Spencer Tracy, Claudette Colbert. MGM, 1940. DVD.

Brokeback Mountain. Dir. Ang Lee. Perfs. Heath Ledger, Jake Gyllenhaal. Paramount, 2005. Film.

Broken Arrow. Dir. Delmer Daves. Perfs. James Stewart, Jeff Chandler, Debra Paget. Twentieth Century Fox, 1950. DVD.

Broken Lance. Dir. Edward Dmytryk. Perfs. Spencer Tracy, Richard Widmark, Robert Wagner. Twentieth Century Fox, 1954. DVD.

The Californians. Dir. Jonathan Parker. Perfs. Noah Wyle, Illeana Douglas. Parker Film Company, 2005. DVD.

The Canadians. Dir. Burt Kennedy. Perfs. Robert Ryan, John Dehner. Twentieth Century Fox, 1961. DVD.

Chato's Land. Dir. Michael Winner. Perf. Charles Bronson, Jack Palance. United Artists, 1971. DVD.

Cheyenne Autumn. Dir. John Ford. Perfs. Richard Widmark, Carroll Baker. Warner Brothers, 1964. DVD.

Cheyenne Warrior. Dir. Mark Griffiths. Perfs. Kelly Preston, Pato Hoffmann. Libra, 1994. DVD.

Chinatown. Dir. Roman Polanski. Perf. Jack Nicholson, Faye Dunaway. Paramount, 1974. DVD.

Chino. Dir. John Sturges. Perfs. Charles Bronson, Jill Ireland. Intercontinental Releasing Corporation, 1973. DVD.

Chisum. Dir. Andrew V. McLaglen. Perfs. John Wayne, Forest Tucker. Warner Brothers, 1970. DVD.

Cimarron. Dir. Wesley Ruggles. Perfs. Richard Dix, Irene Dunn. RKO, 1931. DVD.

Cimarron. Dir. Anthony Mann. Perfs. Glenn Ford, Maria Schell. MGM, 1960. DVD.

Colt .45. Dir. Edwin L. Marin. Perfs. Randolph Scott, Ruth Roman. Warner Brothers, 1950. DVD.

Comes a Horseman. Dir. Alan J. Pakula. Perfs. Jane Fonda, James Caan, Jason Robards. MGM, 1978. DVD.

Conquest of Cheyenne. Dir. R. G. Springsteen. Perfs. Bill Elliott, Robert Blake. Republic, 1946. DVD.

Copper Canyon. Dir. John Farrow. Perfs. Ray Milland, Heddy Lamar. Paramount, 1950. DVD.

The Cowboys. Dir. Mark Rydell. Perfs. John Wayne, Roscoe Lee Browne. Warner Brothers, 1972. DVD.

The Culpepper Cattle Company. Dir. Dick Richards. Perfs. Gary Grimes, Billy Green Bush. Twentieth Century Fox, 1972. DVD.

Daffy Duck in Hollywood. Dir. Tex Avery. Warner Brothers, 1938. DVD.

Dances with Wolves. Dir. Kevin Costner. Perfs. Kevin Costner, Mary McDonnell, Graham Greene. Orion, 1990. DVD.

Devil's Doorway. Dir. Anthony Mann. Perf. Robert Taylor, Louis Calhern. MGM, 1950. DVD.

Dodge City. Dir. Michael Curtiz. Perfs. Errol Flynn, Olivia de Havilland. Warner Brothers, 1939. DVD.

Drums along the Mohawk. Dir. John Ford. Perfs. Claudette Colbert, Henry Fonda. Twentieth Century Fox, 1939. DVD.

Eight Legged Freaks. Dir. Ellory Elkayem. Perfs. David Arquette, Kari Wuhrer. Warner Brothers, 2002. DVD.

El Dorado. Dir. Howard Hawks. Perfs. John Wayne, Robert Mitchum. Paramount, 1966. DVD.

Far and Away. Dir. Ron Howard. Perfs. Tom Cruise, Nicole Kidman. Universal, 1992. DVD.

The Far Country. Dir. Anthony Mann. Perfs. James Stewart, Ruth Roman, John McIntire, Walter Brennan. 1955. DVD.

The Fighting Westerner. Dir. Charles Barton. Perf. Randolph Scott. Paramount, 1935. DVD.

Fort Apache. Dir. John Ford. Perfs. John Wayne, Henry Fonda. RKO, 1948. DVD.

Fort Worth. Dir. Edwin L. Marin. Perfs. Randolph Scott, David Brian, Phyllis Thaxter. Warner Brothers, 1951. DVD.

Geronimo. Dir. Roger Young. Perfs. Joseph Runningfox, Nick Ramus. Turner Pictures, 1993. DVD.

Giant. Dir. George Stevens. Perfs. Elizabeth Taylor, Rock Hudson, James Dean. Warner Brothers, 1956. DVD.

The Gold Rush. Dir. Charles Chaplin. Perf. Charles Chaplin, Mack Swain. United Artists, 1925. DVD.

Gold Rush Daze. Dirs. Cal Dalton, Ben Hardaway. Warner Brothers, 1939. DVD.

Grand Canyon Trail. Dir. William Witney. Perf. Roy Rogers. Republic, 1948. DVD.

The Grapes of Wrath. Dir. John Ford. Perf. Henry Fonda, Jane Darwell, John Carradine. Twentieth Century Fox, 1940. DVD.

The Great Northfield Minnesota Raid. Dir. Philip Kaufman. Perf. Cliff Robertson, Robert Duvall. Universal, 1972. DVD.

Greed. Dir. Erich von Stroheim. Perfs. Gibson Gowland, Jean Hersholt. MGM, 1924. DVD.

Gunfighters. Dir. George Waggner. Perfs. Randolph Scott, Barbara Britton. Columbia, 1947. DVD.

The Harvey Girls. Dir. George Sidney. Perfs. Judy Garland, John Hodiak. MGM, 1946. DVD.

Heaven's Gate. Dir. Michael Cimino. Perfs. Kris Kristofferson, Christopher Walken. United Artists, 1980. DVD.

Hell Town. Dir. Charles Barton. Perfs. John Wayne, Marsha Hunt. Paramount, 1937. DVD.

Hiawatha. Perfs. Joe Biller, Hilde Hadges. States Rights Independent Exchanges, 1913. DVD.

High Plains Drifter. Dir. Clint Eastwood. Perf. Clint Eastwood, Verna Bloom, Geoffrey Lewis. Universal, 1973. DVD.

How the West Was Won. Dirs. John Ford, Henry Hathaway, George Marshall, Richard Thorpe. Perfs. Richard Widmark, George Peppard, James Stewart. MGM, 1962. DVD.

Hud. Dir. Martin Ritt. Perfs. Paul Newman, Melvyn Douglas, Patricia Neal. Paramount, 1960. DVD.

The Indian Fighter. Dir. André De Toth. Perfs. Kirk Douglas, Elsa Martinelli. United Artists, 1955. DVD.

Indian Territory. Dir. John English. Perfs. Gene Autry, Pat Buttram. Columbia, 1950. DVD.

In Old Amarillo. Dir. William Witney. Perf. Roy Rogers. Republic, 1951. DVD.

In Old Oklahoma. Dir. Albert S. Rogell. Perfs. John Wayne, Martha Scott. Republic, 1943. DVD.

The Iron Horse. Dir. John Ford. Perfs. George O'Brien, Madge Bellamy. Fox, 1924. DVD.

Jeremiah Johnson. Dir. Sydney Pollack. Perfs. Robert Redford, Will Geer. Warner Brothers, 1972. DVD.

Jesse James. Dir. Henry King. Perfs. Tyrone Power, Henry Fonda. Twentieth Century Fox, 1939. DVD.

Johnny Guitar. Dir. Nicholas Ray. Perfs. Joan Crawford, Sterling Hayden. Republic, 1954. DVD.

Johnson County War. Dir. David Cass. Perfs. Tom Berenger, Luke Perry. Hallmark Entertainment, 2002. DVD.

Land of the Open Range. Dir. Edward Killy. Perfs. Tim Holt, Ray Whitley. RKO, 1941. DVD.

The Last Hunt. Dir. Richard Brooks. Perfs. Robert Taylor, Stewart Granger, Debra Paget. MGM, 1956. VHS.

The Last of the Mohicans. Dir. George B. Seitz. Perf. Randolph Scott, Binnie Barnes. Edward Small Productions, 1936. DVD.

The Last of the Mohicans. Dir. Michael Mann. Perfs. Daniel Day-Lewis, Madeleine Stowe. Twentieth Century Fox, 1992. DVD.

Legend of the Lost. Dir. Henry Hathaway. Perfs. John Wayne, Sophia Loren. United Artists, 1957. DVD.

Little Big Man. Dir. Arthur Penn. Perfs. Dustin Hoffman, Faye Dunaway. National General, 1970. DVD.

The Long Riders. Dir. Walter Hill. Perfs. David Carradine, James Keach. United Artists, 1980. DVD.

The Lucky Texan. Dir. Robert North Bradbury. Perfs. John Wayne, George Hayes, Yakima Canutt, Lloyd Whitlock, Barbara Sheldon. Lone Star Productions, 1934. DVD.

MacKenna's Gold. Dir. J. Lee Thompson. Perfs. Gregory Peck, Omar Sharif. Columbia, 1969. DVD.

A Man Called Horse. Dir. Elliot Silverstein. Perfs. Richard Harris, Judith Anderson. National General, 1970. DVD.

Man of the Frontier. Dir. B. Reeves Eason. Perf. Gene Autry, Smiley Burnette. Republic, 1936. DVD.

Man without a Star. Dir. King Vidor. Perfs. Kirk Douglas, Jeanne Crain. Universal, 1955. DVD.

McCabe and Mrs. Miller. Dir. Robert Altman. Perfs. Warren Beatty, Julie Christie. Warner Brothers, 1971. DVD.

McClintock! Dir. Andrew V. McLaglen. Perfs. John Wayne, Maureen O'Hara. United Artists, 1963. DVD.

Mexicali Rose. Dir. George Sherman. Perfs. Gene Autry, Smiley Burnette. Republic, 1939. DVD.

The Miracle Rider. Dirs. B. Reeves Eason, Armand Schaefer. Perfs. Tom Mix, Joan Gale. Mascot Pictures, 1935. DVD.

Monty Walsh. Dir. William A. Fraker. Perfs. Lee Marvin, Jeanne Moreau. Cinema Center 100 Productions, 1970. DVD.

Monty Walsh. Dir. Simon Wincer. Perfs. Tom Selleck, Isabella Rosellini. TNT Television, 2003. Television.

Mule Train. Dir. John English. Perfs. Gene Autry, Pat Buttram. Columbia, 1950. DVD.

Mystic River. Dir. Clint Eastwood. Perfs. Sean Penn, Tim Robbins. Warner Brothers, 2003. DVD.

'Neath Arizona Skies. Dir. Harry L. Fraser. Perfs. John Wayne, Sheila Terry. Monogram, 1934. DVD.

Nevada. Dir. Edward Killy. Perfs. Robert Mitchum, Anne Jeffreys. RKO, 1944. DVD.

The New World. Dir. Terrence Malick. Perfs. Colin Farrell, Q'Orianka Kilcher. New Line Cinema, 2005. DVD.

Night Passage. Dir. James Neilson. Perfs. James Stewart, Audie Murphy. Universal, 1957. DVD.

North of the Great Divide. Dir. William Whitney. Perfs. Roy Rogers, Penny Edwards. Republic, 1950. DVD.

North Star. Dir. Nils Gaup. Perfs. James Caan, Christopher Lambert, Catherine McCormack. Warner Brothers, 1996. DVD.

The Oklahoman. Dir. Francis D. Lyon. Perfs. Joel McCrea, Barbara Hale. Allied Pictures, 1957. DVD.

Once Upon a Time in the West. Dir. Sergio Leone. Perfs. Henry Fonda, Claudia Cardinale, Jason Robards, Charles Bronson. Paramount, 1968. DVD.

Open Range. Dir. Kevin Costner. Perfs. Kevin Costner, Robert Duvall, Annette Bening. Touchstone, 2003. DVD.

The Oregon Trail. Dir. Gene Fowler Jr. Perfs. Fred MacMurray, William Bishop. Twentieth Century Fox, 1959. DVD.

The Outlaw Josie Wales. Dir. Clint Eastwood. Perfs. Clint Eastwood, Sandra Locke. Warner Brothers, 1976. DVD.

The Outlaws Is Comin'. Dir. Norman Maurer. Perfs. Joe DeRita, Larry Fine, Moe Howard, Adam West. Columbia, 1965. DVD.

The Painted Desert. Dir. Howard Higgin. Perfs. William Boyd, Helen Twelvetrees, Clark Gable. RKO-Pathe Distributing, 1931. DVD.

Pale Rider. Dir. Clint Eastwood. Perfs. Clint Eastwood, Michael Moriarty, Carrie Snodgrass. Warner Brothers, 1985. DVD.

The Plainsman. Dir. Cecil B. DeMille. Perfs. Gary Cooper, Jean Arthur. Paramount, 1936. DVD.

The Plow that Broke the Plains. Dir. Pare Lorentz. Voice. Thomas Chalmers. Resettlement Administration, 1936. DVD.

Prophecy. Dir. John Frankenheimer. Perfs. Robert Foxworth, Talia Shire. Paramount, 1979. DVD.

Rainbow Valley. Dir. Robert North Bradbury. Perfs. John Wayne, George Hayes, LeRoy Mason, Lucile Browne. Lone Star Productions, 1935. DVD.

Rancho Grande. Dir. Frank McDonald. Perf. Gene Autry, Smiley Burnette. Republic, 1940. DVD.

Range War. Dir. Lesley Selander. Perfs. William Boyd, Russell Hayden. Paramount, 1939. DVD.

The Rare Breed. Dir. Andrew V. McLaglen. Perfs. James Stewart, Maureen O'Hara. Universal, 1966. DVD.

The Red Girl. Dir. D. W. Griffith. Perfs. Florence Lawrence, Charles Insee. American Mutoscope and Biograph, 1908. DVD.

Red River. Dir. Howard Hawks. Perfs. John Wayne, Montgomery Clift. United Artists, 1948. DVD.

Riders of Destiny. Dir. Robert N. Bradbury. Perf. John Wayne. Lone Star Productions, 1933. DVD.

Riders of the Whistling Pines. Dir. John English. Perf. Gene Autry. Columbia, 1949. DVD.

Ride the High Country. Dir. Sam Peckinpah. Perfs. Randolph Scott, Joel McCrea. MGM, 1961. DVD.

Rio Grande. Dir. John Ford. Perfs. John Wayne, Maureen O'Hara. Republic, 1950. DVD.

The River. Dir. Pare Lorentz. Voice. Thomas Chalmers. Farm Security Administration, 1938. DVD.

Roll on Texas Moon. Dir. William Witney. Perfs. Roy Rogers, Dale Evans. Republic, 1946. DVD.

Rovin' Tumbleweeds. Dir. George Sherman. Perfs. Gene Autry, Smiley Burnette. Republic, 1939. DVD.

Run of the Arrow. Dir. Samuel Fuller. Perf. Rod Steiger, Sara Montiel. Globe Enterprises, 1957. DVD.

The Scalphunters. Dir. Sydney Pollack. Perfs. Burt Lancaster, Shelley Winters, Telly Savalas. United Artists, 1968. DVD.

Sea of Grass. Dir. Elia Kazan. Perfs. Spencer Tracy, Katharine Hepburn. Twentieth Century Fox, 1947. DVD.

The Searchers. Dir. John Ford. Perf. John Wayne, Jeffrey Hunter, Natalie Wood. Warner Brothers, 1956. DVD.

Shane. Dir. George Stevens. Perfs. Alan Ladd, Van Heflin, Jean Arthur. Paramount, 1953. DVD.

Shanghai Noon. Dir. Tom Dey. Perfs. Jackie Chan, Owen Wilson. Touchstone, 2000. DVD.

The Sheepman. Dir. George Marshall. Perfs. Glenn Ford, Shirley MacLaine. MGM, 1958. DVD.

She Wore a Yellow Ribbon. Dir. John Ford. Perf. John Wayne, Joanne Dru. RKO, 1949. DVD.

Silver City. Dir. John Sayles. Perfs. Chris Cooper, Danny Huston. New Market Films, 2004. DVD.

"Silver Mining." *Modern Marvels.* History Channel. 21 July 2006. Television.

Smoke Bellew. Dir. Scott Dunlap. Perf. Conway Tearle, Barbara Bedford. Big 4, 1929. DVD.

Smoke Signals. Dir. Chris Eyre. Perfs. Adam Beach, Evan Adams. Miramax, 1998. DVD.

Soldier Blue. Dir. Ralph Nelson. Perfs. Candice Bergen, Peter Strauss. AVCO Embassy Pictures, 1970. DVD.

South of the Border. Dir. George Sherman. Perfs. Gene Autry, Smiley Burnette. Republic, 1939. DVD.

Spoilers of the Plains. Dir. William Witney. Perfs. Roy Rogers, Penny Edwards. Republic, 1951. DVD.

Springtime in the Rockies. Dir. Joseph Kane. Perfs. Gene Autry, Smiley Burnette. Republic, 1937. DVD.

The Storm Rider. Dir. Edward Bernds. Perfs. Scott Brady, Mala Powers. Twentieth Century Fox, 1957. DVD.

Sunset in Wyoming. Dir. William Morgan. Perfs. Gene Autry, Smiley Burnette. Republic, 1941. DVD.

Susanna Pass. Dir. William Witney. Perfs. Roy Rogers, Dale Evans. Republic, 1949. DVD.

The Tall Stranger. Dir. Thomas Carr. Perfs. Joel McCrea, Virginia Mayo. Universal, 1957. DVD.

The Tall T. Dir. Budd Boetticher. Perfs. Randolph Scott, Maureen O'Sullivan, John Hubbard, Richard Boone. Columbia, 1957. DVD.

There Will Be Blood. Dir. Paul Thomas Anderson. Perfs. Daniel Day-Lewis, Paul Dano. Miramax, 2007. Film.

They Rode West. Dir. Phil Karlson. Perfs. Robert Francis, Donna Reed. Columbia, 1954. DVD.

3 Godfathers. Dir. John Ford. Perfs. John Wayne, Pedro Armendariz. MGM, 1948. DVD.

3:10 to Yuma. Dir. Delmer Daves. Perf. Glenn Ford, Van Heflin, and Felicia Farr. Columbia, 1957. DVD.

3:10 to Yuma. Dir. James Mangold. Perf. Russell Crowe, Christian Bale. Lionsgate, 2007. Film.

Thunderheart. Dir. Michael Apted. Perfs.Val Kilmer, Sam Shepard, Graham Greene. Columbia, 1992. DVD.

Tom Horn. Dir. William Wiard. Perfs. Steve McQueen, Linda Evans. Warner Brothers, 1980. DVD.

The Trail Beyond. Dir. Robert North Bradbury. Perf. John Wayne. Lone Star Productions, 1935. DVD.

The Trail of '98. Dir. Clarence Brown. Perfs. Delores del Rio, Ralph Forbes, Harry Carey. MGM, 1928. DVD.

The Treasure of Sierra Madre. Dir. John Huston. Perfs. Humphrey Bogart, Tim Holt, Walter Huston. Warner Brothers, 1948. DVD.

The True Story of Jesse James. Dir. Nicholas Ray. Perfs. Robert Wagner, Jeffrey Hunter. Twentieth Century Fox, 1957. DVD.

Tulsa. Dir. Stuart Heisler. Perfs. Susan Hayward, Robert Preston. Eagle-Lion, 1949. DVD.

Tumbleweeds. Dir. King Baggot. Perfs. William S. Hart, Barbara Bedford. United Artists, 1925. DVD.

Two Rode Together. Dir. John Ford. Perfs. James Stewart, Richard Widmark. Columbia, 1961. DVD.

Ulzana's Raid. Dir. Robert Aldrich. Perfs. Burt Lancaster, Bruce Davison. Universal, 1972. DVD.

Under Nevada Skies. Dir. Frank McDonald. Perfs. Roy Rogers, Gabby Hayes. Republic Pictures, 1946. DVD.

Under Western Skies. Dir. Joseph Kane. Perfs. Roy Rogers, Smiley Burnette. Republic, 1938. DVD.

Unforgiven. Dir. Clint Eastwood. Perfs. Clint Eastwood, Morgan Freeman. Warner Brothers, 1992. DVD.

The Unforgiven. Dir. John Huston. Perfs. Burt Lancaster, Audrey Hepburn. United Artists, 1960. DVD.

Union Pacific. Dir. Cecil B. DeMille. Perfs. Barbara Stanwyck, Joel McCrea. Paramount, 1939. DVD.

The Vanishing American. Dir. George B. Seitz. Perfs. Richard Dix, Lois Wilson. Paramount, 1925. DVD.

Virginia City. Dir. Michael Curtiz. Perf. Errol Flynn, Miriam Hopkins, Randolph Scott. Warner Brothers, 1940. DVD.

Wagon Master. Dir. John Ford. Perfs. Ben Johnson, Ward Bond, Joanne Dru. RKO, 1950. DVD.

Warrior Spirit. Dir. René Manzor. Perfs. Lukas Haas, Alain Musy, Jimmy Herman. Ellipse Productions, 1994. DVD.

Waterhole Number 3. Dir. William A. Graham. Perf. James Coburn. Paramount, 1967. DVD.

Western Union. Dir. Fritz Lang. Perfs. Randolph Scott, Robert Young. Twentieth Century Fox, 1941. DVD.

When the Daltons Rode. Dir. George Marshall. Perfs. Randolph Scott, Kay Francis. Universal, 1940. DVD.

The White Buffalo. Dir. J. Lee Thompson. Perfs. Charles Bronson, Will Sampson. MGM, 1977. DVD.

White Feather. Dir. Robert D. Webb. Perfs. Robert Wagner, John Lund, Debra Paget. Panoramic Productions, 1955. DVD.

The Wild Bunch. Dir. Sam Peckinpah. Perfs. William Holden, Ernest Borgnine, Robert Ryan. Warner Brothers, 1969. DVD.

Works Cited

Adamson, Joni. *American Indian Literature, Environmental Justice, and Ecocriticism: The Middle Place*. Tucson: University of Arizona Press, 2001. Print.

Aleiss, Angela. *Making the White Man's Indian: American Indians and Hollywood Movies*. Westport, CT: Praeger, 2005. Print.

Alexie, Sherman. "Sending Cinematic Smoke Signals: An Interview with Sherman Alexie." By Dennis West and Joan M. West. *Cineaste* 23.4 (1 Jan. 1998). Web. 6 Dec. 2009.

Altman, Rick. "A Semantic/Syntactic Approach to Film Genre." *The Film Genre Reader III*. Ed. Barry Keith Grant. Austin: University of Texas Press, 2003. 27–41. Print.

Ambrose, Stephen E. *Nothing Like it in the World: The Men Who Built the Transcontinental Railroad, 1863–1869*. New York: Simon and Schuster, 2000. Print.

Autry, Gene. "Gene Autry's Cowboy Code." *Geneautry.com.* 2010. Web. 3 Oct. 2010.

Bailey, Ronald. "The Law of Increasing Returns." *National Interest*. Spring 2000. Web. 3 Oct. 2008.

Baird, Robert. "'Going Indian': *Dances with Wolves*." *Hollywood's Indian: A Portrayal of the American Indian in Film*. Ed. Peter C. Rollins and John E. O'Connor. Lexington: University of Kentucky Press, 1998. 153–69. Print.

Barbour, George. "Texas Oil." *Geographical Journal* C.4 (Oct. 1942): 145–55. *JSTOR*. Web. 5 Nov. 2008.

Beatty, Jack. *The Age of Betrayal: The Triumph of Money in America, 1865–1900.* New York: Alfred A. Knopf, 2007. Print.

Benedict, Ruth. *Patterns of Culture.* New York: Houghton Mifflin, 1934. Print.

Billington, Ray Allen. *Westward Expansion: A History of the American Frontier.* 4th ed. New York: Macmillan, 1974. Print.

Borden, Diane M., and Eric P. Essman. "Manifest Landscape/Latent Ideology: Afterimages of Empire in the Western and 'Post-Western' Film." *California History* 79.1 (Spring 2000): 30–41. Print.

Bordwell, David, and Kristin Thompson. *Film Art: An Introduction.* 2nd ed. New York: Knopf, 1986. Print.

Bowles, Samuel. *The Pacific Railroad Open: How to Go: What to See. Guide for Travel to and through Western America.* Boston: Fields, Osgood, 1869. *Openlibrary.org.* Web. 3 Nov. 2008.

Bozzola, Lucia. "*The Far Country* Review." *All Movie Guide.* Web. 1 June 2010.

Briggs, Harold E. "The Development and Decline of Open Range Ranching in the Northwest." *Mississippi Valley Historical Review* 20.4 (Mar. 1934): 521–36. *JSTOR.* Web. 3 Jan. 2008.

Brown, Richard Maxwell. "Western Violence: Structure, Values, Myth." *Western Historical Quarterly* 24.1 (Feb. 1993): 4–20. Print.

Browne, Nick. "The 'Big Bang': The Spectacular Explosion in Contemporary Hollywood Film." 28 Oct. 2006. Web. 3 Nov. 2007.

Buell, Lawrence. *The Future of Environmental Criticism: Environmental Crisis and Literary Imagination.* Oxford, UK: Blackwell, 2005. Print.

Campbell, James T. "Print the Legend: John Wayne and Post-War American Culture." *Reviews in American History* 28.3 (2000): 465–77. Print.

Carson, Rachel. *Silent Spring.* Boston: Houghton Mifflin, 1962. Print.

Cawelti, John G. *Six-Gun Mystique Sequel.* Bowling Green, KY: Bowling Green State University Press, 1999. Print.

Chen, Michelle. "Alaska Gold Mine Threatens Pristine Waters, Wilderness." *The New Standard,* 27 Apr. 2006. Web. 30 Dec. 2007.

Clements, Kendrick A. "Herbert Hoover and Conservation, 1921–1933." *The American Historical Review* 89.1 (Feb. 1984): 67–88. Print.

Cobb, Amanda J. "This Is What it Means to Say *Smoke Signals:* American Indian Cultural Sovereignty." *Hollywood's Indian: A Portrayal of the American Indian in Film.* Ed. Peter C. Rollins and John E. O'Connor. Lexington: University of Kentucky Press, 1998. 206–28. Print.

Condra, G. E. "Opening of the Indian Territory." *Bulletin of the American Geographical Society* 29.6 (1907): 321–40. *JSTOR*. Web. 3 Nov. 2008.

Conley, Robert J. *The Cherokee Nation: A History*. Albuquerque: University of New Mexico Press, 2005. Print.

Cornwall, Warren. "Radioactive Remains: The Forgotten Story of the Northwest's Only Uranium Mines." *Seattle Times,* 24 Feb. 2008. Web. 6 Dec. 2009.

Daggett, Dan. *Beyond the Rangeland Conflict: Toward a West that Works*. Flagstaff, AZ: Good Stewards Project, 1998. Print.

———. *Gardeners of Eden: Rediscovering Our Importance to Nature*. Santa Barbara, CA: Thatcher Charitable Trust, 2005. Print.

Davidson, R. D., and Kenneth Wernimont. "Tenure Arrangements in Oklahoma Oil Fields." *Journal of Land and Public Utility Economics* 19 (1943): 40–58. *JSTOR*. Web. 3 Nov. 2008.

Davis, John P. "The Union Pacific Railroad." *Annals of the American Academy of Political and Social Science* 8 (Sept. 1896): 47–91. *JSTOR*. Web. 4 Oct. 2008.

Debo, Angie. *And Still the Waters Run: The Betrayal of the Five Civilized Tribes*. New ed. Norman: University of Oklahoma Press, 1984. Print.

"*Defending Mother Earth* Book Review." *Midwest Book Review.* 1996. Web. 3 Dec. 2009.

DeMille, Cecil B. *The Autobiography of Cecil B. DeMille*. New York: Prentice Hall, 1959. Print.

Denby, David. "*3:10 to Yuma* Review." *New Yorker,* 3 Sept. 2007. Print.

"Desert Land Act." *American Memory Project*. Library of Congress. 3 Mar. 1877. Web. 3 Mar. 2008.

Diamond, Jared. *Collapse: How Societies Choose to Fail or Succeed*. New York: Viking, 2005. Print.

Doughty, Robin W. *Wildlife and Man in Texas: Environmental Change and Conservation*. College Station: Texas A&M Press, 1989. Print.

Douglas, William O. "Current Legal Literature: Sierra Club v. Morton, 405 U.S. 727." *American Bar Association Journal* (Dec. 1972): 1335. Web. 3 Dec. 2008.

"Drilling Frenzy in West Texas District Draws Hodgepodge of Operators, Service Companies." M-I SWACO, 2005. Web. 3 Oct. 2008.

"*Drums Along the Mohawk* Review." *Variety,* 31 Dec. 1938. Web. 3 Nov. 2007.

Ebert, Roger. "*The Assassination of Jesse James by the Coward Robert Ford* Review." *Chicago Sun Times,* 5 Oct. 2007. Web. 3 Oct. 2008.

———. "*Silver City* Review." *Chicago Sun Times,* 17 Sept. 2004. Web. 4 Oct. 2008.

Frayling, Christopher. "Eastwood on Eastwood." *Clint Eastwood: Interviews.* Ed. Robert E. Kapsis and Kathie Coblentz. Jackson: University Press of Mississippi, 1999. 130–36. Print.

Friedman, Lester, ed. *American Cinema of the 1970s: Themes and Variations.* Piscataway, NJ: Rutgers University Press, 2007. Print.

Gare, Arran E. *Postmodernism and the Environmental Crisis.* London: Routledge University Press, 1995. Print.

Gedricks, Al. "Resource Wars against Native Peoples." *The Quest for Environmental Justices: Human Rights and the Politics of Pollution.* Ed. Robert D. Bullard. San Francisco: Sierra Club Books, 2005. Print.

"The General Mining Law of 1872." *Great Basin Mine Watch.* 16 Nov. 2005. Web. 12 June 2006.

Gladstone, John. "The Romance of the Iron Horse." *Journal of Decorative and Propaganda Arts* 15 (Winter/Spring 1990): 6–37. *JSTOR.* Web. 3 Oct. 2007.

Glotfelty, Cheryl. "Introduction: Literary Studies in an Age of Environmental Crisis." *The Ecocriticism Reader: Landmarks in Literary Ecology.* Ed. Cheryl Glotfelty and Harold Fromm. Athens: University of Georgia Press, 1996. xv–2. Print.

"Gold Fever!: Giant Gold Machines—Hydraulic Mining." 1998. Oakland Museum of California. Web. 10 Aug. 2003.

Gordon, Iain J., and Herbert H. T. Prins. *The Ecology of Browsing and Grazing.* Berlin: Springer, 2008. Print.

Greenswald, John. "Arsenic and Old Mines: As Montanans Battle a New Gold Rush, Californians Are Dealing with the Poisonous Legacy of the Past." *Time,* 25 Sept. 1995: 36. Print.

Hartman, Todd. "Death of Trees 'Catastrophic.'" *Rocky Mountain News,* 15 Jan. 2008. Web. 3 Oct. 2008.

Harvey, Dennis. "*The Californians* Review." *Variety,* 18 Oct. 2005. Web. 3 Oct. 2007.

Hayles, N. Katherine. "Searching for Common Ground." Abstract. *Reinventing Nature? Responses to Postmodern Deconstruction.* Ed. Michael E. Soule and Gary Lease. Washington, DC: Island, 1995. viii. Print.

Hearne, Joanna. "John Wayne's Teeth: Speech, Sound, and Representations in *Smoke Signals* and *Imagining Indians.*" *Western Folklore* 64.3–4 (Summer and Fall 2005): 189–208. *JSTOR.* Web. 4 Sept. 2008.

Howard, William Williard. "The Rush to Oklahoma." *Harper's Weekly,* 18 May 1889, 391. Web. 3 Jan. 2007.

Hoxie, Frederick E., ed. *Encyclopedia of North American Indians.* New York: Houghton Mifflin, 1996. Print.

Hubbard, William. *Narrative of the Indian Wars in New England.* New York: Kraus Reprint, 1969. Print.

Hudak, Mike. "Mike Hudak's Public Lands Ranching Photo Gallery." *Mikehudak.com.* 10 June 2006. Web. 3 Jan. 2007.

Hundley, Norris. "Water and the West in Historical Imagination." *Western Historical Quarterly* 27.1 (Spring 1996): 4–31. *JSTOR.* Web. 3 Oct. 2008.

Hutchins, Wells A. "The Development and Present Status of Water Rights and Water Policy in the United States." *Journal of Farm Economics* 37.5 (Dec. 1955): 866–74. *JSTOR.* Web. 9 Sept. 2008.

Ingram, David. *Green Screen: Environmentalism and Hollywood Cinema.* Exeter, UK: University of Exeter Press, 2000. Print.

Isenberg, Andrew. *The Destruction of the Bison: An Environmental History.* Cambridge, UK: Cambridge University Press, 2001. Print.

Jenkins, David, et al. "Two Faces of American Environmentalism: The Quest for Justice in Southern Louisiana and Sustainability in the Sonoran Desert." *Forging Environmentalism: Justice, Livelihood, and Contested Environments.* Ed. Joanne Bauer. Armonk, NY: M. E. Sharpe, 2006. Print.

Johnson, Arthur. "The Early Texas Oil Industry: Pipelines and the Birth of an Integrated Oil Industry, 1901–1911." *Journal of Southern History* 32.4 (Nov. 1966): 516–28. *JSTOR.* Web. 15 Sept. 2008.

Jowett, Garth. *Film: The Democratic Art.* New York: Focal, 1976. Print.

Kellert, Stephen R. "Concepts of Nature East and West." *Reinventing Nature? Responses to Postmodern Deconstruction.* Ed. Michael Soule and Gary Lease. Washington, DC: Island, 1995. 103–122. Print.

Kindschy, Robert R., et al. "Wildlife Habitats in Managed Rangelands—the Great Basin of Southeastern Oregon: Pronghorns," Gen. Tech. Rep. PNW 145, USDA–Forest Service; USDI-BLM, Portland, OR (1982): 6. Web. 14 Sept. 2008.

King, Geoff. "Spectacular Narratives: *Twister, Independence Day,* and Frontier Mythology in Contemporary Hollywood." *Journal of American Culture* (1999): 25–39. Print.

Kolodny, Annette. *The Land before Her: Fantasy and Experience of the American Frontiers, 1630–1860.* Chapel Hill: University of North Carolina Press, 1984. Print.

———. "Rethinking the Ecological Indian." *Interdisciplinary Studies in Literature and the Environment* 14.1 (Winter 2007): 1–23. Print.

Kreck, Shepard, III. *The Ecological Indian: Myth and History.* New York: Norton, 1999. Print.

Larmer, Forrest M. *Financing the Livestock Industry.* New York: Macmillan, 1926. Print.

Larson, Floyd. "The Role of Bison in Maintaining the Short Grass Plains." *Ecology* 21.2 (Apr. 1940): 113–21. *JSTOR.* Web. 3 Aug. 2009.

Lawrence, John Shelton. "Western Ecological Films: The Subgenre with No Name." *The Landscape of the Hollywood Western: Ecocriticism in an American Film Genre.* Ed. Deborah A. Carmichael. Salt Lake City: University of Utah Press, 2006. 19–50. Print.

Lease, Gary. "Introduction: Nature under Fire." *Reinventing Nature?: Responses to Postmodern Deconstruction.* Ed. Michael E. Soule and Gary Lease. Washington, DC: Island, 1995. 3–16. Print.

Lenihan, John H. *Showdown: Confronting Modern America in the Western Film.* Urbana: University of Illinois Press, 1985. Print.

Leopold, Aldo. *Sand County Almanac and Sketches Here and There.* 1949. London: Oxford University Press, 2000. Print.

Liggett, Lori. "The Wounded Knee Massacre, December 29, 1890: An Introduction." *The Wounded Knee Massacre.* Summer 1998. Web. 3 July 2008. <www.bgsu.edu/departments/acs/1890s/woundedknee/WKIntro.html>.

Limerick, Patricia Nelson. *The Legacy of Conquest: The Unbroken Past of the American West.* New York: Norton, 1987. Print.

MacDonald, Scott. *The Garden in the Machine: A Field Guide to Independent Films about Place.* Berkeley: University of California Press, 2001. Print.

MacLean, Robert. "The Big-Bang Hypothesis: Blowing up the Image." *Film Quarterly* 32.2 (Winter 1978–79): 2–7. Print.

Manfred, Frederick. *Riders of Judgment.* 1957. New York: Signet, 1995. Print.

Mather, E. Cotton. "The American Great Plains." *Annals of the Association of American Geographers* 62.2 (June 1972): 237–57. *JSTOR.* Web. 3 Aug. 2007.

Mathews, John Joseph. *Wah'Kon-Tah: The Osage and the White Man's Road.* Norman: University of Oklahoma Press, 1932. Print.

Mcade, Edward Sherwood. "The Production of Gold since 1850." *Journal of Political Economy* 6.1 (Dec. 1897): 1–26. *JSTOR.* Web. 3 Dec. 2006.

McClure, Robert, and Andrew Schneider. "The General Mining Act of 1872 Has Left a Legacy of Riches and Ruins." *Seattle Post-Intelligencer,* 11 June 2001. Web. 3 Oct. 2007.

McCoy, Joseph G. *Historic Sketches of the Cattle Trade of the West and Southwest.* Kansas City, MO: Ramsey, Millett, and Hudson, 1874. *Google Book Search.* Web. 3 Sept. 2007.

McGee, Patrick. *From* Shane *to* Kill Bill: *Rethinking the Western*. Oxford, UK: Blackwell, 2007. Print.

McHugh, Tom. *The Time of the Buffalo*. New York: Knopf, 1972. *Google Book Search*. Web. 3 Oct. 2008.

Meeker, Joseph. "The Comic Mode." *The Ecocriticism Reader: Landmarks in Literary Ecology*. Ed. Cheryl Glotfelty and Harold Fromm. Athens: University of Georgia Press, 1996. 155–69. Print.

Merrill, Karen R. "Whose Home on the Range?" *Western Historical Quarterly* 27.4 (Winter 1996): 433–51. *JSTOR*. Web. 5 Aug. 2007.

"Midnight Mine." *Mining Law Reform*. 2007. Web. 12 Mar. 2008.

Mihelich, John. "Smoke or Signals?: American Popular Culture and the Challenge of Hegemonic Images of American Indians in American Indian Films." *Wicazo SA Review* (Summer 2001): 129–37. *JSTOR*. Web. 3 Nov. 2008.

"Montana State Constitution, 1972 to Present." 8 Sept. 2005. *Montana History.net*. Web. 3 Oct. 2006.

Murdoch, David Hamilton. *The American West: The Invention of a Myth*. Reno: University of Nevada Press, 2001. Print.

Murphy, Patrick, et al. "Forum on Literatures of the Environment." *PMLA* 114.4 (Oct. 1999): 1089–1104. Print.

Murray, Robin L., and Joseph K. Heumann. *Ecology and Popular Film: Cinema on the Edge*. Albany: SUNY Press, 2009. Print.

———. "Hydraulic Mining Then and Now: The Case of *Pale Rider* (1985)." *The Landscape of the Hollywood Western: Ecocriticism in an American Film Genre*. Ed. Deborah A. Carmichael. Salt Lake City: University of Utah Press, 2006. 94–110. Print.

Nicolar, Joseph. *The Life and Traditions of the Red Man: Reading Line, a Rediscovered Treasure of American Indian Literature*. Durham, NC: Duke University Press, 2007. Print.

Nolley, Ken. "The Representation of Conquest: John Ford and the Hollywood Indian, 1939–1964." *Hollywood's Indian: A Portrayal of the American Indian in Film*. Ed. Peter C. Rollins and John E. O'Connor. Lexington: University of Kentucky Press, 1998. 73–90. Print.

"No to Dumping Toxic Mine Wast." *Care2.com*. 12 Jan. 2006. Web. 1 Oct. 2009.

O'Connor, John E. "The White Man's Indian: An Institutional Approach." *Hollywood's Indian: A Portrayal of the American Indian in Film*. Ed. Peter C. Rollins and John E. O'Connor. Lexington: University of Kentucky Press, 1998. 27–38. Print.

Official Site of the Coeur d'Alene Tribe of Indians. Web. 3 Dec. 2009.

O'Hehir, Andrew. "*Rango* and the Rise of Kidult-Oriented Animation." *Salon.com*. 2 Mar. 2011. Web. 26 Mar. 2011.

Olien, Roger M., and Diana David Olien. *Oil in Texas: The Gusher Age, 1895–1945*. Austin: University of Texas Press, 2002. Print.

Oppermann, Serpil. "Theorizing Ecocriticism: Toward a Postmodern Eco-critical Practice." *Interdisciplinary Studies in Literature and the Environment* 13.2 (Summer 2006): 102–28. Print.

Osborne, Fairfield. *Our Plundered Planet*. Boston: Little Brown, 1948. Print.

Parker, Quanah. "We Fear Your Success." *The Great Chiefs*. Ed. Benjamin Capps. Alexandria, VA: Time-Life Books, 1975. 124. Print.

Phillips, Dana. "Is Nature Necessary?" *The Ecocriticism Reader: Landmarks in Literary Ecology*. Ed. Cheryl Glotfelty and Harold Fromm. Athens: University of Georgia Press, 1996. 204–22. Print.

Pinard, Mary. "Haunted by Waters: The River in American Films of the West." *The Landscape of the Hollywood Western: Ecocriticism in an American Film Genre*. Ed. Deborah A. Carmichael. Salt Lake City: University of Utah Press, 2006. 127–40. Print.

Powell, Brittany R., and Todd Kennedy. "The Day the Gay Cowboy Broke Up with *McCabe & Mrs. Miller: Brokeback Mountain's* Love Affair with Consumerist Conformity." *Intertexts* 10.2 (2006): 113–27. *Project Muse*. Web. 3 Jan. 2008.

Quam-Wickham, Nancy. "'Cities Sacrificed on the Altar of Oil': Popular Opposition to Oil Development in 1920s Los Angeles." *Environmental History* 3.2 (Apr. 1998): 189–209. *JSOR*. 4 Oct. 2006.

"Report of the World Commission on Environment and Development." *United Nations General Assembly*. 11 Dec. 1987. Web. 3 Oct. 2009.

Reps, John W. "Preface." "The Rush to Oklahoma." By William Willard Howard. *Harper's Weekly*, 18 May 1889, 391. Web. Jan. 2007.

Richardson, Heather Cox. *West from Appomattox: The Reconstruction of America after the Civil War*. New Haven, CT: Yale University Press, 2007. Print.

Richter, F. E. "The Copper-Mining Industry in the United States, 1845–1925." *Quarterly Journal of Economics* 41.4 (Aug. 1927): 684–717. *JSTOR*. Web. 3 Jan. 2006.

Riegel, Robert E. *America Moves West*. New York: Henry Holt, 1947. Print.

Rister, Carl Coke. "The Oilman's Frontier." *Mississippi Valley Historical Review* 37.1 (June 1950): 3–16. *JSTOR*. Web. 3 June 2007.

Robbins, Jim. "Bark Beetles Kill Millions of Acres of Trees in West." *New York Times*, 18 Nov. 2008. Web. 1 Jan. 2009.

Rollins, Peter C. "*Tulsa* (1949) as an Oil Field Film: A Study in Ecological Ambivalence." *The Landscape of the Hollywood Western: Ecocriticism in an American Film Genre.* Ed. Deborah A. Carmichael. Salt Lake City: University of Utah Press, 2006. 81–93. Print.

Rooney, David. "*Silver City* Review." *Variety,* 11 Sept. 2004. Web. 3 Oct. 2009.

Rothman. Hal K. *Saving the Planet: The American Response to the Environment in the Twentieth Century.* Chicago: Ivan R. Dee, 2000. Print.

Russell, Edmund P., III. "The Strange Career of DDT: Experts, Federal Capacity, and Environmentalism in World War II." *Technology and Culture* 4 (Oct. 1999): 770–96. *JSTOR.* Web. 3 Jan. 2009.

Ruth, Kent, et al. *Oklahoma: A Guide to the Sooner State.* Norman: University of Oklahoma Press, 1957. Print.

Sandefur, Gary D. "American Indian Reservations: The First Underclass Areas?" *Focus* 12.1 (Summer 1989): 37–41. Web. *JSTOR.* 5 Nov. 2009.

Saunderson, Mont H. "Western Land Use and Conservation Problems." *Journal of Farm Economics* 31.4, pt. 2 (Nov. 1949): 985–94. *JSTOR.* Web. 3 Nov. 2007.

Sawin, Herbert A. "One Hundred Years of California Placer Mining." *Scientific Monthly* 69.1 (July 1949): 56–62. *JSTOR.* Web. 3 Jan. 2007.

Sayre, Nathan. "The Cattle Boom in Southern Arizona: Towards a Critical Political Ecology." *Journal of the Southwest* 41.2 (Summer 1999): 239–71. *JSTOR.* Web. 4 Jan. 2008.

Self, Robert T. *Robert Altman's* McCabe and Mrs. Miller*: Reframing the West.* Lawrence: University Press of Kansas, 2007. Print.

Seton, Robert Thompson. "The American Bison or Buffalo." *Scribner's Magazine* 40.4 (Oct. 1906): 385–405. Web. 9 Oct. 2007.

Shabecoff, Phillip. *Fierce Green Fire: The American Environmental Movement.* New York: Hill and Wang, 1993. Print.

"Silver Mines." *Modern Marvels.* History Channel. 21 July 2006. Television.

Simmon, Scott. *The Invention of the Western Film: A Cultural History of the Genre's First Half-Century.* Cambridge, UK: Cambridge University Press, 2003. Print.

Simon, Stephanie. "Tiny Beetle Chews Way through Millions of Trees." *Wall Street Journal,* 27–28 Dec. 2008, A2. Web. 4 Jan. 2009.

Slethaug, Gordon E. "Hurricanes and Fires: Chaotics in Sherman Alexie's *Smoke Signals* and *The Lone Ranger and Tonto Fistfight in Heaven.*" *Literature Film Quarterly* (1 Jan. 2003): 130–40. *MLA.* Web. 1 Jan. 2009.

Slotkin, Richard. *Gunfighter Nation: The Myth of the Frontier in Twentieth-Century America.* New York: Athenaeum, 1992. Print.

————. *Regeneration through Violence: The Mythology of the American Frontier, 1600–1860.* Norman: University of Oklahoma Press, 2000. Print.

"*Smoke Signals* Review." *Rolling Stone,* 9–23 July 1998: 790–91. Print.

Smyth, J. E. *Reconstructing American Historical Cinema: From Cimarron to Citizen Kane.* Lexington: University of Kentucky Press, 2006. Print.

"Sonoran Desert Conservation Plan." Environmental Justice E.I.S. Issue Paper, 2002. Web. 12 Oct. 2008.

Sontag, Susan. "The Imagination of Disaster." *Commentary* (Oct. 1965): 42–48. Web. 3 Jan. 2006.

Spence, Clark C. "The Golden Age of Dredging: The Development of an Industry and Its Environmental Impact." *Western Historical Quarterly* 11.4 (Oct. 1980): 401–14. *JSTOR.* Web. 1 Oct. 2006.

Sragow, Michael. "*There Will Be Blood* Review." *Baltimore Sun,* 11 Jan 2009. Web. 3 Mar. 2009.

Steinberg, Jay. "*Pale Rider.*" *Turner Classic Movies.* 21 Nov. 2000. Web. 5 Aug. 2003.

Sungsuwan-Patanavanich, Somthawin. "Reforestation as a Carbon Sink: Toward Slowing Global Warming?" *TDRI Quarterly Review* 7.1 (Mar. 1992): 8–14. *JSTOR.* 1 Jan. 2009.

Terrell, John Upton. *Land Grab.* New York: Dial, 1972. Print.

Tompkins, Jane. *West of Everything: The Inner Life of Westerns.* Oxford, UK: Oxford University Press, 1992. Print.

Travers, Peter. "*Appaloosa* Review." *Rolling Stone,* 18 Sept. 2008. Web. 12 Oct. 2009.

————. "*3:10 to Yuma* Review." *Rolling Stone,* 19 Sept. 2007. Web. 12 Oct. 2009.

Tudor, Andrew. "Genre." *Film Genre Reader III.* Ed. Barry Keith Grant. Austin: University of Texas Press, 2003. 3–10. Print.

Turner, Frederick Jackson. *The Frontier in American History.* New York: Henry Holt, 1920. *Gutenberg.org.* Web. 3 Jan. 2008.

United States. Congress. *An Act to Provide for the Sale of Desert Lands in Certain States and Territories.* 44th Cong., 2nd sess., chap. 107. 3 Mar. 1877. Web. 26 Nov. 2008.

USDA Forest Service. "The Postwar Development Era, 1946–1959." *The USDA Forest Service.* 9 June 2008. Web. 2 Oct. 2009.

Vogt, William. *Road to Survival.* New York: Sloane, 1948. Print.

Waage, Frederick O. *Teaching Environmental Literature: Materials, Methods, Resources.* New York: Modern Language Association, 1985. Print.

Walker, Janet, ed. *Westerns: Films through History.* New York: Routledge University Press, 2001. Print.

Walle, Alf H. *The Cowboy Hero and its Audience: Popular Culture as Market Derived Art.* Bowling Green, KY: Bowling Green State University Popular Press, 2000. Print.

Weaver, J. E., and R. W. Darland. "Changes in Vegetation and Production of Forage Resulting from Grazing Lowland Prairie." *Ecology* 29.1 (Jan. 1948): 1–29. *JSTOR.* Web. 1 Jan. 2008.

Weaver, Jace, ed. *Defending Mother Earth: American Indian Perspectives on Environmental Justice.* New York: Orbis, 1996. Print.

Webb, Walter Prescott. *The Great Plains.* 1931. Reprint, Lincoln: University of Nebraska Press, 1981. Print.

Wells, Kristin L. "Discovering Indian Territory Oil." *American Oil and Gas Historical Society* (Summer 2004). Web. 3 Oct. 2007.

Wickett, Murray R. *Contested Territory: Whites, American Indians, and African Americans in Oklahoma, 1865–1907.* Baton Rouge: Louisiana State University Press, 2000. Print.

Wilson, Alexander. *The Culture of Nature: North American Landscape from Disney to Exxon Valdez.* Toronto: Between the Lines, 1991. Print.

Winthrop, John. *Winthrop's Journal: History of New England, 1630–1649.* Ed. James Kendall Hosmer, L.D. New York: Scribner's Sons, 1908. Reprint, New York: Adamant Media, 2001. Print.

Worster, Donald. "Nature and the Disorder of History." *Reinventing Nature? Responses to Postmodern Deconstruction.* Ed. Michael Soule and Gary Lease. Washington, DC: Island, 1995. 65–86. Print.

———. *Rivers of Empire: Water, Aridity, and the Growth of the American West.* New York: Oxford University Press, 1992. Print.

———. *Under Western Skies.* New York: Oxford University Press, 1992. Print.

Wright, Will. *Sixguns and Society: A Structural Study of the Western.* Berkeley: University of California Press, 1975. Print.

Wurbs, R. A. "Water Rights in Texas." *Journal of Water Resource Planning and Management* 121.6 (1995): 447–54. Web. 8 July 2008.

Yergin, Daniel. *The Prize: The Epic Quest for Oil, Money, and Power.* New York: Simon and Schuster, 1991. Print.

Young, Otis E., Jr. "Origins of the American Copper Industry." *Journal of the Early Republic* 3.2 (Summer 1983): 117–37. *JSTOR.* Web. 3 Oct. 2006.

Index

CPSIA information can be obtained at www.ICGtesting.com
Printed in the USA
LVOW041246120312

272649LV00004B/2/P